Developments in Collateralized Debt Obligations

The Frank J. Fabozzi Series

Developments in Collateralized Debt Obligations

New Products and Insights

DOUGLAS J. LUCAS
LAURIE S. GOODMAN
FRANK J. FABOZZI
REBECCA J. MANNING

BICENTENNIAL
1807
WILEY
2007
BICENTENNIAL

John Wiley & Sons, Inc.

ISBN: 978-0-470-13554-9

Printed in the United States of America.

10 9 8 7 6 5 4 3 2 1

DJL
To my wife Elaine and my children Eric and Benjamin

LSG
To my husband Mark and my children
Louis, Arthur, Benjamin, and Pamela

FJF
To my wife Donna and my children
Karly, Patricia, and Francesco

RJM
To my parents Bob and Kathy and my husband Scott

Contents

Preface

Developments in Collateralized Debt Obligations: New Products and Insights is being published less than one year after the publication of the second edition of *Collateralized Debt Obligations: Structures and Analysis* by Lucas, Goodman, and Fabozzi. Someone unfamiliar with the CDO market might well ask, "What is there new to talk about?"

Anyone who is familiar with CDOs knows that change and innovation in the CDO market continues at an increasing pace. The majority of chapters in this book could not have been written one year ago, as their subjects simply did not exist. Take, for example, the recent expansion of synthetic technology across the CDO market. This book has three chapters on totally new topics: the use of both cash and synthetic assets in the same CDO's collateral portfolio, a comparison of subprime mortgage collateral in cash, credit default swap, and index forms, and an explanation of credit default swaps referencing CDOs. Another chapter discusses recent collateral trends in CLOs.

Two chapters discuss CDO ratings and rating methodology changes made in 2006. Another chapter reveals the growing influence CDOs have upon their underlying collateral markets.

CDO technology continues to be applied to new underlying assets and this book discusses two separate cases: (1) trust-preferred securities issued by banks, insurance companies, and REITs; and (2) commercial real estate and commercial real estate CDOs. Because we believe that the latter are slated for increasing issuance, we devote three chapters to them.

As we said in both the first edition (published in 2002) and second edition (published in 2006) of *Collateralized Debt Obligations* "there have been numerous and dramatic changes within the CDO market as it has evolved." That is still true, but even more so. The 13 chapters of this book are divided into four sections:

- Part One: Introduction
- Part Two: Developments in Synthetic CDOs
- Part Three: Emerging CDOs
- Part Four: Other CDO Topics

In Part One we provide the reader with a basic understanding of CDOs necessary to have before reading the other chapters in the book. This part of the book also covers topics applicable to the entire CDO market. Chapter 1 gives an overview of cash and synthetic CDOs. We pay particular attention to cash CDO features such as the cash flow credit structure, credit rating agencies' methodologies, interest rate hedging, and CDO call features. Chapter 2 explains how CDOs have come to dominate their respective underlying collateral markets, particularly those of high-yield loans, subprime mortgages, and trust preferred securities. CDO have contributed to increased issuance and tighter spreads of these assets, but they have also had an impact on the overall U.S. economy that goes well beyond the CDO market. Chapter 3 presents the rating history of 1,300 CDOs and 3,900 CDO tranches across 22 types of CDOs in the United States, Europe, and emerging markets. The analysis compares CDOs by type and vintage and assesses both the frequency and severity of downgrades.

The line between synthetic and cash CDOs has been blurred. Part Two covers the areas where they have been blended the most. Chapter 4 explains the importance of ABS credit default swaps to mezzanine ABS CDOs and the basic workings of the single-name ABCDS and the ABX contracts. We look at how the three different forms of subprime mortgage risk differ and what drives their relative spreads. Finally, we show the difference in mezz ABS CDO equity arbitrage returns with cash and synthetic assets and address the role of the ABX in ABS CDOs. Chapter 5 examines the structural challenges that ABS CDOs face when their assets are made up of cash bonds and credit default swaps. We also provide a quick review of why the hybrid structure has become so popular and likely to spread to other types of CDOs. A comparison between S&P's and Moody's synthetic CDO ratings is provided in Chapter 6. Differences in rating agency synthetic CDO ratings are caused by differences in CDO rating methodologies and differences in underlying reference ratings. At the AAA level, differences in the meaning of S&P and Moody's ratings create a difference of rating opinion that drives rating agency selection. Chapter 7 walks through the documentation of these trades. In a simple, straightforward way, we explain: the five CDO credit problems the documentation recognizes, the two consequences for which CDO CDS documentation provides, and the *three* choices of interest rate cap. We also address miscellaneous CDO CDS terms, the differences between selling protection on a CDS and owning a cash CDO, how one exits a CDO CDS, and rating agency concerns when a CDO enters into a CDO CDS.

In Part Three, we discuss two specific types of CDOs. One fills a niche important to certain regulated entities (trust-preferred CDOs or TruPS CDOs) and the other seems poised for growth (commercial real estate

CDOs). Chapter 8 defines underlying trust preferred securities and describe the issuance trends and structural features of TruPS CDOs. We also show how rating agencies have used historical data in determining default, recovery, and diversification assumptions. In comparison, we show how trust preferred collateral has performed within seasoned CDOs. Finally, in Chapter 8 we provide a listing of all TruPS CDOs and collateral managers through 2006. Chapter 9 reviews different types of commercial real estate loans and securities and their structure. It focuses particular attention on the performance histories of CRE loans and CMBS. The focus of Chapter 10 is on a type of CDO whose issuance has doubled every year from 2004 through 2006 in the United States and whose issuance in Europe seems poised for growth in 2007. This chapter also discusses the evolution, current market trends, and historical performance of CRE CDOs. Chapter 11 compares spreads, subordination levels, and total credit enhancement of different types of CRE CDOs with one another and with more mainstream CDOs.

We begin Part Four by discussing a default study by Moody's showing that the predictiveness of their corporate ratings can be improved by utilizing the credit's outlook status in Chapter 12. The chapter also discusses two changes in CDO rating methodologies and the confusion and fear they sowed. Chapter 13 quantifies two collateral portfolio phenomena: CLOs have more and more of the same credits in common and single-name concentrations in CLOs are getting smaller. We use our own risk measure to assess the trade offs of this situation and determine that CLO debt investors are better off. The positive effect of smaller exposures swamps the negative effect of collateral overlap.

ACKNOWLEDGMENTS

We gratefully acknowledge the expertise and input of UBS securitized products research personnel: Christian Collins, Jeana Curro, Jeffrey Ho, Shumin Li, David Liu, Linda Lowell, Laura Nadler, Greg Reiter, Susan Rodetis, Dipa Sharif, Rei Shinozuka, Wilfred Wong, Victoria Ye, and especially Thomas Zimmerman. Their helpful discussions and ongoing support is very much appreciated. We also would like to thank the rating agencies, Moody's Investors Service, Standard & Poor's, and FitchRatings, for allowing us to draw upon the wealth of data and expertise they provide to CDO investors.

Douglas J. Lucas
Laurie S. Goodman
Frank J. Fabozzi
Rebecca J. Manning

About the Authors

Douglas Lucas is an Executive Director at UBS and head of CDO Research. His team ranks first in *Institutional Investor's* fixed income analyst survey. His prior positions include head of CDO research at JPMorgan, co-CEO of Salomon Swapco, credit control positions at two boutique swap dealers, and structured products and security firm analyst at Moody's Investors Service. Douglas also served two terms as Chairman of the Bond Market Association's CDO Research Committee. While at Moody's from 1987 to 1993, Douglas authored the rating agency's first default and rating transition studies, quantified the expected loss rating approach, and developed Moody's rating methodologies for collateralized debt obligations and triple-A special purpose derivatives dealers. He is also known for doing some of the first quantitative work in default correlation. Douglas has a BA *magna cum laude* in Economics from UCLA and an MBA with Honors from the University of Chicago.

Laurie S. Goodman is cohead of Global Fixed Income Research and Manager of U.S. Securitized Products Research at UBS. Her securitized products research group is responsible for publications and relative value recommendations across the RMBS, ABS, CMBS, and CDO markets. As a mortgage analyst, Laurie has long dominated *Institutional Investor's* MBS categories, placing first in five categories 35 times over the last nine years. In 1993, Laurie founded the securitized products research group at Paine Webber, which merged with UBS in 2000. Prior to that, Laurie held senior fixed income research positions at Citicorp, Goldman Sachs, and Merrill Lynch, and gained buy side experience as a mortgage portfolio manager. She began her career as a Senior Economist at the Federal Reserve Bank of New York. Laurie holds a B.A. in Mathematics from the University of Pennsylvania, and M.A. and Ph.D. degrees in Economics from Stanford University. She has published more than 170 articles in professional and academic journals.

Frank J. Fabozzi is Professor in the Practice of Finance and Becton Fellow in the School of Management at Yale University. Prior to joining the Yale faculty, he was a Visiting Professor of Finance in the Sloan School at MIT. Professor Fabozzi is a Fellow of the International Center for Finance at Yale

University and on the Advisory Council for the Department of Operations Research and Financial Engineering at Princeton University. He is the editor of *The Journal of Portfolio Management* and an associate editor of *The Journal of Fixed Income*. He earned a doctorate in economics from the City University of New York in 1972. In 2002, Professor Fabozzi was inducted into the Fixed Income Analysts Society's Hall of Fame and is the 2007 recipient of the C. Stewart Sheppard Award given by the CFA Institute. He earned the designation of Chartered Financial Analyst and Certified Public Accountant. He has authored and edited numerous books about finance.

Rebecca J. Manning is a research analyst in the CDO Research group at UBS. Prior to joining UBS, Rebecca was an associate at Friedman Billings Ramsey in the real estate investment banking group. While at FBR, Rebecca helped structure and execute over $2 billion in equity and merger transactions for public and private REITs and real estate operating companies. Prior to FBR, Rebecca was a foundation engineer at Clark Construction in Bethesda, Maryland. Rebecca holds an M.B.A. from the Wharton School at the University of Pennsylvania, where she was a Joseph Wharton Grant recipient, and a B.S. in Civil Engineering cum laude from Cornell University.

Introduction

CHAPTER 1

Review of Collateralized Debt Obligations

Throughout this book, we assume that the reader is familiar with collateralized debt obligations (CDOs). In this chapter, we provide a quick review of these instruments.[1] First, we give an overview of cash CDOs. Then we delve in more cash CDO details, including the cash flow credit structure, methodologies of credit rating agencies, interest rate hedging, and CDO call features. Finally, we discuss synthetic CDOs.

Understanding CDOs

A CDO issues debt and equity and uses the money it raises to invest in a portfolio of financial assets such as corporate loans or mortgage-backed securities. It distributes the cash flows from its asset portfolio to the holders of its various liabilities in prescribed ways that take into account the relative seniority of those liabilities. This is just a starting definition; we will fill in the details of this definition over the next few pages.

Four Attributes of a CDO

Any CDO can be well described by focusing on its four important attributes: assets, liabilities, purposes, and credit structures. Like any company, a CDO has assets. With a CDO, these are financial assets such as corporate loans or mortgage-backed securities. And like any company, a CDO has liabilities. With a CDO, these run the gamut of preferred shares to AAA-rated senior debt. Beyond the seniority and subordination of CDO liabili-

---

[1] Those seeking more detail on the basic workings of cash and synthetic CDOs are referred to Chapters 1, 2, 11, and 13 in Douglas L. Lucas, Laurie S. Goodman, and Frank J. Fabozzi, *Collateralized Debt Obligations: Structures and Analysis, Second Edition* (Hoboken, NJ: John Wiley & Sons, 2006).

ties, CDOs have additional structural credit protections, which fall into the category of either *cash flow* or *market value* protections. Finally, every CDO has a purpose that it was created to fulfill, and these fall into the categories of *arbitrage*, *balance sheet*, or *origination*. In this section, we are going to look at the different types of assets CDOs hold, the different types of liabilities CDOs issue, the purposes for which CDOs are created, and the different credit structures CDOs employ.

Assets

CDOs own financial assets such as corporate loans or mortgage-backed securities. A CDO is primarily identified by its underlying assets.

Created in 1987, the first CDOs owned high-yield bond portfolios. In fact, before the term "CDO" was invented to encompass an ever-broadening array of assets, the term in use was "collateralized bond obligation" or "CBO." In 1989, corporate loans and real estate loans were used in CDOs for the first time, causing the term "collateralized loan obligation" or "CLO" to be coined. Generally, CLOs are comprised of performing high-yield loans, but a few CLOs, even as far back as 1988, targeted distressed and nonperforming loans. Some CLOs comprised of investment-grade loans have also been issued.

Loans and bonds issued by emerging market corporations and sovereign governments were first used as CDO collateral in 1994, thus "emerging market CDO" or "EM CDO." In 1995, CDOs comprised of residential mortgage-backed securities (RMBS) were first issued. CDOs comprised of commercial mortgage-backed securities (CMBS) and asset-backed securities (ABS), or combinations of RMBS, CMBS, and ABS followed, but they have never found a universally accepted name. In this book, we use "structured finance CDO" or "SF CDO." However, Moody's champions the term "resecuritizations" and many others use "ABS CDO," even to refer to CDOs with CMBS and RMBS in their collateral portfolios.

Liabilities

Any company that has assets also has liabilities. In the case of a CDO, these liabilities have a detailed and strict ranking of seniority, going up the CDO's capital structure as equity or preferred shares, subordinated debt, mezzanine debt, and senior debt. These *tranches* of notes and equity are commonly labeled Class A, Class B, Class C, and so forth, going from top to bottom of the capital structure. They range from the most secured AAA-rated tranche with the greatest amount of subordination beneath it, to the most levered, unrated equity tranche. Exhibit 1.1 shows a simplified tranche structure for a CLO.

EXHIBIT 1.1 Simple, Typical CLO Tranche Structure

Tranche	Percent of Capital Strucutre	Rating	Coupon
Class A	77.5	AAA	LIBOR + 26
Class B	9	A	LIBOR + 75
Class C	2.75	BBB	LIBOR + 180
Class D	2.75	BB	LIBOR + 475
Preferred shares	8	NR	Residual cash flow

Special purposes entities like CDOs are said to be "bankrupt remote." One aspect of the term is that they are new entities without previous business activities. They therefore cannot have any legal liability for sins of the past. Another aspect of their "remoteness from bankruptcy" is that the CDO will not be caught up in the bankruptcy of any other entity, such as the manager of the CDO's assets, or a party that sold assets to the CDO, or the banker that structured the CDO.

Another very important aspect of a CDO's bankruptcy remoteness is the absolute seniority and subordination of the CDO's debt tranches to one another. Even if it is a certainty that some holders of the CDO's debt will not receive their full principal and interest, cash flows from the CDO's assets are still distributed according to the original game plan dictated by seniority. The CDO cannot go into bankruptcy, either voluntarily or through the action of an aggrieved creditor. In fact, the need for bankruptcy is obviated because the distribution of the CDO's cash flows, even if the CDO is insolvent, has already been determined in detail at the origination of the CDO.

Within the stipulation of strict seniority, there is great variety in the features of CDO debt tranches. The driving force for CDO structurers is to raise funds at the lowest possible cost. This is done so that the CDO's equity holder, who is at the bottom of the chain of seniority, can get the most residual cash flow.

Most CDO debt is floating rate off LIBOR (London interbank offered rate), but sometimes a fixed rate tranche is structured. Avoiding an asset liability mismatch is one reason why floating rate, high-yield loans are more popular in CDOs than fixed rate, high-yield bonds. Sometimes a CDO employs short-term debt in its capital structure. When such debt is employed, the CDO must have a standby liquidity provider, ready to purchase the CDO's short-term debt should it fail to be resold or roll in the market. A CDO will only issue short-term debt if its cost, plus that of the liquidity provider's fee, is less than the cost of long-term debt.

Sometimes a financial guaranty insurer will wrap a CDO tranche. Usually this involves a AAA-rated insurer and the most senior CDO tranche. Again, a CDO would employ insurance if the cost of the tranche's insured coupon plus the cost of the insurance premium is less than the coupon the tranche would have to pay in the absence of insurance. To meet the needs of particular investors, sometimes the AAA tranche is divided into *senior* AAA and *junior* AAA tranches.

Some CDOs do not have all their assets in place when their liabilities are sold. Rather than receive cash that the CDO is not ready to invest, tranches might have a delay draw feature, where the CDO can call for funding within some specified time period. This eliminates the negative carry that the CDO would bear if it had to hold uninvested debt proceeds in cash. An extreme form of funding flexibility is a revolving tranche, where the CDO can call for funds and return funds as its needs dictate.

Purposes

CDOs are created for one of three purposes:

1. *Balance Sheet*. A holder of CDO-able assets desires to (1) shrink its balance sheet, (2) reduce required regulatory capital, (3) reduce required economic capital, or (4) achieve cheaper funding costs. The holder of these assets sells them to the CDO. The classic example of this is a bank that has originated loans over months or years and now wants to remove them from its balance sheet. Unless the bank is very poorly rated, CDO debt would not be cheaper than the bank's own source of funds. But selling the loans to a CDO removes them from the bank's balance sheet and therefore lowers the bank's regulatory capital requirements. This is true even if market practice requires the bank to buy some of the equity of the newly created CDO.
2. *Arbitrage*. An asset manager wishes to gain assets under management and management fees. Investors wish to have the expertise of an asset manager. Assets are purchased in the marketplace from many different sellers and put into the CDO. CDOs are another means, along with mutual funds and hedge funds, for an asset management firm to provide its services to investors. The difference is that instead of all the investors sharing the fund's return in proportion to their investment, investor returns are also determined by the seniority of the CDO tranches they purchase.
3. *Origination*. Banks, insurance companies, and REITs wish to increase equity capital. Here the example is a large number of smaller-size banks issuing trust-preferred securities[2] directly to the CDO simultaneous with the CDO's issuance of its own liabilities. The bank capital notes would not be issued but for the creation of the CDO to purchase them.

---

[2] Trust-preferred securities are unsecured obligations that are generally ranked lowest in the order of repayment.

Three purposes differentiate CDOs on the basis of how they acquire their assets and focus on the motivations of asset sellers, asset managers, and trust preferred securities issuers. From the point of view of CDO investors, however, all CDOs have a number of common purposes, which explain why many investors find CDO debt and equity attractive.

One purpose is the division and distribution of the risk of the CDO's assets to parties that have different risk appetites. Thus, a AAA investor can invest in speculative-grade assets on a loss-protected basis. Or a BB investor can invest in AAA assets on a levered basis.

For CDO equity investors, the CDO structure provides a leveraged return without some of the severe adverse consequences of borrowing via repo from a bank. CDO equity holders own stock in a company and are not liable for the losses of that company. Equity's exposure to the CDO asset portfolio is therefore capped at the cost of equity minus previous equity distributions. Instead of short-term bank financing, financing via the CDO is locked in for the long term at fixed spreads to LIBOR.

Credit Structures

Beyond the seniority and subordination of CDO liabilities, CDOs have additional structural credit protections, which fall into the category of either *cash flow* or *market value* protections.

The *market value credit structure* is less often used, but easier to explain, since it is analogous to an individual's margin account at a brokerage. Every asset in the CDO's portfolio has an *advance rate* limiting the amount that can be borrowed against that asset. Advance rates are necessarily less than 100% and vary according to the market value volatility of the asset. For example, the advance rate on a fixed rate B-rated bond would be far less than the advance rate on a floating rate AAA-rated bond. Both the rating and floating rate nature of the AAA bond indicate that its market value will fluctuate less than the B-rated bond. Therefore, the CDO can borrow more against it. The sum of advance rates times the market values of associated assets is the total amount the CDO can borrow.

The credit quality of a market value CDO derives from the ability of the CDO to liquidate its assets and repay debt tranches. Thus, the market value of the CDO's assets are generally measured every day, advance rates applied, and the permissible amount of debt calculated. If this comes out, for example, to $100 million, but the CDO has $110 million of debt, the CDO must do one of two things. It can sell a portion of its assets and repay a portion of its debt until the actual amount of debt is less than the permissible amount of debt. Or the CDO's equity holders can contribute more cash to the CDO. If no effective action is taken, the entire CDO portfolio is liquidated, all debt is repaid, and residual cash given to equity holders. The market value credit structure is analogous to an individual being faced with a collateral call at his (or her) brokerage account. If he does not post additional collateral, his portfolio is at least partially liquidated.

The *cash flow credit structure* does not have market value tests. Instead, subordination is sized so that the *after-default cash flow* of assets is expected to cover debt tranche principal and interest with some degree of certainty. Obviously, the certainty that a AAA CLO tranche, with 23% subordination beneath it, will receive all its principal and interest is greater than the certainty a BB CLO tranche, with only 8% subordination beneath it, will receive all its principal and interest.

Most cash flow CDOs have overcollateralization and interest coverage tests. These tests determine whether collateral cash flow is distributed to equity and subordinate debt tranches or instead diverted to pay down senior debt tranche principal or used to purchase additional collateral assets. We will discuss these tests in detail later in this chapter, but their purpose is to provide additional credit enhancement to senior CDO debt tranches.

A CDO Structural Matrix

Exhibit 1.2 shows the four CDO building blocks and a variety of options beneath each one. Any CDO can be well described by asking and answering the four questions implied by the exhibit:

- What are its assets?
- What are the attributes of its liabilities?
- What is its purpose?
- What is its credit structure?

EXHIBIT 1.2   CDO Structural Matrix

Assets	Liabilities	Purpose	Credit Structure
High-yield loans	Fixed/floating rate	Arbitrage	Cash flow
High-grade structured finance	PIK/non-PIK	Balance sheet	Market value
Mezzanine structured finance	Guaranteed/unenhanced	Origination	
Capital notes	Short term/long term		
High-yield bonds	Delayed draw/revolving		
Emerging market debt			
Synthetic assets	Unfunded super senior		

This way of looking at CDOs encompasses all the different kinds of CDOs that have existed in the past and all the kinds of CDOs that are currently being produced. By adding "synthetic asset option" and "unfunded super senior" to the matrix, the matrix also encompasses synthetic CDOs, a type of CDO we discuss in detail later in this chapter.

Parties to a CDO

A number of parties and institutions contribute to the creation of a CDO.

CDO Issuer and Coissuer

A CDO is a distinct legal entity, usually incorporated in the Cayman Islands. Its liabilities are called CDOs, so one might hear the seemingly circular phrase "the CDO issues CDOs." Offshore incorporation enables the CDO to more easily sell its obligations to United States and international investors and escape taxation at the corporate entity level. When a CDO is located outside the U.S., it will typically also have a Delaware coissuer. This entity has a passive role, but its existence in the structure allows CDO obligations to be more easily sold to U.S. insurance companies.

Asset Manager (Collateral Manager)

Asset managers (or *collateral managers*) select the initial portfolio of an arbitrage CDO and manage it according to prescribed guidelines contained in the CDO's *indenture*. Sometimes an asset manager is used in a balance sheet CDO of distressed assets to handle their workout or sale. A variety of firms offer CDO asset management services including hedge fund managers, mutual fund managers, and firms that specialize exclusively in CDO management.

Asset Sellers

Asset sellers supply the portfolio for a balance sheet CDO and typically retain its equity. In cash CDOs, the assets involved are usually smaller-sized loans extended to smaller-sized borrowers. In the United States, these are called "middle market" loans and in Europe these are called "small and medium enterprise" (SME) loans.

Investment Bankers and Structurers

Investment bankers and *structurers* work with the asset manager or asset seller to bring the CDO to fruition. They set up corporate entities, shepherd the CDO through the debt rating process, place the CDO's debt and equity with investors, and handle other organizational details. A big part of this job involves structuring the CDO's liabilities: their size and ratings, the cash diversion features of the structure, and, of course, debt tranche coupons. To obtain the cheapest funding cost for the CDO, the structurer must know when to use short-term debt or insured debt or senior/junior AAA notes, to name just a few structural options. Another part of the structurer's job is to negotiate an acceptable set of eligible assets for the CDO. These tasks obviously involve working with and balancing the desires of the asset manager or seller, different debt and equity investors, and rating agencies.

Insurers/Guarantors

Monoline bond insurers or *financial guarantors* typically only guarantee the senior-most tranche in a CDO. Often, insurance is used when a CDO invests in newer asset types or is managed by a new CDO manager.

Rating Agencies

Rating agencies approve the legal and credit structure of the CDO, perform due diligence on the asset manager and the trustee, and rate the various seniorities of debt issued by the CDO. Usually two or three of the major rating agencies (Moody's, S&P, and Fitch) rate the CDO's debt. DBRS is a recent entrant in CDO ratings and A. M. Best has rated CDOs backed by insurance company trust preferred securities.

Trustees

Trustees hold the CDO's assets for the benefit of debt and equity holders, enforce the terms of the CDO indenture, monitor and report upon collateral performance, and disburse cash to debt and equity investors according to set rules. As such, their role also encompasses that of collateral custodian and CDO paying agent.

CASH FLOW CDOs

As explained earlier, arbitrage CDOs are categorized as either cash flow transactions or market value transactions. The objective of the asset manager in a cash flow transaction is to generate cash flow for CDO tranches without the active trading of collateral. Because the cash flows from the structure are designed to accomplish the objective for each tranche, restrictions are imposed on the asset manager. The asset manager is limited in his or her authority to buy and sell bonds. The conditions for disposing of issues held are specified and are usually driven by credit risk management. Also, in assembling the portfolio, the asset manager must meet certain requirements set forth by the rating agency or agencies that rate the deal.

In this section, we review cash flow transactions. Specifically, we look at the distribution of the cash flows, restrictions imposed on the asset manager to protect the noteholders, and the key factors considered by rating agencies in rating tranches of a cash flow transaction. We focus on establishing a basic understanding of cash flow CDO deals using examples.[3]

Distribution of Cash Flows

In a cash flow transaction, the cash flows from income and principal are distributed according to rules set forth in the prospectus. The distribution of the cash flows is referred to as the "waterfall." We describe these rules below and will use a representative CDO to illustrate them.

The representative CDO deal we will use is a $300 million cash flow CDO with a "typical" cash flow structure. The deal consists of the following:

- $260 million (87% of the deal) Aaa/AAA (Moody's/S&P) floating rate tranche.
- $27 million ($17 million fixed rate + $10 million floating rate) Class B notes, rated A3 by Moody's.
- $5 million (fixed rate) Class C notes, rated Ba2 by Moody's.
- $8 million in equity (called "preference shares" in this deal).

The collateral for this deal consists primarily of investment-grade, CMBS, ABS, REIT, and RMBS; 90% of which must be rated at least "Baa3" by Moody's or BBB− by S&P.[4] The asset manager is a well-respected money management firm.

Exhibit 1.3 illustrates the priority of interest distributions among different classes for our sample deal. Interest payments are allocated first to high priority deal expenses such as fees, taxes, and registration, as well as monies owed to the asset manager and hedge counterparties. After these are satisfied, investors are paid in a fairly straightforward manner, with the more senior bonds paid off first, followed by the subordinate bonds, and then the equity classes.

---

[3] For a discussion of deals based by other types of collateral, see Chapters 3 through 9 in Lucas, Goodman, and Fabozzi, *Collateralized Debt Obligations: Structures and Analysis, Second Edition.*

[4] At the time of purchase, the collateral corresponded, on average, to a Baa2 rating.

EXHIBIT 1.3 Interest Cash Flow "Waterfall"

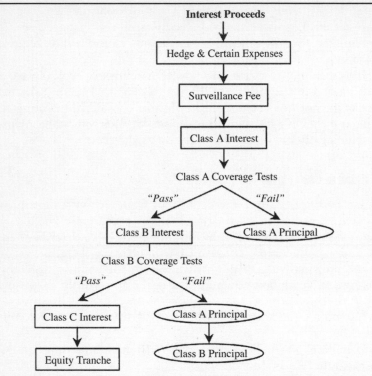

Note the important role in the waterfall played by what is referred to as the *coverage tests*. We explain these shortly. They are important because, before any payments are made on Class B or Class C bonds, coverage tests are run to assure the deal is performing within guidelines. If that is not the case, consequences to the equity holders are severe. Note from Exhibit 1.3 if the Class A coverage tests are violated, then excess interest on the portfolio goes to pay down principal on the Class A notes, and cash flows will be diverted from all other classes to do so. If the portfolio violates the Class B coverage tests, then interest will be diverted from Class C and the equity tranche to pay down first principal on Class A, or, if Class A is retired, Class B principal.

Exhibit 1.4 shows the simple principal cash flows for this deal. Principal is paid down purely in class order. Any remaining collateral principal from overcollateralization gets passed on to the equity piece.

EXHIBIT 1.4   Principal Cash Flow Waterfall

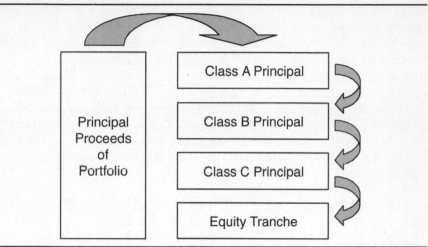

Restrictions on Management: Safety Nets

Noteholders have two major protections provided in the form of tests. They are coverage tests and quality tests. We discuss each type in this section.

Coverage Tests

Coverage tests are designed to protect noteholders against a deterioration of the existing portfolio. There are actually two categories of tests—*overcollateralization tests* and *interest coverage tests*.

Overcollateralization Tests   The overcollateralization or O/C ratio for a tranche is found by computing the ratio of the *principal* balance of the collateral portfolio over the *principal* balance of that tranche and all tranches senior to it. That is,

$$\text{O/C ratio for a tranche} = \frac{\text{Principal (par) value of collateral portfolio}}{\text{Principal of tranche} + \text{Principal of all tranches senior to it}}$$

The higher the ratio, the greater protection for the note holders. Note that the overcollateralization ratio is based on the principal or par value of the assets.[5] (Hence, an overcollateralization test is also referred to as a *par*

---

[5] For market value CDOs, overcollateralization tests are based on market values rather than principal or par values.

value test.) An overcollateralization ratio is computed for specified tranches subject to the overcollateralization test. The overcollateralization test for a tranche involves comparing the tranche's overcollateralization ratio to the tranche's required minimum ratio as specified in the CDO's guidelines. The required minimum ratio is referred to as the *overcollateralization trigger*. The overcollateralization test for a tranche is passed if the overcollateralization ratio is greater than or equal to its respective overcollateralization trigger.

Consider our representative CDO. There are two rated tranches subject to the overcollateralization test—Classes A and B. Therefore, two overcollateralization ratios are computed for this deal. For each tranche, the overcollateralization test involves first computing the overcollateralization ratio as follows:

$$\text{O/C ratio for Class A} = \frac{\text{Principal (par) value of collateral portfolio}}{\text{Class A principal}}$$

$$\text{O/C ratio for Class B} = \frac{\text{Principal (par) value of collateral portfolio}}{\text{Class A principal} + \text{Class B principal}}$$

Once the overcollateralization ratio for a tranche is computed, it is then compared to the overcollateralization trigger for the tranche as specified in the guidelines. If the computed overcollateralization ratio is greater than or equal to the overcollateralization trigger for the tranche, then the test is passed with respect to that tranche.

For our representative deal, the overcollateralization trigger is 113% for Class A and 101% for Class B. Note that the lower the seniority, the lower the overcollateralization trigger. The Class A overcollateralization test is failed if the ratio falls below 113% and the Class B overcollateralization test is failed if the ratio falls below 101%.

Interest Coverage Test The interest coverage or I/C ratio for a tranche is the ratio of scheduled interest due on the underlying collateral portfolio to scheduled interest to be paid to that tranche and all tranches senior to it. That is,

$$\text{I/C ratio for a tranche} = \frac{\text{Scheduled interest due on underlying collateral portfolio}}{\text{Scheduled interest to that tranche} + \text{Scheduled interest to all tranches senior}}$$

The higher the interest coverage ratio, the greater the protection. An interest coverage ratio is computed for specified tranches subject to the interest coverage test. The interest coverage test for a tranche involves comparing the tranche's interest coverage ratio to the tranche's *interest coverage trigger* (i.e., the required minimum ratio as specified in the guidelines). The interest coverage test for a tranche is passed if the computed interest coverage ratio is greater than or equal to its respective interest coverage trigger.

For our representative deal, Classes A and B are subject to the interest coverage test. The following two interest coverage ratios are therefore computed:

$$\text{I/C ratio for Class A} = \frac{\text{Scheduled interest due on underlying collateral portfolio}}{\text{Class A scheduled interest}}$$

$$\text{I/C ratio for Class B} = \frac{\text{Scheduled interest due on underlying collateral portfolio}}{\text{Class A scheduled interest} + \text{Class B scheduled interest}}$$

In the case of our representative deal, the Class A interest coverage trigger is 121%, while the Class B interest coverage trigger is 106%.

PIK-ing Occurs When Coverage Tests are Not Met   We showed in Exhibit 1.3 that if the Class A coverage tests are violated, the excess interest on the portfolio goes to pay down principal on the Class A notes, and cash flows is diverted from the other classes to do so. In this case, what happens to the Class B notes?

They have a *pay-in-kind* or PIK feature. This is a clearly disclosed structural feature in most CDOs where, instead of paying a current coupon, the par value of the bond is increased by the appropriate amount. So if a $5 coupon is missed, the par value increases, say from $100 to $105. The next coupon is calculated based on the larger $105 par amount. The PIK concept originated in the high-yield market, and was employed for companies whose future cash flows were uncertain. The option to pay-in-kind was designed to help these issuers conserve scarce cash or even avoid default. It was imported to the CDO market as a structural feature to enhance the more senior classes.

The PIK-ability of subordinate tranches and the diversion of cash flows to cause early amortization of the Class A tranche naturally strengthens the Class A tranche. The Class A tranche can therefore either achieve a higher rating, or its size can be increased while still maintaining its original rating. CDO equity holders benefit from an overall lower cost of funds: They either have a lower coupon on the Class A tranche; or the Class A tranche, which enjoys the CDO's lowest funding cost, is larger. Either case lowers interest costs to the CDO and thus increases return to equity holders.

The effectiveness of PIK-ing in bolstering the credit quality of the Class A tranche depends upon the amount of collateral cash flow that exists in excess of Class A coupon. The higher the coupon on collateral, and the longer the tenor of collateral, then the more cash flow potentially available for diversion to pay down Class A principal. The effectiveness of PIK-ing (in bolstering the Class A tranche) also depends upon the looseness or tightness of the overcollateralization and interest coverage tests. The tighter the coverage tests are to the CDO's original par and coupon ratios, the sooner a deterioration in those ratios will cause cash flow to be diverted to repay Class A principal.

The effect of cash diversion to the Class A tranche in a high-yield-backed CDO can be dramatic. It is not unusual for subordinate tranches of a CDO to have been downgraded (and to be PIK-ing without any chance of ultimate payment) while the CDO's Aaa tranche maintains its credit quality and rating. That is due to the outlook for Class A receiving full principal and interest because of the diversion of cash to Class A principal.

In determining its optimal capital structure, CDO equity must weigh reduction in the overall cost of CDO debt against the potential for equity to receive less cash flow in severe default scenarios. Distribution of collateral cash flow amongst tranches in a CDO is a zero-sum game. And since equity receives residual cash flow after debt tranches are satisfied, PIK-ing and the diversion of cash flows to Class A principal affects it the most. First, the CDO's average cost of funds increases. Second, the CDO becomes more delevered. Finally, less cash reaches the equity tranche, and that which does is delayed.

Quality Tests

After the tranches of a CDO deal are rated, the rating agencies are concerned that the composition of the collateral portfolio may be adversely altered by the asset manager over time. Tests are imposed to prevent the asset manager from trading assets so as to result in a deterioration of the quality of the portfolio and are referred to as *quality tests*. These tests deal with maturity restrictions, the degree of diversification, and credit ratings of the assets in the collateral portfolio.

Credit Ratings

There are three key inputs to cash flow CDO ratings: collateral diversification, likelihood of default, and recovery rates. While each rating agency uses a slightly different methodology, they reach similar conclusions. For this analysis, we use a variation of Moody's methodology, as it is the most transparent and allows us to change inputs to show the import and impact of each.

Moody's uses the same objective process for developing liability structures regardless of the type of collateral. Moody's determines losses on each tranche under different default scenarios, and probability-weight those results. The resulting "expected loss" is then compared to the maximum permitted for any given rating. While that whole iterative process makes for a tedious analysis, it does help highlight why, for example, a deal backed by investment-grade corporate bonds will have a very high proportion of triple A tranches and a low proportion of equity compared to a deal backed by high-yield corporate bonds.

Collateral Diversification

Moody's methodology reduces the number of credits in the CDO portfolio to a smaller number of homogenous, uncorrelated credits. For example, for CDOs backed by corporate bonds, a *diversity score* is calculated by dividing the bonds into different industry classifications. Each industry group is assumed to have zero correlation with other industry groups. Two securities from different issuers within the same industry group are assumed to have some correlation to each other. At the extreme, two securities from the same issuer are treated as having 100% correlation and thus providing zero diversification.

Reducing the portfolio to the number of independent securities allows the use of a binomial probability distribution. This is the distribution that allows one to figure out the probability of obtaining 9 "heads" in 10 flips of the coin. This distribution can also be applied to a weighted coin, where the probability of "heads" is substantially different than the probability of tails. Intuitively, each asset is a separate flip of the coin, and the outcomes ("heads" and "tails") corresponds to "no default" and "default." The use of this probability distribution makes it possible to define the likelihood of a given number of securities in the portfolio defaulting over the life of a deal.

One factor concerning investors in CDOs is the potential for the default on one bond to wipe out the equity. In fact, in addition to the general diversification methodology, there are single-name concentration rules that protect against too large a concentration within securities issued by any single entity. It is customary for issuer exposure to be no more than 2%. To allow asset managers some flexibility, a few exceptions are permitted. In one actual deal, for example, four positions could be as large as 3%, as long as no more than two of these exposures were in the same industry. If two of the exposures greater than 2% were in the same industry, additional restrictions apply.

Historical Defaults

Likelihood of default is provided by the *weighted average rating factor* (WARF). This is a rough guide to the asset quality of a portfolio and is meant to incorporate the probability of default for each of the bonds backing a CDO. To see where this comes from, we need to look at actual default experience on corporate bonds.

Exhibit 1.5 shows actual average cumulative default rates from 1 to 10 years based on Moody's data from 1983 to 2004. These data show that bonds with an initial rating of Baa3 experienced average default rates of 5.36% after 7 years, and 7.20% after 10 years. Compare that to the B1 default rate of 35.69% after 7 years and 47.43% after 10 years. Generally, as would be expected, bonds with lower ratings exhibit higher default patterns. Moreover, defaults rise exponentially, not linearly, as rating decline.

However, it is difficult to use these data to construct a stylized default pattern, as some anomalies appear. For example, over some time periods,

EXHIBIT 1.5 Average Issuer-Weighted Cumulative Default Rates by Alphanumeric Rating, 1983–2004 Moody's

Cohort Rating	Time Horizon (Years)									
	1	2	3	4	5	6	7	8	9	10
Aaa	0.00	0.00	0.00	0.06	0.18	0.24	0.32	0.40	0.40	0.40
Aa1	0.00	0.00	0.00	0.15	0.15	0.25	0.25	0.25	0.25	0.25
Aa2	0.00	0.00	0.04	0.13	0.28	0.34	0.40	0.48	0.57	0.67
Aa3	0.00	0.00	0.05	0.11	0.18	0.26	0.26	0.26	0.26	0.33
A1	0.00	0.00	0.19	0.30	0.38	0.47	0.50	0.58	0.67	0.84
A2	0.03	0.08	0.22	0.47	0.68	0.89	1.05	1.34	1.59	1.69
A3	0.03	0.21	0.37	0.50	0.65	0.86	1.19	1.38	1.55	1.69
Baa1	0.17	0.50	0.84	1.14	1.46	1.69	1.92	2.05	2.21	2.31
Baa2	0.12	0.40	0.81	1.52	2.11	2.74	3.39	3.98	4.62	5.49
Baa3	0.41	1.07	1.70	2.66	3.60	4.49	5.36	6.15	6.68	7.20
Ba1	0.66	2.07	3.55	5.23	6.76	8.67	9.70	10.85	11.61	12.38
Ba2	0.62	2.22	4.48	6.84	8.82	10.11	11.85	13.13	14.20	14.66
Ba3	2.23	6.10	10.62	15.03	19.14	23.05	26.56	30.00	33.35	36.24
B1	3.03	8.89	14.81	20.09	25.27	30.29	35.69	39.97	43.98	47.43
B2	5.93	13.73	20.58	26.58	31.24	34.54	37.39	39.60	42.19	44.48
B3	10.77	20.43	29.01	36.82	43.55	49.74	54.46	58.40	61.02	62.32
Caa-C	22.24	35.80	46.75	54.60	60.40	65.15	68.30	72.36	75.38	78.81
Investment grade	0.08	0.23	0.43	0.71	0.96	1.21	1.43	1.65	1.84	2.03
Speculative grade	5.26	10.84	16.06	20.63	24.54	28.00	31.04	33.63	35.87	37.66
All rated	1.79	3.66	5.38	6.89	8.13	9.17	10.04	10.75	11.35	11.83

Source: Exhibit 17 in David T. Hamilton, Praveen Vama, Sharon Ou, and Richard Cantor, *Default and Recovery Rates of Corporate Bond Issuers: 1920–2004*, Moody's Investors Service (January 2005), p. 17.

Aaa bonds default more frequently than do Aa1 bonds. And Aa2 bonds default more frequently than either Aa3 or A1 bonds, while A2 bonds default more frequently than A3 bonds. Correspondingly, B2 bonds default less frequently than either Ba3 or B1 bonds.

Moody's smooths these data and constructs a *weighted average rating factor* (WARF), shown in Exhibit 1.6. Thus, a bond with a Baa1 rating has a Moody's score of 260, while one rated Baa3 would have a WARF score of 610. Note that these scores exhibit the same pattern as did actual default numbers: Scores are nonlinear and increase exponentially as ratings decline. These scores are also dollar-weighted across the portfolio to deliver a WARF for the portfolio.

The weighted average rating factor for the portfolio translates directly into a cumulative probability of default. The cumulative probability of default will be larger the longer the portfolio is outstanding. A WARF score of 610 means that there is a 6.1% probability of default for each of the independent, uncorrelated assets defaulting in a 10-year period. (In general, the WARF score translates directly into the 10-year "idealized" cumulative default rate.) The same 610 WARF would correspond to a 4.97% probability of default after eight years, or a 5.57% probability of default after nine years.

When the desired rating on the CDO tranche is the same as the rating on the underlying collateral, Moody's uses the probability of default derived from the WARF score. For CDO ratings higher than the ratings on their underlying collateral, Moody's will use a higher default rate. The multiple applied to the idealized cumulative default rate is referred to as a *stress factor*. Thus, for example, in an investment-grade deal (Baa-rated collateral),

EXHIBIT 1.6 Moody's Weighted Average Rating Factor

Rating	WARF	Rating	WARF	Rating	WARF
Aaa	1	Baa1	260	Caa1	4,770
Aa1	10	Baa2	360	Caa2	6,500
Aa2	20	Baa3	610	Caa3	8,070
Aa3	40	Ba1	940	Ca/C	10,000
A1	70	Ba2	1,350		
A2	120	Ba3	1,780		
A3	180	B1	2,220		
		B2	2,720		
		B3	3,490		

Source: Moody's Investors Service.

Moody's uses a factor of 1.0 to rate a Baa tranche. If the rating on the CDO tranche is Aaa, Aa, or A, then Moody's uses a higher factor to stress the default rates.

Recovery Rates

Moody's recovery rates are dependent on the desired rating of the CDO tranche. To obtain the highest ratings (Aaa and Aa), Moody's generally assumes recovery rates of 30% on unsecured corporate bonds. To obtain an A or Baa rating, recovery assumptions are slightly higher, at 33% and 36%, respectively. It should be understood that actual average recovery rates are higher than these assumptions. A Moody's study covering the period 1981 to 2004 showed that the median, or midpoint, recovery rate for senior unsecured debt was $45.20 ($44.90 average or mean). For subordinated unsecured debt, the median recovery rate was $33.40 ($32.00 average). The bottom line is this: Moody's is again conservative, as it uses a recovery value consistent with subordinated unsecured debt on debt that is in most cases senior—and that builds in "extra" protection for the investors.

Putting It All Together

Moody's has an expected loss permissible for each CDO rating. That expected loss is derived as follows:

Expected loss

$$= \sum_{i=1}^{n}\left(\text{Loss in default scenario } i\right)\times\left(\text{Probability of scenario } i \text{ ocurring}\right)$$

The following example, using an investment-grade corporate CDO, helps clarify this formula. Assume a typical CDO deal with 45 independent assets. Assume further that we are looking at a 10-year deal in which each asset has a probability of default of 5% corresponding to a WARF score of 500, which is well within the category of Baa-rated assets. Moreover, we assume a capital structure with 85% of the bonds Aaa-rated, 10% Baa-rated, and 5% equity. The recovery rate is assumed to be 30%.

To create an example that can be replicated with a simple spreadsheet, we assume all interim cash flows are distributed, and all defaults occur at the end of the life of the deal. Moody's actually runs each scenario through its CDO cash flow model in order to determine the loss to each bond in the CDO structure. Then Moody's assumes a number of different loss schedules and select the most detrimental.

We have simplified that whole analytical process to make it more transparent. Our methodology overstates losses to the bondholders, since we ignored all overcollateralization and interest coverage tests. As the portfolio deteriorated, those two tests kick in and would cut off cash flow to the equity tranche, redirecting cash flows to pay down the higher-rated tranches. We have also ignored the excess spread on these deals, which provides a very important cushion to the noteholders.

The probability of a scenario in which none of the 45 securities default is (probability of no default)^{45}, or $(0.95)^{45}$. This is equal to 9.94%. If there are zero defaults, there is obviously no loss. The probability of only one loss is found as follows:

$$\left[\left(\text{Probability of no default}\right)^{44} \times \left(\text{Probability of 1 default}\right) \times 45 \right]$$
$$= \left(0.95\right)^{44} \times 0.95 \times 45 = 23.55\%$$

This frequency distribution for a selected number of defaults is shown in the column of Exhibit 1.7, labeled "Probability."

With one default, the defaulted bond comprises 1/45 of the portfolio, or 2.22%. However, since a 30% recovery rate is assumed, that loss is lowered to 1.56% (2.22 × 0.7). Thus, the "Portfolio Loss" column of Exhibit 1.7 shows that the loss with one default would be 1.56%. But the 5% equity in the deal acts as a buffer, and there would be no loss to the BBB bond. In order to impact the BBB bond, losses must total more than 5%.

Assume four defaults among the 45 assets. This means that 8.89% of the assets (4/45) are defaulting, and portfolio loss becomes 6.22% (8.89% × 0.7). The probability of this occurring is 11.37%. If that case does occur, the Baa bond would lose 12.22% of its value. That is, the equity would be eliminated, and the $10 Baa tranche ($10 per $100 par value) would be reduced by ($6.22 − $5.00), or $1.22, for a 12.22% reduction. Thus,

[(Baa loss) × (Probability of loss)] = 1.38%

or

[(11.37% probability of scenario) × (12.22% loss if scenario materializes)]

Similarly, if there were five defaults (a 4.92% probability), the portfolio loss would be 7.78%. This corresponds to a loss of 27.78% on the Baa bond. The expected loss to the Baa bond in this scenario is (4.91 × 27.78), or 1.3629%. Note that if portfolio losses total more than 15%, the Baa bond is eliminated, and only then does the Aaa bond start incurring losses.

EXHIBIT 1.7   Expected Loss on BBB Class, Investment-Grade CDO Deal (Given 45 Assets)

No. of securities: 45
Default probability: 5%
Loss given default: 70%
Portfolio loss for single default: 1.56% (1/45 × 70%)
Expected BBB loss: 3.9205%

No. of Defaults	Portfolio Loss (%)	Probability (%)	BBB Loss (%)	BBB Loss × Probability (%)
0	0.00	9.94	0.00	0.0000
1	1.56	23.55	0.00	0.0000
2	3.11	27.27	0.00	0.0000
3	4.67	20.57	0.00	0.0000
4	6.22	11.37	12.22	1.3895
5	7.78	4.91	27.78	1.3629
27	42.00	0.00	100.00	0.0000
28	43.56	0.00	100.00	0.0000
29	45.11	0.00	100.00	0.0000
30	46.67	0.00	100.00	0.0000
31	48.22	0.00	100.00	0.0000
32	49.78	0.00	100.00	0.0000
42	65.33	0.00	100.00	0.0000
43	66.89	0.00	100.00	0.0000
44	68.44	0.00	100.00	0.0000
45	70.00	0.00	100.00	0.0000

Adding expected losses in each of the scenarios across the binomial probability distribution, we find that the expected loss on this Baa CDO tranche is 3.92%. Realize again that this example is for illustrative purposes and will overstate losses to the bondholders. It ignores overcollateralization and interest coverage ratios and the excess spread in the deal.

Importance of Diversification   We can now readily show the importance of diversification. No matter how many assets we have, if the probability of default on each is 5% and recovery is 30%, then the expected loss on the portfolio is 3.5%. However, this does not address the distribution of losses, which is certainly important to the bondholders.

In fact, the Baa bondholders are concerned about the likelihood of losses exceeding the amount of equity in the deal, while the Aaa bondholders are concerned about the likelihood of losses exceeding the amount of equity and Baa bonds. The greater the number of assets, the greater the likelihood that losses on those assets will cluster around 3.5% and the lower the likelihood that losses will exceed the 5% equity cushion and impact the Baa piece. On the flipside, the smaller the number of assets, the greater the likelihood that losses exceed the 5% equity cushion and will hit the Baa bonds.

Exhibit 1.8 shows probability distributions for losses on pools of 15, 30, and 45 securities. Note that the fewer the number of assets, the greater likelihood that losses will exceed a 5% equity cushion.

Exhibit 1.9 supports the point that with fewer assets, expected losses to the Baa-rated tranche are much higher. Thus, for 15 assets, the loss to the Baa tranche is 9.15%; for 30 assets it is 5.62%. For 45 assets, the loss to the Baa tranche is 3.92%; and for 60 assets, it is 2.92%. Note also that the benefits of diversification diminish as more assets are added. The loss to the Baa tranche is 5.5% lower in moving from 15 to 30 assets. It only drops 1.7% in moving from 30 to 45 assets and only 1% from 45 to 60 assets.

EXHIBIT 1.8   Benefits of Diversification

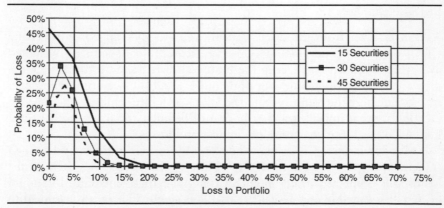

EXHIBIT 1.9   Diversity and Expected Losses, %

No. of Securities	15	20	25	30	45	60
Aaa losses	0.0273	0.0091	0.0032	0.0012	0.0001	0.0000
Baa losses	9.1520	8.5074	6.8720	5.6216	3.9205	2.9262

What's "Too Much" Diversification? The above analysis suggests that greater diversification is always better, since it means less variation of collateral returns. However, a higher diversity score also means that it may be likely the asset manager pushed for, and achieved, less equity in the deal. In fact, with a diversity score of 60, the same losses on the Aaa and Baa bonds could have been achieved with less equity (on the order of 4.5% rather than the 5% required on a deal with a diversity score of 45).

Is there any such thing as too much of a diversification "good thing"? That depends on the asset manager. A large, broad-based asset manager may have considerable strength across all sectors and should be able to handle the analysis—and risks—of a highly diverse portfolio. Even here, a very high diversity score can limit flexibility by requiring an asset manager with broad expertise to invest in an industry he does not like. Whether or not flexibility is being limited too much by a very high diversity score is dependent on the range of assets employed and the strengths of a particular asset manager.

Too much diversification is even more a major problem for a smaller asset manager, where the portfolio may have selective strengths in fewer industries. This asset manager may be stretching to take on additional diversity to achieve a lower required equity. Investors should certainly be wary of deals in which very high diversity scores are achieved by managers straying from their fields of expertise.

Loss Distribution Tests

As can be seen from the discussion above, Moody's approach to rating CDOs involves (1) developing a diversity score; (2) calculating a weighted average rating factor; (3) using the binomial distribution to determine the probability of a specific number of defaults; and (4) calculating the impact of those defaults on bonds within the CDO structure. One element needed to calculate that impact is a distribution of defaults and losses across time. Let us look at this distribution of defaults and losses.

Moody's stresses CDOs via six different loss distributions, and a CDO tranche must pass each test. Moody's basic approach assumes 50% of the losses will occur at a single point in time, and that remaining losses are evenly distributed over a 5-year period. This single 50% loss is assumed to occur at a different point in each of the six tests.

Liability Structure

The structure of the liabilities will be primarily determined by the credit quality of the assets, the amount of diversification, and excess spread. That is, the combination of credit quality, diversification of assets, and excess spread dictate expected losses on each tranche. That is then compared to losses allowed to achieve a given rating. Realize that the structures have been optimized. If a structurer sees one of the tranches passing expected loss tests by a large margin, that means there is room to improve the arbitrage. That can be accomplished by leveraging the structure more (i.e., reducing equity, reducing the amount of mezzanine bonds, or both).

Uses of Interest Rate Swaps and Caps in CDO Transactions

We have mentioned that a wide variety of collateral can be used to back CDO deals. Some of this collateral (high-yield bonds, investment-grade bonds) have fixed rate coupons, some (high-yield loans) have floating-rate coupons. SF collateral may be fixed or floating. CDO liabilities are usually LIBOR-based floating instruments. To convert a fixed rate asset into a floating rate liability, it is necessary to use either an interest rate swap or a cap.

Exhibit 1.10 shows how this is done. The CDO enters into a swap with an interest rate swap counterpart. The CDO pays a fixed rate coupon to the swap counterparty, and receives a LIBOR-based coupon from the swap counterparty. Exhibit 1.11 shows a bond-backed CDO using an interest rate cap. With an interest rate cap, the CDO makes an upfront payment, and receives a payment only if LIBOR is over a certain prespecified level.

EXHIBIT 1.10 Bond-Backed CDO and Interest Rate Swap

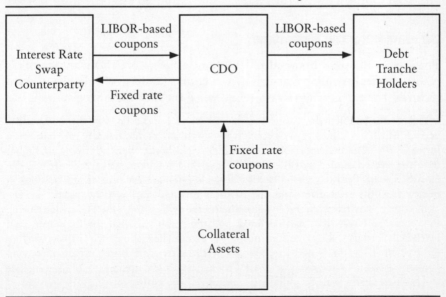

EXHIBIT 1.11   Bond-Backed CDO and Interest Rate Cap

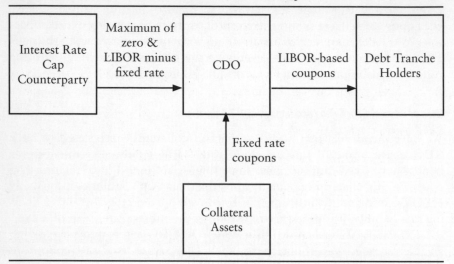

This protects the deal against the scenario in which LIBOR spikes, and the fixed rate coupons on the assets are insufficient to cover the cash flow on the liabilities.

The use of an interest rate swap or cap requires assumptions about the cash flows on the assets. If the assets run off more quickly than anticipated, the CDO can be left with the swaps in place, and no assets.[6]

Call Provisions in CDO Transactions

The commonly used optional redemption features in CDO transactions is where the deal is callable at par by the equity holders, after a prespecified lockout. The call is generally exercised when the deal is doing very well, and

---

[6] This was a problem for a number of high-yield bond CDOs in the 2001–2002 period, which has used swaps to convert fixed rate assets into floating rate liabilities. In the 2001–2002 recession, defaults on high-yield bonds were considerably higher than the levels assumed by the structure. Since the collateral was fixed rate and the liabilities were floating, virtually all the deals had interest rate swaps or caps in place. When the assets defaulted, the CDOs which had employed swaps still had the obligation to pay fixed and receive floating on the swaps. With the Fed easing during this period, interest rates had declined, and the result was that the fixed rate paid by the CDOs was well above current market rates. Their choice was to keep paying it, or to buy back the swap by making a one-time payment to the interest rate swap counterparty. Since that experience CDOs have employed greater use of floating rate assets (high-yield loans, SF collateral) and have been conservative in the number of swaps used in CDO transactions.

the collateral can be liquidated at a healthy net profit. The deal is more apt to be called when the spreads on the debt tranches have narrowed. That is, the equity holders are looking at the possibility of liquidating the deal, paying off the debt holders, and putting the collateral into a new deal where the debt holders are paid a narrower spread. When evaluating CDOs that have been outstanding for a few years and are being traded in the secondary market, call provisions can be important to the valuation of the securities.

Call Protection for Bond Investors

There are many different variations of the basic CDO structure in which the deal is callable at par after a preset lockout period. Two of the most common variations protecting bondholders are prepayment penalties and coupon step-ups.

Prepayment penalties can take two forms: Either the investor is compensated with a premium call, or there is a "make-whole" provision. The most typical premium call is an amount equal to one-half the annual coupon, which steps down over time. Essentially, the effect of the prepayment penalties is to make the call less attractive to the asset manager.

Coupon step-ups are somewhat rare in deals. If the tranche is not called on a certain date, the coupon "steps up" to a higher level. A coupon step-up is only used if the asset manager wants to signal to investors that it is unlikely that the deal will extend beyond a certain point. For example, deals backed by collateral with long legal final maturities are more apt to have a coupon step up to quell investor concerns about extension risk.

Variations of Call Provisions that Benefit Equity Holders

Not all call provisions will be exercised because the deal is going well. Sometimes if the deal is going very poorly, the equity holders may choose to liquidate because the deal is worth more "dead" than alive. This is particularly true towards the end of the deal because the expenses of running a small deal with low leverage are too high and a "clean-up call" is beneficial.

There are also customized call provisions to protect the equity holders from the whims of an asset manager. Some CDO deals have "partial calls," which allows each group of equity holders to exercise authority over their own piece of the deal. This is different from typical structures, in which the deal is only callable in whole by a majority of the equity interests. It is clear that the value of the deal on an ongoing basis will be different for the asset manager (who earns management fees) and an equity holder (who does not). In certain rare cases, a majority of equity holders may replace the asset manager. This is most common in those deals in which the asset manager does not own a piece of the equity. Both of these call provisions are meant to protect the equity holder (who is not the asset manager) at the expense of the asset manager.

Synthetic Arbitrage CDOs

In this section, we review synthetic CDOs. More specifically, our focus is on synthetic arbitrage CDOs. A synthetic CDO does not actually own the portfolio of assets on which it bears credit risk. Instead, it gains credit exposure by selling protection via credit default swaps. In turn, the synthetic CDO buys protection from investors via the tranches it issues. These tranches are responsible for credit losses in the reference portfolio that rise above a particular attachment point; each tranche's liability ends at a particular detachment or exhaustion point. The motivation in an arbitrage synthetic CDO is investors' desire to assume tranched credit risk in return for spread.

Synthetic arbitrage CDOs come in the following forms:

- The oldest are *full-capital structure CDOs* that include a full complement of tranches from super senior to equity. These CDOs have either static reference portfolios or a manager who actively trades the underlying portfolio of credit default swaps (CDS).
- *Single-tranche CDOs* are newer, and are made possible by dealers' faith in their ability to hedge the risk of a CDO tranche through single-name CDS. Single tranche CDOs often allow CDO investors to substitute credits and amend other terms over the course of the CDOs' life.
- *Standard tranches of credit default swap indices* are the most liquid type of CDOs. These instruments allow long-short strategies that appeal to certain types of investors.

Next we outline the features of these types of synthetic arbitrage CDOs.

Full-Capital Structure Synthetic Arbitrage CDOs

Full capital structure synthetic arbitrage CDOs come in many forms. The best way to explain the differences is to focus on two CDO types that represent the range of structural variations.

The first has a static reference portfolio of 100 investment-grade names which we will refer to as CDO #1. The second, which we refer to as CDO #2, is managed with roughly the same underlying credit quality as CDO #1. Salient features of each of the two CDOs, including capital structures and spreads, are shown in Exhibit 1.12.

EXHIBIT 1.12 Synthetic CDO Spectrum

		CDO #1		CDO #2	
Reference pool amount:		$1 billion		$1 billion	
Number of reference entities:		100		100	
Management:		Static		Managed	
Class	Capital Structure	Amount ($ million)	Spread (bps)	Amount ($ million)	Spread (bps)
	Super Senior	870	6	890	6
Class A	AAA	50	50	30	48
Class B	AA	30	90	30	85
Class C	A	5	175	14	125
Class D	BBB	15	400	20	275
Class E	Equity	30		16	
Coverage Test		None		Cash collateral / (Class A+B+C+D) >111%	
Final maturity		5 years		5 years	
Write-down provisions		Immediately upon default		At end of life of deal	
Swap settlement		Cash		Physical	

Static versus Managed

Synthetic arbitrage CDOs can be done as static pools or as managed trans-actions. The advantage to static CDOs is that the investor can examine the proposed portfolio before closing and know that the portfolio will not change. The investors can ask that certain credits be removed from the port-folio or can decide not to invest in the CDO at all. There are also no ongoing management fees. The disadvantage to a static deal becomes apparent if an underlying credit begins to deteriorate, because no mechanism exists for the CDO to rid itself of the problem credit, which remains in the portfolio and may continue to erode.

Capital Structure

Observe from Exhibit 1.12 that static synthetic CDO #1 has much higher equity (3% versus 1.6%) and no coverage tests. The higher equity percent-age is a reflection of the absence of coverage tests. The key to understanding the smaller size of the equity tranche in CDO #2 is the structure of its inter-est waterfall.

First the trustee fee, the senior default swap fee, and the senior advisory fee are all paid out of the available collateral interest and CDS premium receipts. Next interest is paid to the various note holders, from Class A to Class D, in order of their seniority. Then a coverage test is conducted. If the coverage test is passed, remaining funds are used to pay the subordinate advisory fee, and the residual cash flow goes to equity holders.

But if the coverage test is failed, cash flow is trapped in a reserve account. Cash in the CDO's reserve account is factored into the coverage test, helping the CDO to meet its required ratio. If the coverage test comes back into compliance, future excess cash flows can be released to the sub-ordinate advisory fee and to equity holders. At the CDO's maturity, cash in the reserve account becomes part of the principal waterfall and helps to pay off tranches in order of their seniority.

Despite the different proportions of equity in the two CDOs, the credit protection enjoyed by rated tranches in each CDO is about equal. This is so because credit protection is measured not only by the amount of subordina-tion below a tranche, but also by how high credit losses can be on the under-lying portfolio before the tranche's cash flows are affected. In this case, the rated tranches from both CDOs can survive approximately the same level of default losses; the lower amount of equity in CDO #2 is compensated for by its coverage test and cash trap mechanism.

Settlement on Credit Default Swaps

Note in Exhibit 1.12 that CDO #1 uses cash settlement on the reference pool of assets, while CDO #2 uses physical settlement. There are advantages and disadvantages to both. Cash settlement is simple and final, thus one generally sees cash settlement in static deals. With physical settlement, the CDO has to deal with the defaulted debt that has been delivered to it. In a managed CDO, however, the manager can decide whether to sell the debt immediately or hold it in hope of realizing a higher market value later. Physical settlement tends is more common than cash settlement in managed deals.

Equity Cash Flows and the Timing of Write-Downs

In CDO #1, equity is paid a fixed coupon, and thus has no claim on the residual cash flows of the CDO. Equity holders receive interest only on the outstanding equity balance. In CDO #2, the equity holders have a claim on all residual cash flows of the CDO.

The timing of write-downs is very different for the two CDOs. In CDO #1, there is a cash settlement whenever a credit event occurs. Thus, when a credit event occurs (1) that credit is removed from the pool; (2) the CDO pays default losses; and (3) the lowest tranche in the CDO is written down by the amount of default losses. If equity is written down to zero, further losses are written down against the next most junior tranche and so on, moving up the CDO's capital structure.

By contrast, when a credit event occurs in CDO #2, physical settlement occurs. The security can be sold, but there is no write-down until the end of the deal. At that time, the principal cash flows go through the principal waterfall, paying off first the Class A note holders and then those in Class B, C, and D. After note holders are paid, remaining funds go to the equity holders.

Because of these structural differences and investor taste, the BBB and lower classes in CDO #1 generally sell wider than they do in CDO #2. In Exhibit 1.12, the BBB tranche is shown at LIBOR + 400 in CDO #1; it is only LIBOR + 275 in CDO #2. In CDO #1, the write-downs are immediate, and there is no way to recoup losses by better performance later in the deal's life. Moreover, if any of the classes (including the equity) incur losses, their interest is reduced accordingly.

How "Arbitrage" Are Synthetic Arbitrage CDOs?

We have called the CDOs discussed "arbitrage" CDOs. We now look at that label more closely. In some synthetic CDOs, particularly in static portfolio

CDOs, the selection of underlying credits is constrained by the availability of risk at the specific bank putting together the CDO.

What do we mean by this? By this we mean that potential equity investors in a synthetic CDO go to a bank with a list of credits on which they want to sell first loss protection. In practice, the final selection of the portfolio depends upon names that the bank either is exposed to already or can become exposed to quickly.

If the bank has an imbalance in its single-name CDS book (which was caused by having sold more protection on a particular name than it has purchased), it will be interested in buying protection on that name from an "arbitrage" CDO. Sometimes the bank's desire to buy credit protection on a particular name derives from exposures built up in other activities. For example, the bank might be exposed to a certain counterparty on interest rate and currency derivatives. In that case, the bank may be interested in buying protection from a CDO. Sometimes the bank can sell protection on a particular name, thereby creating the need to buy protection from a CDO.

The issue of the availability of credit exposure gives these "arbitrage" CDOs a certain balance sheet feel. This is less true in the case of managed synthetic CDOs, where the manager can offer to sell credit protection to a number of banks. Another "arbitrage" synthetic CDO with a balance sheet favor is the CDO driven by a bank's desire to lay off the credit risk of a bond portfolio it owns. The bank thereafter becomes the funder of the bond portfolio without being the owner of its credit risk.

Single-Tranche CDOs

Single-tranche CDOs are notable for what they are not: the placement of a complete capital structure complement of tranches, from equity to super senior. Instead, a protection seller enters into one specific CDO tranche with a CDS dealer in isolation.

This arrangement creates an imbalanced position for the CDS dealer. For example, it might have bought protection on the 3% to 7% tranche of a synthetic CDO comprising 150 underlying investment-grade names. The CDS dealer will sell protection on these names in the single-name CDS market, varying the notional amount of protection it buys from name to name, in a process called *delta hedging*.

While there are concerns with using delta hedging, because CDS dealers believe in its efficacy, protection sellers enjoy great flexibility in choosing the terms of single tranche CDOs.[7] Protection sellers can choose the portfolio they wish to reference, as well as the attachment and detachment points of

---

[7] Any losses dealers incur in delta hedging do not affect the terms or economics of the single-tranche CDO.

the tranche they wish to sell protection on. These factors will imply a price for that protection.

Alternatively, the protection seller can start with a premium in mind and then negotiate other terms to create a transaction furnishing that premium. Because there are only two parties to the transaction, execution can be quicker than it would be with a full-capital structure CDO encompassing many constituencies.

The single-tranche synthetic CDO can also provide flexibility over its life. As reference credits in the underlying portfolio either erode or improve in credit quality, the value of the CDO changes. If, for example, reference credits have all been severely downgraded, the value of credit protection increases because it is more likely there will be default losses. A protection seller of such a single-tranche CDO might be willing to pay a fee to terminate the CDO early rather than be exposed to default losses later.

Single-tranche CDO investors can go back to the original dealer to reverse out of a trade, or they can reverse the trade with another dealer. If investors have sold protection to dealer A, for example, they can buy protection on the exact terms from dealer B. This would leave them with offsetting trades. In many cases, dealers will allow the investor to step out of the trades completely, and the two dealers will face each other directly.

Many single-tranche synthetic CDOs have a feature where terms of the CDO are adjustable over its life. Recall the example where underlying credits have severely deteriorated. Protection sellers might be allowed to replace a soured credit with a better one for a fee. Or, instead of paying a fee, the terms of the CDO tranche might change. In exchange for getting rid of a troubled underlying credit, the attachment point might be decreased, or the detachment point might be increased, or the premium might decrease.

Standard Tranches of CDS Indices

The last type of synthetic CDO we will discuss are those whose underlyings are indices of credit default swaps. The terms of these CDO tranches are so standardized and their trading is so liquid that they are typically sold directly from the dealer's trading desk, rather than marketed via term sheets, pitch books, memorandums, and road shows. In fact, pricing on more custom synthetic CDOs often reflects prices in the standard tranche market. The reason standard tranches are so liquid is that they are based on liquid credit default swap indices.

The desire of market participants to go long or short a portfolio of underlying names at the same time led to the establishment in 2003 of rival CDS indices, Trac-X and iBoxx. These indices merged in early 2004, deepening the liquidity of the consolidated indices. New indices and subindices

EXHIBIT 1.13 Credit Default Swap Indices

Geographic Concentration	Main Index Name	Main Index Composition	Subindices
North America investment grade	Dow Jones CDX NA IG	125 corporate names	5 Industries: Consumer, Energy, Financials, Industrials, and Technology/Media/Telecom High Volatility
North American high yield	Dow Jones CDX NA HY	100 corporate names	BB-rated B-rated High Beta
Europe	Dow Jones iTraxx Europe	125 corporate names	9 Industries: Autos, Consumer, Consumer Cyclicals, Consumer Non-Cyclicals, Energy, Senior Financials, Subordinate Financials, Industrials, and Technology/Media/Telecom Largest Corporates Lower Rated (aka Crossover) High Volatility
Japan	Dow Jones iTraxx CJ Japan	50 corporate names	3 industries: Capital Goods, Financials, Technology High Volatility
Asia ex-Japan	Dow Jones iTraxx Asia ex-Japan	50 corporate and sovereign names	3 Geographies: China and Taiwan, Korea, and the rest of ex-Japan Asia
Australia	Dow Jones iTraxx Australia	25 corporate names	None
Emerging market	Dow Jones CDX EM	15 sovereign names	None
Emerging market diversified	Dow Jones CDX EM Diversified	40 sovereign and corporate names	3 Geographies: Asia, EEMEA, Latin America

have since been added. The composition of the indices and subindices is provided at www.mark-it.com. Each name in an index is equally weighted in the indices.[8] These broad indices are available in maturities from one to 10 years, with the greatest liquidity at 5-, 10-, and, to a lesser extent, 7-year maturities. A new index series is created every six months. At that time, the specific composition of credits in each new series is determined and a new premium level determined for each maturity. Premiums on indices are exchanged once a quarter on the 20th of March, June, September, and December. Over the life of the index, the index's premium remains fixed. To compensate for changes in the price of credit protection, an upfront payment is exchanged. This upfront payment can be regarded as the present value of the difference between the index's fixed premium and the current market premium for the index.

Indices are static and as credit events occur, protection sellers make protection payments to protection buyers, and the notional amount of the index then decreases. It is important to realize that CDS index trades are bilateral agreements. There is no exchange and only recently have there been attempts to centralize the determination of protection payments. Otherwise, protection payments are subject to individual physical settlements.

We begin with a description of how the tranches of the CDS indices are quoted and traded like liquid synthetic CDO tranches. As shown in Exhibit 1.14, the Dow Jones CDX.NA.IG is divided up into 0% to 3%, 3% to 7%, 7% to 10%, 10% to 15%, and 15% to 30% tranches. The lower and higher percentage for each tranche represents that tranche's *attachment point* and *detachment point*, respectively. When the cumulative percentage loss of the portfolio of reference entities reaches the attachment points, investors in that tranche begin to lose their principal, and when the cumulative percentage loss of principal reaches the detachment point, those investors lose all their principal and no further loss can occur to them. For example, in Exhibit 1.14, the Tranche 3 has an attachment point of 7% and a detachment percentage of 10%. The tranche will be used to covered the cumulative loss during the life of a CDO in excess of 7% (its attachment point) and up to a maximum of 10% (its detachment point).

For the investment-grade indices, equity tranches require an upfront payment from the protection buyer to the protection seller. After that, a fixed 500 bps per annum is exchanged. For the high-yield index, the first two tranches require upfront payments but have no running fee. The higher

---

[8] For the North American indices, only Bankruptcy and Failure to Pay are credit events even though Modified Restructuring is commonly a credit event in the North American market. For the European indices, Bankruptcy, Failure to Pay, and Modified-Modified Restructuring are credit events.

EXHIBIT 1.14   Standard Tranches of CDS Indices

CDX NA IG

	Attachment/ Detachment Points	Upfront Payment	Running Premium
Tranche 1	0%–3%	Yes	500 bps
Tranche 2	3%–7%	No	Yes
Tranche 3	7%–10%	No	Yes
Tranche 4	10%–15%	No	Yes
Tranche 5	15%–30%	No	Yes

iTraxx Europe, iTraxx Asia (ex Japan), iTraxx Japan

	Attachment/ Detachment Points	Upfront Payment	Running Premium
Tranche 1	0%–3%	Yes	500 bps
Tranche 2	3%–6%	No	Yes
Tranche 3	6%–9%	No	Yes
Tranche 4	9%–12%	No	Yes
Tranche 5	12%–22%	No	Yes

CDX NA HY

	Attachment/ Detachment Points	Upfront Payment	Running Premium
Tranche 1	0%–10%	Yes	No
Tranche 2	10%–15%	Yes	No
Tranche 3	15%–25%	No	Yes
Tranche 4	25%–35%	No	Yes
Tranche 5	35%–100%	No	Yes

tranches of the indices trade solely on their running fees. Exhibit 1.14 gives details of tranche structure for various CDS indices.

Investors in standard tranches often engage in various forms of long/ short trades. The tranche's liquidity makes them ideal for bets on relative price relationships among the tranches. Investors might sell protection on an equity or first-loss tranche and buy protection on a more senior tranche of the same index. In market parlance, they are said to be long the equity tranche and short the more senior tranche. Being long a tranche can be confusing to some investors because one has sold protection on it, but the situation is analogous to being long a bond. When one is long a bond or long a standard tranche (having sold protection), an investor abhors a default and does not want cash or synthetic credit spreads to widen.

Another popular long/short trade is to sell protection on a tranche in a longer maturity and then to buy protection on the same tranche from the same index in a shorter maturity. Hedge funds are big participants in long/short strategies via the standard tranches of credit default swap indices.

Conclusion

CDOs incorporate ever-evolving structures that have rapidly gained acceptance in the market. In this chapter, we provide an overview of cash and synthetic CDOs, with special attention to the cash flow credit structure, credit rating agencies' methodologies, interest rate hedging, and CDO call features. No doubt, other forms of CDOs will be invented and current forms will fall into disuse. But at least for now, our CDO Structural Matrix in Exhibit 1.2 provides a good way to categorize the different features of CDOs.

CHAPTER 2

Impact of CDOs on Collateral Markets

With annual issuance breaking $100 billion in 1998 and outstanding of $1.2 trillion as of 2006, CDOs were the fastest growing investment vehicle of the last decade. In this chapter, we explain how the CDO market has become so large that it dominates the respective underlying collateral markets, particularly for high-yield loans, mezzanine mortgage asset-backed securities, and trust-preferred debt. These three collateral types are important to U.S. CDOs, as they comprise 55% of the underlying collateral in cash CDOs issued in 2006 (high-yield loans, 30%; mezzanine mortgage ABS, 20%; and trust-preferred debt, 5%). Issuance of CDOs backed by these assets has steadily increased and has led to both an increase in the underlying's issuance and a tightening of the underlying's spreads.

COLLATERALIZED LOAN OBLIGATIONS AND THE HIGH-YIELD BANK LOAN MARKET

Exhibit 2.1 shows the two factors that drive the purchases of high-yield bank loans by CLOs. The lower portion of the stacked bars shows the amount of new CLO issuance in a given year. New issuance has expanded from $13 billion in 1999 to $87 billion in 2006. All of these newly issued CLOs obviously need to purchase loan collateral to fill their portfolios. However, the volume of new issue CLOs does not capture the full extent of CLO loan purchases in any given year. Because loans prepay and otherwise amortize, seasoned CLOs need to constantly purchase new loans to refill their portfolios. The top part of each stacked bar in Exhibit 2.1 shows new loan purchases by seasoned CLOs. Depending on loan prepayment rates, seasoned CLO loan purchases have been twice that of newly issued CLO loan purchases. In 2006, new and previously existing CLOs purchased $133 billion of loans. Compared to loan issuance that year, CLOs bought 63%

EXHIBIT 2.1 U.S. CLO Issuance and Additional Loan Purchases

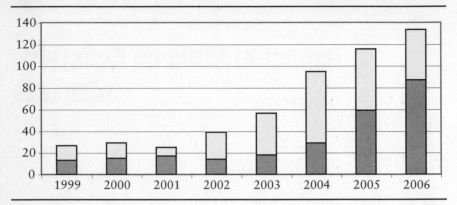

Source of data: Standard & Poor's LCD.

EXHIBIT 2.2 Bank and Institutional Loan Share, %

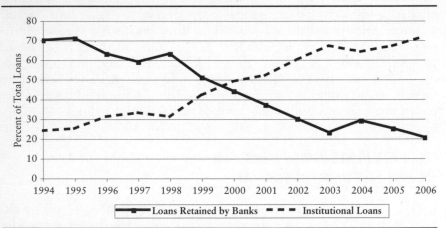

Note: Percentages do not sum to 100% because firm and finance company purchases of pro rata loans are excluded.
Source: Standard & Poor's LCD.

of "institutional loans" (the kind of loans held by nonbank investors) and 42% of all loans (both institutional loans and "pro rata loans," the latter being the kind of loans held by banks).

The bid for high-yield loans from CLOs has had fairly major implications. CLOs have helped fuel the growth of the institutional loan market and diminished the role of banks as holders of loans. Exhibit 2.2 shows that the share of institutional loans has grown from 24% in 1994 to 72% in 2006.

The figure also shows that bank retention of pro rata loans has shrunk from 70% in 1994 to 20% in 2006.[1] The primary role of banks in the loan market is now as loan originators and distributors, not as portfolio lenders.

The impact on loan spreads has been dramatic, as well. Taking into account upfront fees, institutional loans used to trade wider than pro rata loans. This was logical, because, in comparison to the pro rata loans held by banks, institutional loans have longer maturities without significant amortization before their maturity. Exhibit 2.3, however, shows the steady erosion of this spread differential since 1998. From as high as +89 basis points for BB- and BB—rated loans and as high as +67 basis points for B+ and B-rated loans, institutional loans traded right on top or even below pro rata loans in 2005 and 2006. The demand for institutional loans by CLOs has greatly contributed to this tightening.

The disintermediation of banks as holders of credit risk has been going on for quite some time, for both consumer loans as well as commercial and industrial (C&I) loans. With respect to C&I loans, investment-grade firms usually bypass commercial banks and go straight to the capital markets for funding. We have seen how CLOs have contributed to the disintermediation of banks for high-yield loans. Exhibit 2.4 shows the extent of this disintermediation. The figure shows C&I loans as a percent of total U.S. bank assets.

EXHIBIT 2.3   Institutional minus Pro Rata All-In Spreads

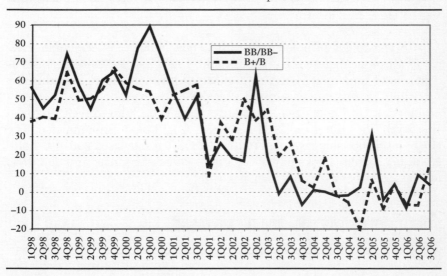

Source: Standard & Poor's LCD.

---

[1] Note that the numbers in Exhibit 2.2 do not add up to 100%. This is because we have excluded security firm and finance company purchases of pro rata loans, which have been pretty stable over the years at 5% to 11%.

EXHIBIT 2.4   U.S. Bank C&I Loan Holdings and Recessions

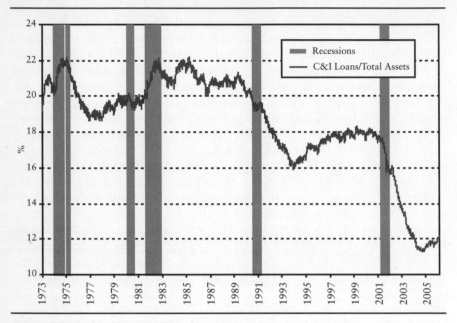

Source: The Federal Reserve Board.

C&I lending is a Conference Board lagging indicator of economic activity. One can see that after recessions in the 1970s and 1980s, C&I loans as a percent of bank total assets first declined and then increased until the next recession. That pattern was halted after the 1991 recession when we see, in Exhibit 2.4, C&I holdings never quite making it back up to their prerecession level. Then, after the 2001 recession, C&I holdings plummeted. The rise of institutional loans, supported by CLOs, has displaced banks as holders of loan assets. Banks now more often serve to originate and distribute loan assets rather than hold loan assets.

STRUCTURED FINANCE CDOs AND THE MEZZANINE MORTGAGE ABS MARKET

Structured finance (SF) collateralized debt obligations are CDOs backed by asset-backed securities (ABS), residential mortgage-backed securities

(RMBS), commercial mortgage-backed securities, and other CDOs.[2] (A CDO consisting of other CDOs is referred to as a "CDO squared".) SF CDOs grew from $15 billion in 2001 to $180 billion in 2006. According to estimates by UBS, in 2006, $100 billion, or 57%, of all SF CDOs were backed by high-grade (AAA and AA) ABS, CMBS, or RMBS collateral. $48 billion, or 30%, of SF CDOs were backed by mezzanine (A, BBB, and BB) collateral. CMBS and CDOs backed $30 billion, or 13%, of SF CDO issuance in 2005.

Yet, even though SF CDOs bought more high-grade collateral, SF CDO purchases of mezzanine subprime home equity loan or "resi. B&C" securitizations.[3] This is because of the relative size of high-grade versus mezzanine issuance. Exhibit 2.5 shows the rating breakdown of Resi. B&C securitizations issued in 2005. Note that the vast majority (91%) of the structure consists of AAA- and AA-rated tranches. Only 8% of the structure consists of A-, BBB-, and BB-rated tranches. In aggregate, there were $385 billion of AAA- and AA-rated Resi. B&C tranches issued and $33 billion of A-, BBB-, and BB-rated tranches issued in 2005. So the $50 billion that SF CDOs spent on high-grade collateral was a fraction of AAA- and AA-rated Resi. B&C issuance, let alone the other types of AAA- and AA-rated assets purchased by SF CDOs in 2005. However, the $27 billion of mezzanine collateral purchased by SF CDOs was a sizable amount of the $33 billion of A-, BBB-, and BB-rated Resi. B&C issuance.

Exhibit 2.6 displays our process of estimating the amount of Resi. B&C A-, BBB-, and BB-rated tranches purchased by SF CDOs. The first and second columns show the distribution of underlying collateral ratings in a typical mezzanine SF CDO. In the third column of the table, we assume that 65% of the collateral portfolio is comprised of Resi. B&C collateral. We multiply column two by 0.65 to get the percent of Resi. B&C collateral in a mezzanine SF CDO by rating category. In the fourth column, we multiply column three by the $27 billion of mezzanine SF CDOs issued in 2005 to get the dollar amount of Resi. B&C collateral purchased by mezzanine SF CDOs in 2005. In the fifth column we restate Resi. B&C production from Exhibit 2.5. Column six is column four divided by column five to get the share of Resi. B&C production purchased by mezzanine SF CDOs.

The conclusion from Exhibit 2.6 is that mezzanine SF CDOs bought 27% of Resi. B&C A tranches in 2005, 94% of BBB-rated tranches, and 49% of BB-rated tranches. As high-grade SF CDOs also buy A-rated Resi.

---

[2] For a further discussion of structured finance CDOs, see Chapter 8 in Douglas J. Lucas, Laurie S. Goodman, and Frank J. Fabozzi, *Collateralized Debt Obligations: Structures and Analysis, Second Edition* (Hoboken, NJ: John Wiley & Sons, 2006).

[3] Just to be clear, the collateral for subprime residential mortgage loans may be low rated but, when structured, some tranches in the securitization have ratings that are investment-grade ratings.

EXHIBIT 2.5   2005 Residential B and C Issuance by Tranche

S&P Rating	$ Million	$ Million	Percent
AAA	345,025	345,025	82.3
AA+	17,273		
AA	17,487	40,957	9.8
AA-	6,197		
A+	6,768		
A	7,716	19,251	4.6
A-	4,768		
BBB+	4,668		
BBB	4,258	12,054	2.9
BBB-	3,128		
BB+	1,091		
BB	661	1,784	0.4
BB-	32		
B+	27		
B	27	74	0.0
B-	20		
NA	29,072	34,178	8.1
NR	5,086		
Total	453,303	453,303	100.0

Source: MCM Structured Finance Watch.

EXHIBIT 2.6   Resi. B&C Production Purchased by Mezzanine SF CDOs

	Collateral Rating Distribution in Mezz. SF CDOs	Times 65% of Resi. B&C in Mezz. SF CDOs	Times $27 Billion of Mezz. SF CDOs Production	2005 Resi. B&C Production	2005 Resi. B&C Production Purchased by Mezz. SF CDOs
A	30%	20%	$5.3	$19.3	27%
BBB	65%	42%	$11.4	$12.1	94%
BB	5%	3%	$0.9	$1.8	49%

Source: UBS Estimates.

B&C tranches, the percent of A-rated tranches purchased by all types of SF CDOs is higher, we think it is as much as 70%.

The SF CDO bid for mezzanine tranches of subprime mortgage securitizations has contributed to the amazing expansion of that product. Exhibit 2.7 shows that whereas subprime mortgage production was a single-digit share of total mortgage production as recently as 2003, it was 22% of mortgage production in 2005. Very few subprime mortgages are held in portfolio, as most are securitized in senior-subordinate structures. SF CDOs offer the best bids for mezzanine tranches of subprime mortgage securitizations, thereby facilitating the growth of the product.

The dependence of mezzanine Resi. B&C tranches on the SF CDO bid has lead to some significant technical spread movements. As shown in Exhibit 2.8, spreads of BBB-rated Resi. B&C structures have been much more volatile than those of prime jumbo mortgages. Part of the upward blip of 2002 Resi. B&C spreads was caused by concerns about the credit quality of U.S. consumers and the stress these structures might come under in a rising interest rate environment. However, the extent of the spread widening was caused by SF CDOS shifting their allocations out of BBB Resi. B&C tranches and into A-rated Resi. B&C tranches, which had also widened. The collapse of Resi. B&C spreads in late 2003 was caused by a massive amount of SF CDO issuance in October of that year. Similarly, the tighten-

EXHIBIT 2.7   Growth of Subprime Mortgage Issuance

	Total MBS Issuance	Subprime Issuance	
Year	$ Millions	$ Millions	Percent
1995	318,058	17,772	6%
1996	440,541	30,769	7%
1997	487,016	56,921	12%
1998	929,163	75,830	8%
1999	832,977	55,852	7%
2000	605,165	48,145	8%
2001	1,354,819	87,053	6%
2002	1,858,381	122,681	7%
2003	2,718,170	194,959	7%
2004	1,883,033	362,549	19%
2005	2,151,635	464,990	22%
3Q2006	1,539,776	341,903	22%

Source: Inside MBS & ABS, based on SEC filings and industry surveys.

EXHIBIT 2.8 BBB Spreads on Residential B and C versus BBB Prime (Jumbo) Securities

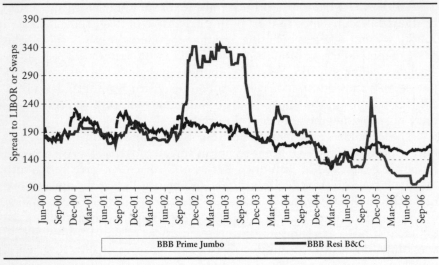

Source: UBS CDO Research.

ing of Resi. B&C spreads during the first half of 2006 was also due to SF CDO demand.

TRUST-PREFERRED SECURITIES CDOs AND THEIR COLLATERAL MARKET

A bank trust-preferred security (commonly denoted by TruPS) is cumulative preferred stock issued via a special purpose vehicle. The advantage of a bank TruPS is that it combines the the Tier 1 capital treatment of equity with the interest deductability allowed for debt funding. Exhibit 2.9 shows the growth of trust-preferred-backed CDOs to $10 billion since the CDO category began in 2000. The exhibit also shows how bank-issued TruPS in CDOs were joined by insurance company TruPS in 2002 and by REIT TruPS in 2005. Prior to these instruments being packaged and distributed in CDOs, trust-preferred issuance was limited to larger bank holding companies. An issuance size of around $100 million was necessary to make the fixed cost of issuance efficient. TruPS CDOs have allowed smaller-sized entities to pool their issuance together and gain economies of scale. Since the TruPS CDO market began, 1,500 banks have used the mechanism to issue Tier 1 capital eligible TruPS. These entities would not have been able to access the efficiencies of the capital market except via the CDO structure.

EXHIBIT 2.9 Trust-Preferred CDO Issuance

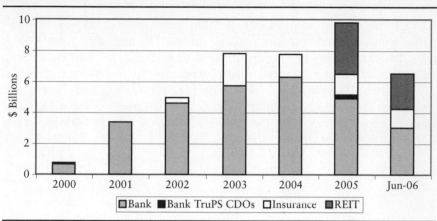

Source: FitchRatings, UBS Calculations.

EXHIBIT 2.10 Bank Trust-Preferred CDO Issuance and Trust-Preferred Spreads

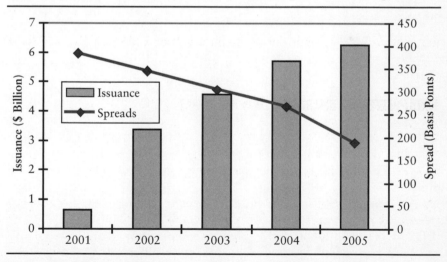

Source: UBS CDO Research.

Exhibit 2.10 shows how bank TruPS spreads have tightened as a result of the CDO bid for these assets. In 2001, the average spread over LIBOR of bank TruPS in CDOs was 390 basis points. In 2005, that spread had come down to 220 basis points. As with bank loans and Resi. B&C tranches, the CDO bid has contributed to underlying asset spread tightening.

CONCLUSION

CDO issuance is up sharply in high-yield loans, mezzanine structured finance collateral, and trust-preferred securities. The huge amount of CDOs done has contributed to the expansion of those collateral markets and the tightening of collateral spreads. By contributing to the disintermediation of C&I loans, the rise of subprime mortgage borrowing, and the efficient placement of Tier 1 capital by small banks and insurance companies, CDO have also had an impact on the overall economy that goes far beyond the CDO market.

CHAPTER 3

CDO Rating Experience

In this chapter, we provide is a vintage-by-vintage comparison of the frequency and severity of cumulative CDO rating downgrades across different types of CDOs, including an analysis of the most severe downgrades as well as an analysis of the severity of AAA downgrades.

We are conscious that in looking at rating changes, we reflect only what rating analysts *express* about the credit quality of the CDOs they monitor. And what analysts publicly express through rating actions does not necessarily reflect either the CDO's *actual* credit quality or even the rating analyst's up-to-date *view* of the CDO's actual credit quality. Nevertheless, despite issues of timeliness and subjectivity surrounding ratings, no other CDO performance statistic has the *potential* to encompass all the quantitative and qualitative factors that comprise a CDO's credit quality as does a formally issued rating.

We find that most of the CDOs that experienced high downgrade frequency and severity suffered from one of two problems. For many arbitrage CDOs, poor performance was the result of an imbalance between collateral spreads on one hand and CDO debt spreads and targeted equity returns on the other. The difficulty of satisfying all CDO constituents tempted CDO managers into low-quality, high-yielding, and misrated assets. For many balance sheet CDOs, poor performance was the result of using the CDO structure to offload credit risk upon unsuspecting CDO investors. But both of these specific manifestations arose out of a more fundamental CDO problem: poor management of the conflict of interest between CDO classes.

Our analysis indicates that most of the CDOs that experienced low downgrade frequency and severity had one of two advantages. For loan and low diversity structured finance-backed CDOs, good performance resulted from timely and conservative collateral ratings. When collateral credit quality is underestimated, CDO debt investors benefit from relative overprotectiveness in the CDO structure. For market value CDOs, good debt rating performance naturally arises from the forced liquidation of collateral assets in the event of a violation of market value coverage tests. But an exception exists when collateral liquidation is not automatic. It is our understanding that in all the cases of market value CDO downgrades, senior debtholders exercised their veto over collateral liquidation.

Finally, our study identifies three turnaround situations in CDO performance. Some CDOs and CDO managers took advantage of wide collateral spreads that were available following default disasters in emerging market debt, high-yield bond CBOs, and, ironically enough, CDOs. CDOs backed by these assets have experienced complete reversals of their fortunes for the better.

CDO RATING DOWNGRADE DATA

Exhibit 3.1 shows the distribution of the 1,361 CDOs and 3,933 CDO tranches that we analyzed. This information was obtained from Moody's ratings databases across different CDO types and years of issuance or "vintage."

Given Moody's descriptions of the CDOs they rate, we categorized CDOs in Exhibit 3.1 by the domicile of their assets (U.S., Europe, or emerging markets), their purpose (arbitrage or balance sheet), their structure (cash flow, synthetic, or market value), and their underlying assets (high-yield bonds, investment-grade bonds, high-yield loans, or structured finance assets). Structured finance-backed CDOs are further divided into those comprised of ABS, CMBS, RMBS, and REIT debt and having diversity scores less than or greater than 18, or CDOs backed by other CDOs.

In Exhibit 3.1, and in our other exhibits presenting CDO rating downgrades later in this chapter, we eliminated insured and principal-protected CDO tranches. This was done to focus on actual CDO performance rather than the credit quality of financial insurers and Treasury securities. We also eliminated combo tranches and tranches from the same CDO having the same rating histories, including tranches that are pari passu in seniority. We did this so that tranche downgrade rates are not influenced by CDOs that issued large numbers of tranches.

Note that the CDO population in Exhibit 3.1 is skewed toward U.S. arbitrage cash flow and European synthetic CDOs. This is due to the pattern of Moody's public CDO ratings, and not any selection preferences on our part. And, with the exception of bank and insurance company preferred stock-backed CDOs and fund of funds-backed CDOs, we feel that our capture of Moody's public CDO ratings is pretty complete. However, we note with chagrin the 130 CDOs tranches, including many commercial loan master trust CDOs, whose ratings became private. Furthermore, the disappearance of a public rating seems to be associated with previous rat-

EXHIBIT 3.1 Number of CDOs/Tranches in Study, by Type of CDO and Vintage

	1996	1997	1998	1999	2000	2001	2002	2003	2004	All Vintages
U.S. ACF HYB	10/25	18/44	25/72	49/151	31/99	34/108	5/14	2/4	1/3	175/520
U.S. ACF HYL	3/6	6/14	17/49	26/71	32/106	26/97	37/147	30/129	57/241	234/860
U.S. ACF IGB			3/6	4/10	11/29	13/33	5/17		1/3	37/98
U.S. ACF Low-D SF				2/10	5/18	9/28	19/54	15/46	37/134	87/290
U.S. ACF High-D SF			1/2		13/36	19/60	20/64	18/61	18/64	89/287
U.S. ACF CDO^2				1/3	2/5	5/16	4/15	2/6	4/15	18/60
U.S. BS		1/2		5/18	4/9	2/2	4/13		5/19	22/67
U.S. Market Value			5/14	11/35	8/23	6/24	1/4		3/7	34/107
U.S. Syn Arb Managed					1/2	6/20	21/70		18/45	46/137
U.S. Syn Arb Static					1/3	4/15	15/45	4/7	20/28	44/98
U.S. Syn BS		1/2	5/15	1/4	7/28	4/14			6/10	24/73
Europe ACF HYB				1/4	6/15	5/11		1/2		13/32
Europe ACF HYL						4/12	6/15	10/42	18/65	38/134
Europe ACF IGB						1/3	2/4		1/1	4/8
Europe ACF SF				1/5		1/1	4/12	5/17	10/34	21/69
Europe BS			3/11	6/18	8/21	9/29	2/4	3/6	5/6	36/95
Europe BS SME Loans				1/2	2/5	1/2	6/14	7/24	3/14	20/61
Europe Syn Arb Managed						5/15	17/49	20/52	12/25	54/141
Europe Syn Arb Static				1/3	1/3	21/35	34/75	68/88	16/21	141/225
Europe Syn BS			1/3	5/19	17/59	13/51	12/58	12/40	2/6	62/236
Europe Syn SF			1/3		2/3	5/12	17/34	50/99	57/121	132/272
Emerging Market	4/5	7/13	5/7	6/16	2/5	3/8	3/9			30/63
Yearly Issuance	17/36	33/75	66/184	121/371	153/469	196/596	234/717	247/623	294/862	1361/3933

Abbreviations: ACF = arbitrage cash flow; BS = balance sheet; CDO^2 = CDOs of CDOs; HYB = high-yield bonds; HYL = high-yield loans; IGB = investment-grade bonds; SF = structured finance (ABS, CMBS, RMBS); Syn = synthetic.
Source: UBS calculations from Moody's rating data.

ing downgrades those CDOs experienced. In any event, we were unable to include these secretive CDOs in our analysis.[1]

CDO AND TRANCHE RATING DOWNGRADE FREQUENCY

Focusing on cumulative downgrades provides a picture of ratings performance over the life of the CDO. Calculating downgrades by vintage eliminates the dampening effect that new issuance has on overall downgrade rates. For example, if all CDOs issued in previous years have been downgraded, but an equal number of new CDOs are issued, then the downgrade rate for all CDOs is 50%. But a downgrade figure of 100% is more descriptive of the performance of seasoned vintages. For that reason, in Exhibit 3.1 and throughout the analysis described in this chapter, we exclude 2005 CDO issuance altogether.

Exhibit 3.2 shows the percent of CDOs with at least one downgraded tranche. This exhibit shows the cumulative frequency of CDO downgrades, irrespective of downgrade severity or the number of rating notches that tranches have been downgraded. For example, the top row of the exhibit contains cumulative downgrade rates for arbitrage cash flow CDOs backed by U.S. high-yield bonds issued from 1996 through 2004. We see that 90% of such CDOs issued in 1996 have had at least one tranche downgraded. The equivalent figure is 100% for 1997, 96% for 1998, and so on. The "All Vintages" column in the exhibit calculates the percentages of downgraded CDOs across all vintages from 1996 through 2004. That number is 74% for arbitrage cash flow CDOs backed by U.S. high-yield bonds. The "Yearly Issuance" row provides the percentage of downgraded CDOs across all types of CDOs in any particular vintage; it was 76% for CDOs issued in 1996.

In calculating cumulative downgrade frequency in Exhibit 3.2—and later in this chapter when we calculate downgrade severity—we focus on the lowest rating to which a CDO tranche has been downgraded. For example, if a Aa2 tranche is downgraded to A2 and then subsequently upgraded to Aaa, we treat this as a downgraded tranche with a rating migration from Aa2 to A2 rather than an upgraded tranche from Aa2 to Aaa.

We note that the frequent upgrading of previously downgraded CDO tranches as a phenomenon unique to CDOs. The rating rational is that once a troubled CDO goes into early amortization, the senior tranche is often repaid quickly and its overcollateralization rises above that tranche's origi-

---

[1] It seems to us that if a CDO enjoys the public announcement of its ratings, then that CDO's bankers and managers should allow the public monitoring of its ratings, whatever their course.

EXHIBIT 3.2 Percent of CDOs with One or More Tranches Downgraded, by Type of CDO and Vintage

	1996	1997	1998	1999	2000	2001	2002	2003	2004	All Vintages
U.S. ACF HYB	90	100	96	88	74	38	0	0	0	74
U.S. ACF HYL	67	83	82	4	13	4	3	0	2	12
U.S. ACF IGB			33	75	73	62	0	0	0	54
U.S. ACF Low-D SF				0	40	22	21	0	0	9
U.S. ACF High-D SF				100	92	79	40	0	0	40
U.S. ACF CDO^2				100	100	20	0	0	0	22
U.S. BS			0	40	0	0	0			9
U.S. Market Value		0	20	27	13	0	0	0	0	15
U.S. Syn Arb Managed					100	67	24		0	22
U.S. Syn Arb Static					100	100	13	0	5	18
U.S. Syn BS		100	80	100	71	100		0	17	67
Europe ACF HYB				0	67	20		0		38
Europe ACF HYL						0	0	0	0	0
Europe ACF IGB						100	0	0	0	25
Europe ACF SF				100		0	0	0	0	5
Europe BS			0	17	38	22	0	0	0	17
Europe BS SME Loans				0	0	100	0	0	0	5
Europe Syn Arb Managed						80	24	0	0	15
Europe Syn Arb Static				100	100	95	53	22	13	40
Europe Syn BS			100	40	35	15	0	0	0	18
Europe Syn SF			100		50	40	0	0	9	7
Emerging Market	50	71	40	0	0	0	0			30
Yearly Issuance	76	88	73	50	48	43	18	6	3	28

Source: UBS calculations from Moody's rating data.

nal overcollateralization at issuance. We rationalize our pessimistic methodology of not giving credit to upgrades that follow downgrades by likening downgrades to the finality of death, or at least that of getting fired. If an asset manager loses his job over the poor performance of his CDO portfolio, he is unlikely to be rehired if/when amortizing tranches are subsequently upgraded. Only if a CDO is upgraded without previously being downgraded do we give the CDO credit for the upgrade in our study. In our database, half of the CDO upgrades follow downgrades, and are thus ignored in our analysis.

Exhibit 3.3 shows the cumulative percent of CDO tranches downgraded by CDO type and vintage. Again, this is the frequency of tranche downgrades. For example, in the top row of the exhibit, we see downgrade rates for arbitrage cash flow CDO tranches backed by U.S. high-yield bonds issued from 1996 through 2004. The exhibit shows that 76% of these CDO tranches issued in 1996 have been downgraded. The equivalent figures are 95% for 1997, 86% for 1998, and so on. Again, the "All Vintages" column in the exhibit provides the percentages of downgraded tranches across all vintages and the "Yearly Issuance" row provides the percentage of downgraded tranches across all types of CDOs in any particular vintage.

CDO DOWNGRADE PATTERNS

Whether by CDO or CDO tranche, clear patterns emerge in Exhibits 3.2 and 3.3. High rates of downgrade plague:

- U.S. arbitrage cash flow CDOs backed by high-yield and investment-grade bonds
- U.S. synthetic balance sheet CDOs
- European static synthetic arbitrage CDOs

On the other hand, downgrades are rare among:

- U.S. and European balance sheet CDOs
- Low-diversity U.S. and European structured finance CDOs
- U.S. and European high yield loan-backed CDOs
- U.S. market value CDOs

Put into perspective, these overall downgrade rates are such that those of the first group are much higher than the corporate downgrade rate while those of the second group are much lower than the corporate downgrade rate. We estimate that the multiyear corporate downgrade rate, compara-

EXHIBIT 3.3 Percent of CDO Tranches Downgraded, by Type of CDO and Vintage

	1996	1997	1998	1999	2000	2001	2002	2003	2004	All Vintages
U.S. ACF HYB	76	95	86	87	65	29	0	0	0	67
U.S. ACF HYL	67	57	49	3	9	3	1	0	1	6
U.S. ACF IGB			17	60	62	52	0	0	0	43
U.S. ACF Low-D SF				0	28	18	22	0	0	8
U.S. ACF High-D SF				100	81	65	22	0	0	29
U.S. ACF CDO^2				100	100	19	0	0	0	18
U.S. BS		0	0	11	0	0	0	0	0	3
U.S. Market Value			7	17	4	0	0		0	7
U.S. Syn Arb Managed					50	45	13		0	14
U.S. Syn Arb Static					100	93	18	0	4	27
U.S. Syn BS		100	67	50	61	93			10	62
Europe ACF HYB				0	47	18	0	0	0	28
Europe ACF HYL						0	0	0	0	0
Europe ACF IGB						67	0	0	0	25
Europe ACF SF				60		0	0	6	0	6
Europe BS				6	24	10	0	0	0	9
Europe BS SME Loans			0	0	0	50	0	0	0	2
Europe Syn Arb Managed						53	12	0	0	10
Europe Syn Arb Static				100	100	91	44	19	10	40
Europe Syn BS			100	26	29	14	0	0	0	14
Europe Syn SF			67		33	33	0	0	7	6
Emerging Market	40	69	29	0	0	0	0			21
Yearly Issuance	69	81	57	45	40	32	12	3	2	22

Source: UBS calculations from Moody's rating data.

ble to the "All Vintage" columns above, is around 25%. Thus on average, CDOs and CDO tranches experience about the same percentage of downgrades as corporate credits. But for the CDOs cited in the first set of bullet points immediately above, tranche downgrade rates vary between 40% and 67%. For the CDOs within the second set of bullet points immediately above, tranche downgrade rates range from 0% to 9%.

WHY DOWNGRADE PATTERNS?

We chalk up poor performing CDOs to the following causes. U.S. bond spreads were extremely tight during much of the time studied, especially when collateralized bond obligation (CBO) issuance was high. Tighter spreads caused high-yield and investment-grade CBO managers to reach for higher yielding (and poorer quality) assets to achieve targeted equity returns. But once high-yield and investment-grade CBO assets shrank because of defaults and forced liability paydowns, the CBOs became overhedged in losing interest rate swap positions. European high-yield CBOs also suffered from being overinvested in telecom and the fact that the fledging European high-yield bond market was, in some cases, the funding source of last resort for poor-quality issuers.

U.S. synthetic balance sheet CDOs worked the way they were intended, if one interprets that as being a vehicle for banks to transfer the risk of their weakest loans to the capital market. European static synthetic arbitrage CDOs did poorly because many had a balance sheet flavor to them, in that they included credit risks that someone wanted to get rid of, not necessarily credit risks that someone consciously chose to become exposed to. It is significant that managed synthetic arbitrage CDOs, where risk positions are truly selected and managed, have done relatively well.[2]

A fundamental problem underlies both the imprudent pursuit of collateral yield in bond-backed CDOs and the opportunistic transfer of credit risk in balance sheet CDOs. This problem is the mismanagement (or lack of management) of conflicts of interest between CDO classes. In the past, the advantage in a CDO structure has been with managers and equity holders in arbitrage CDOs, and asset sellers in balance sheet CDOs. CDO debt holders

---

[2] We point out that there is nothing inherently wrong with synthetic CDOs, either static or managed, that lack the bells and whistles of cash diversion mechanisms (i.e., synthetic CDO versions of cash flow interest and par coverage tests). In fact, we view the lack of cash flow diversion features, and the concomitant increase in subordination, as a superior structure. Subordination is a surer source of credit protection than cash flow diversion mechanisms that can be (and have been) manipulated and defeated by motivated managers. Synthetic balance sheet CDO performance problems were not caused by structure, but by reference asset selection.

often bore a disproportionate amount of the CDO's risk. This was due to the failure of adequate structural safeguards, either because of their absence or because they could be got around by CDO managers. In 2002, the struggle started to create better protection for debt holders and a better balance among the interests of parties in a CDO.

The reason for the disparity in performance between synthetic and cash flow U.S. balance sheet CDOs eludes us. A plausible explanation for the much better performance of cash flow balance sheet CDOs is that these CDOs are more often done for funding reasons or regulatory capital reasons, whereas synthetic balance sheet CDOs are usually effected to achieve credit risk transfer. But while we like this explanation, we cannot present any evidence to support it.

One reason that high-yield collateralized loan obligations (CLOs) have done well is because their underlying credits are vetted by commercial banks. We also feel that public loan ratings are more timely than bond ratings and private loan ratings are more conservative than bond ratings. For whatever reason, loans historically default about half as frequently as equally rated bonds, a fact not taken into account in CLO rating methodologies.

Low-diversity structured finance CDOs, focused on CMBS, REIT debt, RMBS, and residential mortgage-related ABS, had the advantage of underlying assets with exemplary credit histories. And as in the case of high-yield loans, this exemplary credit history goes unrewarded in the CDO rating process. This causes structured finance CDO debt investors to be relatively overprotected as the credit protection of the CDO's structure over compensates for the risk of the CDO's assets. In contrast, high diversity SF CDOs reached for yield in all the wrong places: manufactured housing, aircraft leases, 12b-1 fees, and franchise loans.

Market value CDOs really should never be downgraded. Rather, if the aggregate market price of their assets decline, assets should be sold and liabilities redeemed until the CDO regains its previous market value coverage of assets to liabilities. If this happens, CDO credit quality is maintained. The market value CDOs that have been downgraded contained a structuring flaw where the sale of assets was not automatic, but instead required the approval of senior debt holders who were in a much safer position than subordinate debt holders and decided to waive collateral liquidation.

Exhibits 3.2 and 3.3 also show three CDO sectors that have apparently reformed themselves. While every tranche of the three CDOs of CDOs issued before 2001 has been downgraded, only one of the 15 CDOs of CDOs issued since has suffered a downgrade among its tranches. Nor have there been any tranche downgrades of the 14 emerging market CDOs issued after 1998. Finally, there has not been a downgrade of the eight high-yield CBOs issued after 2001.

The turnaround in the experience of these CDOs shows the importance of timing to the fortunes of a CDO. This affords an example directly opposite to that of CDO collateral managers reaching for the yield on low quality speculative and investment grade bonds to make the arbitrage work for CBO equity. In the case of emerging market CDOs, the bursting of emerging market prices in the fall of 1998 meant that emerging market CDO managers could fulfill targeted equity returns and still be very picky about credit. For CDOs of CDOs, low secondary CDO prices over much of this period also allowed managers to acquire good assets cheaply. The same can also be said of the high-yield CBOs issued since 2001.

DOWNGRADE SEVERITY

Exhibit 3.4 looks at CDO downgrade activity by factoring in the severity of downgrades along with their frequency. The exhibit shows cumulative average rating migration by type of CDO and year of issuance. Positive numbers mean that, on average, CDO tranches experienced a downgrade; negative numbers mean that, on average, tranches were upgraded. We compute rating migration as the change in rating in terms of number of rating notches. A "rating notch" in Moody's symbol system is the difference, for example, between a Aa2 and a Aa3 rating or between a A3 and a Baa1 rating. Exhibit 3.4 shows that U.S. high-yield bond-backed CDO tranches issued in 1996 have suffered cumulative average downgrades of 5.0 ratings notches since issuance. For example, that would be a downgrade from A2 to Ba1. The equivalent rating migration figure is 8.3 for 1997, 6.5 for 1998, and so on. The "Average Drift/Year" column shows average *annual* rating migration experience across vintages, weighting each vintage equally.

The CDOs doing well or poorly with respect to downgrade frequency in Exhibits 3.2 and 3.3 generally fare the same with respect to downgrade severity in Exhibit 3.4. To put that exhibit into perspective, we estimate that over the same period, corporate credits have been downgraded an average of 0.4 of a rating notch a year, which is about equal to CDOs taken as a whole. However, the annual downgrade severity for different types of CDOs ranges from –0.2 to 0.9.

EXTREME RATING DOWNGRADES

Exhibit 3.5 provides an overall picture of CDO downgrades in a *rating transition matrix*. Initial tranche ratings are shown on the left of the graph; current tranche ratings (or, according to our methodology, the lowest rating

EXHIBIT 3.4 Cumulative Rating Notch Change in Rating, by Type of CDO and Vintage

	1996	1997	1998	1999	2000	2001	2002	2003	2004	Avg Drift/ Year
U.S. ACF HYB	5.0	8.3	6.5	7.0	3.9	0.8	0.0	0.0	0.0	0.5
U.S. ACF HYL	2.7	3.4	2.3	0.0	0.4	0.0	0.0	0.0	0.0	0.1
U.S. ACF IGB			0.7	3.4	3.6	3.8	0.0		0.0	0.3
U.S. ACF Low-D SF				-1.3	2.5	0.7	1.7	0.0	0.0	0.1
U.S. ACF High-D SF				8.5	7.8	5.1	1.2	-0.1	0.0	0.7
U.S. ACF CDO^2				10.7	6.0	1.6	0.0	0.0	0.0	0.5
U.S. BS		-1.0		0.2	-0.6	-4.5	-0.4		0.0	-0.2
U.S. Market Value			0.1	0.8	0.2	0.0	0.0		0.0	0.0
U.S. Syn Arb Managed					1.0	1.3	0.2		0.0	0.1
U.S. Syn Arb Static					6.3	4.7	0.6	0.0	0.0	0.5
U.S. Syn BS		2.5	5.9	0.5	3.6	7.0			0.1	0.6
Europe ACF HYB				0.0	3.5	1.6	0.0	0.0		0.2
Europe ACF HYL						0.0	0.0	0.0	0.0	0.0
Europe ACF IGB						1.3	0.0		0.0	0.1
Europe ACF SF				5.4		0.0	0.0	0.0	0.0	0.2
Europe BS			-2.3	-1.1	0.9	0.3	0.0	0.0	0.0	0.0
Europe BS SME Loans				0.0	0.0	1.0	0.0	0.0	0.0	0.0
Europe Syn Arb Managed						2.4	0.2	0.0	0.0	0.1
Europe Syn Arb Static				7.7	10.0	7.2	1.4	0.2	0.3	0.9
Europe Syn BS			4.3	0.7	1.7	0.4	-0.1	0.0	0.0	0.2
Europe Syn SF			4.0		1.7	1.1	-0.1	0.0	0.2	0.2
Emerging Market	1.4	2.2	1.3	0.0	0.0	0.0	0.0		0.0	0.1
Yearly Issuance	4.1	5.9	3.7	3.3	2.6	1.8	0.4	0.0	0.0	0.4

Source: UBS calculations from Moody's rating data.

EXHIBIT 3.5 Rating Migration of CDO Tranches

Initial Rating	Aaa	Aa1	Aa2	Aa3	A1	A2	A3	Baa1	Baa2	Baa3	Ba1	Ba2	Ba3	B1	B2	B3	Caa1	Caa2	Caa3	Ca	C	Number of Tranches
Aaa	88.1	2.0	2.0	1.6	1.4	0.8	1.4	0.7	0.4	0.6	0.3	0.2	0.1	0.2	0.2		0.2					1018
Aa1	3.6	81.2	0.7	0.7	2.9	3.6	1.4		1.4	2.2	0.7	0.7		0.7								138
Aa2	1.7	0.7	75.2	4.4	3.1	1.7	1.5	1.1	1.1	2.6	1.3	1.5	0.2	0.4	0.7	0.4		0.6	0.7	0.7	0.4	540
Aa3	2.1	1.4	2.1	62.8	4.1	5.5	2.1	4.1	2.1	2.8	2.8	0.7	3.4	1.4		1.4				0.7	0.7	145
A1	0.8	1.7	0.8	1.7	84.2	1.7	2.5	0.8	0.8		1.7		0.8		1.7							120
A2	0.9	0.3	0.9	0.6	0.3	86.2	0.6	1.5	2.1	1.2	0.9	0.3	0.3	0.3	0.6		0.3	0.9	1.5	0.3	0.3	341
A3	0.4		0.4	0.4		0.4	74.6	3.3	2.5	2.9	2.9	1.3	0.4	1.7	1.3	1.3	0.8	1.7	0.8	1.3	1.7	240
Baa1					2.5		2.5	84.8						1.3	1.3	2.5		2.5	1.3	1.3		79
Baa2		0.2	0.2		0.2		1.0		72.2	3.0	2.8	1.5	1.5	0.8	1.2	1.8	1.0	2.1	1.5	5.6	3.3	608
Baa3	0.5	0.5			0.5			0.5		45.9	1.5	7.2	7.2	5.7	1.5	1.0	2.1	3.1	5.7	11.9	10.8	194
Ba1							1.7				85.0	1.7					1.7		5.0	1.7	1.7	60
Ba2						0.4	0.4		0.8	0.4	0.4	70.3	2.4	2.0	2.4	2.0	1.2	1.6	1.2	5.6	8.8	249
Ba3										1.5	1.5		59.1	1.5	0.8	3.8	1.5	2.3	3.8	9.1	16.7	132
B1														6.7					6.7	10.0	76.7	30
B2												4.2			79.2				4.2	4.2	8.3	24
B3															6.7	33.3		6.7	13.3	6.7	33.3	15

Source: UBS calculations from Moody's rating data.

the tranche ever had or the tranche's rating before its rating was withdrawn) are shown across the top. The percentages in the body of the exhibit show rating migration from the tranche's initial rating to its current rating. For example, 88% of tranches initially rated Aaa have remained Aaa, 2% have been downgraded to Aa1, 2% to Aa2, and so forth. The rightmost column in the exhibit shows how many tranches had a particular initial rating. For example, 1,018 CDO tranches were initially rated Aaa after eliminating insured, principal-protected, combo, and pari passu tranches.

Exhibit 3.5 gives a good picture of the distribution and extremes of ratings downgrades. For example, 93.6% of tranches initially rated Aaa have remained Aa3 or better. Only 1.2% of Aaa tranches have been downgraded below investment grade. And only two Aaa tranches (2/1,018 rounds to 0%) have been downgraded below B2. The paucity of Aaa CDO tranches falling below investment grade and below B2 in the exhibit should be of assurance to the majority of CDO investors who participate at this level of the CDO's capital structure. The Aaa rating category really seems to be a safe harbor rating, even for volatile CDOs.

The lowest rating to which each type of CDO has been downgraded is reported in Exhibit 3.6. For example, in the exhibit's top row, we see the lowest rating to which any arbitrage cash flow CDO tranche backed by U.S. high-yield bonds has been downgraded. The row shows these ratings according to the original rating of the tranche. Thus, the lowest rating a Aaa tranche has been downgraded to is B2. For Aa tranches the lowest rating is C, for A tranches the lowest rating is C, and so on.

In looking at the exhibit, remember that each cell in the CDO type and initial rating matrix displays the *worst* current rating. For example, U.S. arbitrage cash flow low-density structured finance CDOs have generally done well, but one Aaa tranche happens to have been downgraded to Caa1. On the other hand, it seems amazing to us, given how poorly they have fared in general, that the lowest a Aaa U.S. investment-grade arbitrage cash flow CBO has been downgraded to is A3.

So what have been the very worst CDOs? It's a tie between two U.S. high-yield bond CBO tranches that have both fallen 18 rating notches since issuance. From 1998 and 1999, respectively, these tranches both fell from Aa2 to C, Moody's lowest rating. Three more U.S. high-yield bond CDOs have fallen from Aa2 to Ca.

CDO "DEFAULTS" AND NEAR "DEFAULTS"

CDO default studies are extremely difficult. One reason is the private nature of the securities. Another reason is that even with perfect information, it is

EXHIBIT 3.6 Worst Current CDO Tranche Ratings, by CDO Type and Original Tranche Rating

	Aaa	Aa	A	Baa	Ba	B
U.S. ACF HYB	B2	C	C	C	C	C
U.S. ACF HYL	Aa2	Baa1	Ba2	Ca	C	Ca
U.S. ACF IGB	A3	B3	Caa3	Ca	Ca	Caa3
U.S. ACF Low-D SF	Caa1	Baa2	Ca	C	C	B2
U.S. ACF High-D SF	B2	Ca	C	C	C	
U.S. ACF CDO^2	Baa2	Baa3	Ca	C	C	
U.S. BS	Aaa	Aa2	A3	Ba3	Ba3	
U.S. Market Value	A2	Aa2	A3	Caa2	Ca	C
U.S. Syn Arb Managed	Aa1	A2	B1	Ba1	B2	
U.S. Syn Arb Static	Aa3	Baa1	Ba2	Caa2	C	B2
U.S. Syn BS	Ba2	C	C	C	C	C
Europe ACF HYB	Baa1	Aa2	Caa1	C	C	
Europe ACF HYL	Aaa	Aa3	A3	Baa3	Ba3	
Europe ACF IGB	Aaa	Aa3	Baa1	Ba2		
Europe ACF SF	Caa1	Aa3	A3	Caa3	Ca	
Europe BS	Ba1	A1	Ba1	Ba3	Caa2	
Europe BS SME Loans	Aaa	A2	A2	Baa3	Ba3	B2
Europe Syn Arb Managed	A1	Ba3	Ba1	Ca	Ba3	B3
Europe Syn Arb Static	Baa2	Ba3	Caa3	C	C	
Europe Syn BS	A3	Ba3	Caa2	Ca	Caa3	B3
Europe Syn SF	Aa3	Ba1	Ba1	B1	Ba1	Ca
Emerging Market	Aaa	A2	Baa2	Ca	Ba3	B2

Source: UBS calculations from Moody's rating data.

hard to determine whether a tranche has defaulted or is certain to default in the future. For example, it is often unclear whether a PIKing tranche is going to catch up on missed coupons and pay in full. It can also be unclear whether a non-PIKing performing tranche from a distressed CDO will pay back principal.

We take, as our proxy for "default," downgrades to ratings below B3: Caa1, Caa2, Caa3, Ca, and C. The Ca and C ratings are traditionally reserved by Moody's for defaulted credits. Thus, by including the Caa rating categories in our definition of default, we add the wounded to the count of the dead. Of the 3,933 tranches in our study, 331 tranches have "achieved" these ratings: 21 Caa1; 39 Caa2; 47 Caa3; 99 Ca; and 125 C.

Exhibit 3.7 shows the cumulative percent of "defaulted" CDO tranches by CDO type and rating. The second column of the exhibit shows that across all types of CDOs, 0.2% of Aaa tranches have been downgraded below B3. In other rating categories, the figures are 1.8% of Aa tranches, 3.7% of A tranches, 17.1% of Baa tranches, 21.8% of Ba tranches, and 59.4% of B tranches. This is the "lifetime" default rate of CDOs that have been outstanding between 1 to 10 years, for a weighted average of 4 years.

Exhibit 3.7 confirms the results of our earlier exhibits that looked at CDO downgrades by frequency and severity. U.S. arbitrage cash flow CDOs backed by high-yield and investment-grade bonds, and U.S. synthetic balance sheet CDOs all have high default rates. In addition, so do U.S. arbitrage cash flow high-diversity structured finance CDOs, U.S. CDOs of CDOs, and European arbitrage cash flow CDOs backed by high-yield bonds. In contrast, balance sheet cash flow CDOs, low diversity U.S. structured finance CDOs, U.S. managed synthetic arbitrage CDOs, high-yield loan-backed CDOs, and U.S. market value CDOs all have low default rates.

A more detailed look at the performance of different ratings within different types of CDOs is shown in our Exhibits 3.8 through 3.13. First we consider the Aaa tranches. Exhibit 3.8 shows that across all different types of CDOs and CDO vintages, 121 Aaa CDO tranches have been downgraded. Exhibit 3.9 shows that in percentage terms, across all types of CDOs and vintage years, 12% of Aaa CDOs have been downgraded. This statistic encompasses CDOs issued from 1996 through 2004, so the CDOs studied have been outstanding at least 1 year and as many as 10 years. The 12% "lifetime" downgrade rate for Aaa CDOs works out to a rate of 3% per year. Meanwhile, between 1970 and 2003, Moody's has downgraded Aaa corporates at a rate of 10% per year.

However, downgrade statistics vary greatly by type of CDO. Exhibit 3.9 shows that Aaa downgrades were most common among U.S. synthetic balance sheet CDOs (44% lifetime downgrades across all vintage years), U.S. high-yield bond CBOs (39%), European static synthetic arbitrage CDOs (38%), U.S. CDOs of CDOs (18%), and U.S. arbitrage cash flow high-diversity synthetic CDOs (18%). Yet, eight types of Aaa CDOs experienced 1% or fewer lifetime downgrades.

For Aaa CDO investors who are a little less sensitive to downgrades, we show the percent of Aaa CDO tranches downgraded below Baa3 in Exhibit 3.10. Twelve Aaa tranches have experience downgrades this severe, which is about 1% of all Aaa tranches. Exhibit 3.11 shows the less severe case of Aaa CDO tranches downgraded below Aa3. In total, 65 tranches have been downgraded from Aaa to Aa3. In percentage terms, such downgrades

EXHIBIT 3.7 Percent of CDO Tranche Defaults (Downgraded Below B3)

	All	U.S. ACF HYB	U.S. ACF HYL	U.S. ACF IGB	U.S. ACF Low-D SF	U.S. ACF High-D SF	U.S. ACF CDO^2	U.S. BS	U.S. Market Value	U.S. Syn Arb Managed	U.S. Syn Arb Static	U.S. Syn BS
Aaa	0.2	0.0	0.0	0.0	1.2	0.0	0.0	0.0	0.0	0.0	0.0	0.0
Aa	1.8	13.4	0.0	0.0	0.0	4.2	0.0	0.0	0.0	0.0	0.0	10.0
A	3.7	18.2	0.0	7.1	3.6	16.1	7.1	0.0	0.0	0.0	0.0	18.8
Baa	17.1	49.4	3.8	27.6	9.5	32.1	28.6	0.0	4.3	0.0	13.6	30.8
Ba	21.8	59.6	6.0	80.0	8.7	31.6	25.0	0.0	7.1	0.0	40.0	53.3
B	59.4	94.3	33.3	100.0	0.0	na	na	na	18.2	na	0.0	66.7

	Europe ACF HYB	Europe ACF HYL	Europe ACF IGB	Europe ACF SF	Europe BS	Europe BS SME Loans	Europe Syn Arb Managed	Europe Syn Arb Static	Europe Syn BS	Europe Syn SF	Emerging Market
Aaa	0.0	0.0	0.0	4.8	0.0	0.0	0.0	0.0	0.0	0.0	0.0
Aa	0.0	0.0	0.0	0.0	0.0	0.0	0.0	0.0	0.0	0.0	0.0
A	25.0	0.0	0.0	0.0	0.0	0.0	0.0	9.3	2.2	0.0	0.0
Baa	42.9	0.0	0.0	6.3	0.0	0.0	3.8	17.9	4.3	0.0	11.8
Ba	33.3	0.0	na	25.0	9.1	0.0	0.0	33.3	10.0	0.0	0.0
B	na	na	na	na	na	0.0	0.0	na	0.0	100.0	0.0

Source: UBS calculations from Moody's rating data.

EXHIBIT 3.8   Number of Aaa CDO Tranches Ever Downgraded, by Type of CDO and Vintage

	Cumulative Downgrades									
	1996	1997	1998	1999	2000	2001	2002	2003	2004	All Vintages
U.S. ACF HYB			6	28	9	2				45
U.S. ACF HYL			1							1
U.S. ACF IGB					2	2				4
U.S. ACF Low-D SF				1						1
U.S. ACF High-D SF				1	7	8				16
U.S. ACF CDO^2				1	2					3
U.S. BS										
U.S. Market Value				1						1
U.S. Syn Arb Managed						1	1			2
U.S. Syn Arb Static						3	1			4
U.S. Syn BS	1		1		2	3				7
Europe ACF HYB					2					2
Europe ACF HYL										
Europe ACF IGB										
Europe ACF SF				1				1		2
Europe BS					2					2
Europe BS SME Loans										
Europe Syn Arb Managed						1	1			2
Europe Syn Arb Static				1		8	10	3		22
Europe Syn BS			1		3	2				6
Europe Syn SF						1				1
Emerging Market										
Yearly Issuance	1	9	33	30	31	13	4			121

Source: UBS calculations from Moody's rating data.

were most common among U.S. synthetic balance sheet CDOs (31% lifetime downgrades), European static synthetic arbitrage CDOs (21%), U.S. high-yield bond CBOs (21%), U.S. arbitrage cash flow high-diversity CDOs (13%), and U.S. CDOs of CDOs (12%). Exhibit 3.11 also shows 10 types of Aaa CDOs that have experience 1% or fewer lifetime downgrades.

Exhibit 3.12 shows the percentage of tranches initially rated Aa that have been downgraded below Baa3. Exhibit 3.13 shows the percentage of tranches initially rated A and Baa that have been downgraded below B3.

EXHIBIT 3.9 Percent of Aaa CDO Tranches Ever Downgraded, by Type of CDO and Vintage

	Cumulative Downgrades									
	1996	1997	1998	1999	2000	2001	2002	2003	2004	All Vintages
U.S. ACF HYB	0	0	46	67	36	7	0	0	0	39
U.S. ACF HYL	0	0	7	0	0	0	0	0	0	0
U.S. ACF IGB			0	0	22	25	0	0	0	14
U.S. ACF Low-D SF				0	20	0	0	0	0	1
U.S. ACF High-D SF				100	54	44	0	0	0	18
U.S. ACF CDO^2				100	100	0	0	0	0	18
U.S. BS			0	0	0	0	0	0	0	0
U.S. Market Value				20	0	0	0	0	0	7
U.S. Syn Arb Managed					0	20	6		0	5
U.S. Syn Arb Static						75	9	0	0	17
U.S. Syn BS		100	50	0	33	75		0	0	44
Europe ACF HYB				0	33	0		0		20
Europe ACF HYL						0	0	0	0	0
Europe ACF IGB						0	0			0
Europe ACF SF				100			0	17	0	10
Europe BS			0	0	22	0	0	0	0	6
Europe BS SME Loans				0	0	0	0	0	0	0
Europe Syn Arb Managed						20	8	0	0	5
Europe Syn Arb Static				100		89	43	14	0	38
Europe Syn BS			100	0	20	17	0	0	0	11
Europe Syn SF			0	0	0	33	0	0	0	1
Emerging Market	0	0	0	0			0			0
Yearly Issuance	0	20	22	34	23	21	7	2	0	12

Source: UBS calculations from Moody's rating data.

EXHIBIT 3.10 Percent of Aaa CDO Tranches Ever Downgraded Below Baa3, by Type of CDO and Vintage

	Cumulative Downgrades Below Baa3									
	1996	1997	1998	1999	2000	2001	2002	2003	2004	All Vintages
U.S. ACF HYB	0	0	8	10	4	0	0	0	0	5
U.S. ACF HYL		0	0	0	0	0	0	0	0	0
U.S. ACF IGB			0	0	0	0	0	0	0	0
U.S. ACF Low-D SF				0	20	0	0	0	0	1
U.S. ACF High-D SF				0	15	0	0	0	0	2
U.S. ACF CDO^2				0	0	0	0	0	0	0
U.S. BS			0	0	0	0	0			0
U.S. Market Value				0	0	0	0	0	0	0
U.S. Syn Arb Managed					0	0	0	0	0	0
U.S. Syn Arb Static						0	0	0	0	0
U.S. Syn BS		0	0	0	0	25	0	0	0	6
Europe ACF HYB				0	0	0	0	0	0	0
Europe ACF HYL						0	0	0	0	0
Europe ACF IGB						0	0	0	0	0
Europe ACF SF				100		0	0	0	0	5
Europe BS			0	0	11	0	0	0	0	3
Europe BS SME Loans					0	0	0	0	0	0
Europe Syn Arb Managed						0	0	0	0	0
Europe Syn Arb Static				0		0	0	0	0	0
Europe Syn BS			0	0	0	0	0	0	0	0
Europe Syn SF			0		0	0	0	0	0	0
Emerging Market	0	0	0	0			0	0	0	0
Yearly Issuance	0	0	2	5	4	1	0	0	0	1

Source: UBS calculations from Moody's rating data.

EXHIBIT 3.11 Percent of Aaa CDO Tranches Ever Downgraded Below Aa3, by Type of CDO and Vintage

	Cumulative Downgrades Below Aa3									
	1996	1997	1998	1999	2000	2001	2002	2003	2004	All Vintages
U.S. ACF HYB	0	0	23	43	12	0	0	0	0	21
U.S. ACF HYL		0	0	0	0	0	0	0	0	0
U.S. ACF IGB			0	0	11	13	0	0	0	7
U.S. ACF Low-D SF				0	20	0	0	0	0	1
U.S. ACF High-D SF				100	38	28	0	0	0	13
U.S. ACF CDO^2				100	50	0	0	0	0	12
U.S. BS			0	0	0	0				0
U.S. Market Value				20	0	0				7
U.S. Syn Arb Managed					0	0				0
U.S. Syn Arb Static					0	0	0			0
U.S. Syn BS		0	0	0	33	75	0	0	0	31
Europe ACF HYB				0	17	0	0	0		10
Europe ACF HYL						0	0	0	0	0
Europe ACF IGB						0	0	0		0
Europe ACF SF				100			0	17	0	10
Europe BS			0	0	11	0	0	0	0	3
Europe BS SME Loans						0	0	0	0	0
Europe Syn Arb Managed					0	20	0	0	0	2
Europe Syn Arb Static				100		78	13	5	0	21
Europe Syn BS			0	0	7	8	0	0	0	4
Europe Syn SF			0		0	0	0	0	0	0
Emerging Market	0	0	0	0			0			0
Yearly Issuance	0	0	7	24	12	12	2	1	0	6

Source: UBS calculations from Moody's rating data.

EXHIBIT 3.12 Percent of Aa CDO Tranches Ever Downgraded Below Baa3, by Type of CDO and Vintage

	Cumulative Downgrades Below Baa3									
	1996	1997	1998	1999	2000	2001	2002	2003	2004	All Vintages
U.S. ACF HYB	25	47	46	50	14	0	0	0	0	35
U.S. ACF HYL	0	0	0	0	0	0	0	0	0	0
U.S. ACF IGB			0	0	25	22	0	0	0	15
U.S. ACF Low-D SF				0	0	0	0	0	0	0
U.S. ACF High-D SF					63	37	0	0	0	17
U.S. ACF CDO^2						0	0	0	0	0
U.S. BS							0			0
U.S. Market Value		0	0		0	0	0	0	0	0
U.S. Syn Arb Managed						0	0		0	0
U.S. Syn Arb Static					0	0	0	0	0	0
U.S. Syn BS			100		40	33			0	40
Europe ACF HYB				0	0	0	0	0	0	0
Europe ACF HYL						0	0	0	0	0
Europe ACF IGB							0	0	0	0
Europe ACF SF				0			0	0	0	0
Europe BS			0		0	0		0	0	0
Europe BS SME Loans						0	0	0	0	0
Europe Syn Arb Managed						20	0	0	0	3
Europe Syn Arb Static						40	5	0	0	4
Europe Syn BS				0	17	11	0	0	0	7
Europe Syn SF		0	100		0	0	0	0	0	1
Emerging Market	0	0	0	0	0	0	0	0	0	0
Yearly Issuance	14	29	28	21	16	14	1	0	0	7

Source: UBS calculations from Moody's rating data.

EXHIBIT 3.13 Percent of A and Baa CDO Tranches Ever Downgraded Below B3, by Type of CDO and Vintage

	Cumulative Downgrades Below B3									
	1996	1997	1998	1999	2000	2001	2002	2003	2004	All Vintages
U.S. ACF HYB	50	94	61	71	25	0	0	0	0	42
U.S. ACF HYL	33	67	16	0	0	0	0	0	0	2
U.S. ACF IGB			0	33	25	31	0	0	0	21
U.S. ACF Low-D SF				0	25	10	19	0	0	7
U.S. ACF High-D SF				100	93	63	14	0	0	28
U.S. ACF CDO^2				100	67	14	0	0	0	18
U.S. BS		0	0	0	0	0	0	0	0	0
U.S. Market Value			0	7	0	0	0	0	0	2
U.S. Syn Arb Managed					0	0	0	0	0	0
U.S. Syn Arb Static					50	29	0	0	0	7
U.S. Syn BS			29	0	20	60			0	24
Europe ACF HYB				0	60	20				36
Europe ACF HYL						0	0	0	0	0
Europe ACF IGB						0	0	0		0
Europe ACF SF				50		0	0	0	0	4
Europe BS			0	0	0	0	0	0	0	0
Europe BS SME Loans						0	0	0	0	0
Europe Syn Arb Managed					0	20	0	0	0	2
Europe Syn Arb Static				0	67	47	0	0	0	13
Europe Syn BS			0	0	10	5	0	0	0	3
Europe Syn SF				0	0	0	0	0	0	0
Emerging Market	0	14	33	0	0	0	0	0	0	7
Yearly Issuance	43	69	31	30	22	15	3	0	0	11

Source: UBS calculations from Moody's rating data.

We picked these combinations of initial ratings and downgrade thresholds to focus on severe downgrades. Once again, we see the safety of Aaa tranches in Exhibits 3.8 through 3.11. Aa tranches have also suffered few downgrades below Baa3. But the relative abundance, in certain types of CDOs, of A and Baa tranches falling below B3 in Exhibit 3.13 is a concern.

SUMMARY

Overall, the frequency and severity of CDO downgrades have been equivalent to those of corporates. However, the performance of specific types of CDOs has been extremely variable. As of January 2006, the outstanding performers have been U.S. and European cash flow balance sheet CDOs, low-diversity U.S. and European structured finance CDOs, U.S. and European high-yield loan-backed CLOs, and U.S. market value CDOs. The good performance of structured finance and loan-backed CDOs is a result of more timely and more conservative collateral ratings not being given credit in the CDO rating process. The good performance of market value CDOs is a result of their being naturally resistant to downgrade. We also admit our inability to explain the good performance of cash flow balance sheet CDOs.

The poor CDO performers have been U.S. arbitrage cash flow CDOs backed by high-yield and investment-grade bonds, U.S. synthetic balance sheet CDOs, and European static synthetic arbitrage CDOs. For bond-backed CDOs, the problem was that low collateral spreads tempted CDO managers into lower-quality assets to achieve targeted CDO equity returns. For synthetic CDOs, the problem was the use of the CDO structure to offload poor credit risks.

The difference in good- and poor-performing CDOs often reflects the fundamental conflict of interest in the CDO structure that must be managed. This conflict becomes apparent in arbitrage CDOs when collateral spreads are low and managers stretch into riskier assets to meet CDO equity return targets. CDO debt investors find they are financing riskier assets without any increase in CDO protections. This was the case with many types of poor performing CDO types. In contrast, when collateral spreads are wide, this conflict of interest remains concealed. Thus, arbitrage CDO managers can be pickier about credit and still meet CDO equity return targets.

The importance of collateral yield is well illustrated in the histories of CDOs of assets that have experienced high default rates and significant spread widening. The performance of emerging market CDOs and CDOs of CDOs radically changed from poor to good over their histories as CDO managers took advantage of wide collateral spreads to select good credit assets.

Two

Developments in Synthetic CDOs

CHAPTER 4

ABS CDO Collateral Choices: Cash, ABCDS, and the ABX

CDO managers can now take on subprime mortgage risk in three different forms:

- Traditional cash tranches of subprime mortgage deals.
- Single-name credit default swaps that reference cash tranches.
- Indices of credit default swaps.

The introduction in 2005 of *asset-backed credit default swaps* (ABCDS) and the ABX index of ABCDS has profoundly affected mezzanine ABS CDOs. ABCDS has provided much needed collateral to CDO managers, boosted issuance, and enabled quicker ramp-up of larger mezzanine ABS CDOs. Accommodating this synthetic collateral has led to changes in the mezzanine ABS CDO structure which have reduced funding costs and improved equity tranche arbitrage. (See Chapter 5 for details on the hybrid CDO structure.)

In this chapter, we explain the importance of ABCDS to mezzanine ABS CDOs and the basic workings of the ABCDS and ABX contracts. We look at how the three different forms of subprime mortgage risk listed above differ and what drives their relative spreads. We explain spread differences from two different perspectives: (1) given their credit and cash flow characteristics, how the three forms of subprime risk should trade relative to one another and (2) given supply and demand technicals, how the three forms of subprime risk actually trade relative to one another. Next, we show the difference in mezzanine ABS CDO equity arbitrage returns with cash and synthetic assets. Finally, we address the role of the ABX in ABS CDOs.

GROWTH OF THE SUBPRIME SYNTHETIC MARKET

While one-off, highly customized transactions were done much earlier, the single-name ABCDS market grew rapidly after the June 2005 release of the

International Swaps and Derivatives Association (ISDA) standard pay-as-you go (PAUG) template. The ABX Index, an index of 20 credit default swaps, debuted in January 2006. Trading of standardized tranches off the index debuted in January 2007, although there has already been considerable activity in customized tranches.

The need for ABCDS arises directly from the growth of the subprime mortgage market. Exhibit 4.1 tells the story. From 1995 to 2003, Agency (GNMA, Fannie Mae, and Freddie Mac) share of total mortgage originations was 75% to 85%. But it dropped to 54% in 2004, 45% in 2005, and 43% in Q1–Q3 2006. This declining issuance share reflects the fact that while rates rose and prime mortgage refinancing abated, the subprime and Alt-A markets continued to grow. To date in 2006, the subprime market represents 39% of non-Agency issuance, whereas it only accounted for 30% in 2002.

Looking at sheer size, the subprime market grew from $48 billion in 2000 to $465 billion in 2005. In addition, the margin between subprime and prime lending shrunk 50 to 75 basis points the past few years, as originators tried to maintain volumes. Both of these trends pressured subprime loan originators, conduits, and securitizers to more effectively hedge the credit risk of their warehouses and pipelines by buying protection on subprime mortgages via ABCDS. These hedging needs were a major demand driver in the original growth of the ABCDS market in 2005. Later, macroeconomic hedge funds looking to short the housing market became important buyers of protection, and have at times dominated the market. From the point of view of protection selling, the supply of single-name ABCDS credit protection has always been driven by ABS CDOs.

IMPORTANCE OF ABCDS TO CDO MANAGERS

ABCDS is very important to mezzanine ABS CDOs. Prior to the release of the PAUG template in June 2005, mezzanine ABS CDOs averaged $300 to $400 million in deal size, and took an average of eight to nine months to ramp. However, the demand to buy protection in the single-name ABCDS market has enable CDO managers to ramp mezzanine ABS CDO deals in two to five weeks, with sizes as much as three times that of pre-June 2005 deals. In other words, CDO managers can now ramp deals by assembling a portfolio of single-name ABCDS, on which they have sold protection, instead of accumulating a portfolio of subprime cash bonds.

In addition to reducing ramping time, ABCDS enables greater mezzanine ABS CDO issuance, as dealers are no longer constrained by the amount of available cash collateral. Through early November, 2006, $42 billion of mezzanine ABS CDOs were issued, up from $28 billion for all of 2005. This deal volume could not have occurred in the absence of the ABCDS market.

EXHIBIT 4.1 Growth of the Subprime Market

Year	Production		Share (%)		Nonagency			Subprime/Nonagency (%)
	Agency	Nonagency	Agency	Nonagency	Subprime	Alt-A	Jumbo & Other	
1995	269,132	48,926	84.6	15.4	17,772	498	30,656	36.3
1996	370,648	69,893	84.1	15.9	30,769	1,803	37,321	44.0
1997	367,884	119,132	75.5	24.5	56,921	6,518	55,694	47.8
1998	725,952	203,211	78.1	21.9	75,830	21,236	106,145	37.3
1999	685,078	147,899	82.2	17.8	55,852	12,023	80,025	37.8
2000	479,011	126,154	79.2	20.8	48,145	14,696	63,313	38.2
2001	1,087,499	267,320	80.3	19.7	87,053	11,374	168,894	32.6
2002	1,444,426	413,955	77.7	22.3	122,681	53,463	237,811	29.6
2003	2,131,953	586,217	78.4	21.6	194,959	74,151	317,107	33.3
2004	1,018,871	864,162	54.1	45.9	362,549	158,586	343,027	42.0
2005	966,319	1,191,310	44.8	55.2	465,036	332,323	393,950	39.0
2006 Q1–Q3	675,363	868,392	43.7	56.3	342,373	269,470	256,549	39.4

Note: MBS are backed by 1 to 4 family mortgage loans. Agency CMO/REMICs are backed by FNMA, FHLMC or GNMA collateral. Starting January 2001, Nonagency MBS include private-label Jumbo and Alt-A transactions, plus mortgage-related ABS, including subprime HEL, second liens, HELOCs, high LTV loans and manufactured housing loans. ABS data pre-2001 includes some mortgage-related collateral.

Source: Inside MBS & ABS, based on SEC filings, and industry surveys.

Exhibit 4.2 shows that through early November 2006, subprime origination totaled $415 billion. The exhibit also demonstrates that only 2.9% of this amount was rated BBB+/BBB/BBB–, and only 1.7% was BBB and BBB–, those two ratings being most desired by mezzanine ABS CDO managers. That is, of the 2.9% in the BBB range, 1.2% was BBB+, 0.9% was BBB, and 0.8% was BBB–. In fact, if every BBB and BBB– produced in 2006 ($7.2 billion) went into mezzanine ABS CDOs, and this segment of the market comprised only 65% of their collateral, mezzanine ABS CDO capacity would only have been $11 billion ($7.2 billion/0.65). And adding all $5.0 billion of BBB+ collateral would only have produced $19 billion ($12.2 billion/0.65) in total CDO volume.

In fact, of the $42 billion in deal volume through early November 2006, ABCDS underlyings constituted $31 billion. This has allowed for sev-

EXHIBIT 4.2 2006 Home Equity Issuance by Ratings as of 11/10/06

S&P Ratings	Amount	Total
AAA	311,178,671,010	75.0%
AA+	18,123,057,003	4.4%
AA	16,913,160,009	4.1%
AA–	6,715,993,011	1.6%
A+	6,626,660,031	1.6%
A	6,965,487,069	1.7%
A–	5,015,548,041	1.2%
BBB+	5,041,978,058	1.2%
BBB	3,767,798,061	0.9%
BBB–	3,374,821,081	0.8%
BB+	1,889,368,433	0.5%
BB	828,987,018	0.2%
BB–	40,294,001	0.0%
B+	18,966,000	0.0%
B	34,576,002	0.0%
B–	26,861,003	0.0%
N.A.	27,142,279,009	6.5%
NR	1,008,332,003	0.2%
Grand Total	414,712,836,843	100.0%

Source: MCM, UBS CDO Research Calculations.

EXHIBIT 4.3 Residential B&C: Percentage & Rating Distribution in ABS CDOs

CDO Vintage	Resi B&C and Subprime/ High LTV	Rating Distribution				
		A	BBB+	BBB	BBB–	BB
Early 2005	65%–70%	30	22	22	21	5
Late 2006	85%	2	5	52	38	3

Source: UBS CDO Research.

eral changes in the composition of CDO deals, as illustrated in Exhibit 4.3. The exhibit clearly shows two major changes in mezzanine ABS CDOs.

1. The residential B&C collateral in mezzanine ABS CDOs has increased. The percent of residential B&C and subprime/high LTV collateral in mezzanine ABS CDOs has historically ranged from 65% to 70%. Obtaining this collateral was so much of an issue that equivalently rated collateral from other asset classes was also used extensively. Thanks to the use of ABCDS, mezzanine ABS CDOs are now 85% residential B&C.
2. The ratings distribution of collateral now used in mezzanine ABS CDOs is more concentrated in BBB and BBB–. This is very different from the case historically, as cash bonds were simply unavailable. In early 2005, approximately 25% to 30% of CDO collateral was rated A, 65% to 70% rated BBB, and 5% to 10% rated BB. In a sample of recent CDOs, we found 2% of the collateral rated A, 3% rated BB, 5% rated BBB+, and 90% rated BBB or BBB–.

We believe these points are very important in explaining the explosion in mezzanine ABS CDO volumes in the face of static subprime issuance. Moreover, the use of synthetic assets in ABS CDOs bodes well for the future growth of this market in a world in which home price appreciation may slow, cash out refinancings slump, and subprime origination drop.

Not only does the synthetic market allow for greater volumes, it also gives the CDO manager more flexibility in managing the deal. New issuance is very light at certain times, and a CDO manager may not necessarily be able to find issuer names that he likes. The ABCDS market allows ABS CDO managers to sell protection on subprime mortgage tranches of their choosing, as long as they find willing buyers of protection.

ABCDS

The explosive growth of the single-name ABCDS market can be directly traced to ISDA's June 2005 release of a standard PAUG template for documenting single-name ABCDS trades. This standardized the documentation process for single-name ABCDS trades and eliminated most of the basis risk that can result from putting on offsetting trades with different terms. As a parallel, ISDA's 1999 publication of a standard corporate CDS template enabled the tremendous growth of that market, from next-to-nothing in 1999 to an estimated $2.5 trillion notional in 2005.

The ISDA PAUG template defines three basic floating amount and credit events:[1]

- *Failure to pay.* The underlying reference obligation fails to make a scheduled interest or principal payment.
- *Writedown.* The principal component of the underlying reference obligation is written down and deemed irrecoverable.
- *Distressed Ratings Downgrade.* The underlying reference obligation is downgraded to a rating of Caa2/CCC or lower.

Since an ABS is typically issued from a bankruptcy remote trust, the template focuses on issues related to cash flow adequacy, as opposed to potential bankruptcy. In a single-name ABCDS, the reference obligation is always a specified security, identified by CUSIP.

In a single-name ABCDS, the protection buyer pays the protection seller a periodic fixed CDS premium in exchange for protection. Exhibit 4.4 illustrates a basic single-name ABCDS transaction for a subprime ABS. The protection seller is contractually responsible for covering any cashflow short-

EXHIBIT 4.4   Single-Name PAUG ABCDS for ABS Rated BBB+

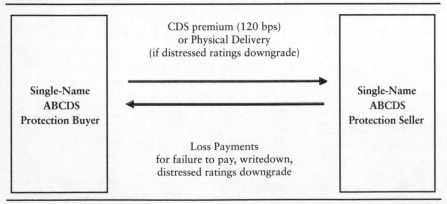

Source: UBS CDO Research.

---

[1] Maturity Extension was a credit event in the original June 2005 PAUG template; it was removed in January 2006.

falls that result from failures to pay or writedowns. For writedowns that are ultimately reversed (if the performance of the underlying reference obligation improves), the protection buyer is required to return the writedown payments to the protection seller. Settlement for failure to pay or writedown credit events is assumed to be PAUG, but can be changed to physical delivery (i.e., the protection buyer tenders the cash subprime security to the protection seller in exchange for par) at the option of the protection buyer. A distressed ratings downgrade can only be settled in physical form.

The PAUG template includes three additional provisions covering (1) how to handle interest payment shortfalls for an ABS with an available funds cap (AFC); (2) whether to make an initial exchange of cash when a reference obligation is trading at a premium or discount to par; and (3) whether the CDS premium will step up if the underlying's 10% cleanup call is not exercised. The options for each provision are:

1. *AFC interest payment shortfall.* The options are (a) variable cap applicable (which would cover AFC risk up to LIBOR plus the protection premium the buyer pays each period); (b) fixed cap applicable (which would cover AFC Risk only up to the protection premium); or (c) cap not applicable. This last option corresponds to the long cash ABS position, as the protection seller (equivalent to the cash bond purchaser) would essentially pay the protection buyer the entire coupon if the underlying cash instrument does not pay interest. If it is necessary for the protection seller to make an interest shortfall payment, that payment is netted against the protection premium the buyer pays the protection seller. The protection seller is better off with either of the first two alternatives. Market practice is to stipulate "fixed cap applicable," as it allows the seller of protection to limit his gross interest protection payments to the protection premium. After netting, the protection seller never has to make a payment to the protection buyer for an interest shortfall; he is only at risk for the incoming protection premium.

2. *Initial cash exchange for discount/premium reference obligations.* The options are (a) initial cash exchange or (b) no initial cash exchange. Single-name ABCDS market practice is no initial cash exchange. Instead, the protection premium is set in recognition of the premium or discount of the underlying. That is, the protection premium tends to decrease if the cash underlying is trading at a premium and increase if the cash underlying is trading at a discount.

3. *10% cleanup call stepup.* The options are (a) applicable or (b) non-applicable. If "applicable" is chosen, the CDS premium will step up unless the protection buyer exercises the option to cancel the CDS within five days of noncall notification. If "not applicable" is chosen,

then no stepup in CDS premium will occur and the CDS cannot be canceled. The market standard is coupon stepup applicable.

To review, the standard choices for most single-name ABCDS are: fixed cap applicable, no initial cash flow exchange, and coupon stepup applicable. The terms "premium squeeze to zero" and "par trade" are often used interchangeably with the terms "fixed cap applicable" and "no initial cash flow exchange." Since the CDO is the seller of protection under ABCDS, fixed cap applicable (limiting the seller's payment in an event of an AFC shortfall) is CDO friendly. No initial cash exchange flow is also CDO friendly because the CDO does not wish to buy assets at a premium.

THE ABX INDEX

The ABX.HE indices began trading on January 19, 2006. The ABX.HE indices consist of five separate subindices, one for each of the rating categories AAA, AA, A, BBB, and BBB–. Appropriately, the names for each of the subindices are ABX.HE.AAA, ABX.HE.AA, ABX.HE.A, ABX.HE.BBB, and ABX.HE.BBB–. Each set of indices are backed by 20 cash subprime deals, with each deal represented once in each subindex. Thus, the BBB tranche of each of the 20 included subprime deals will be in the ABX.HE.BBB. A new set of ABX indices is launched every six months on January 19 and July 19 of each year. These are referred to as index "roll dates."

In order for a subprime deal to be eligible for inclusion in the semiannual ABX.HE indices, the deal must be in excess of $500 million and:

- Have a weighted average FICO score of no more than 660 as of its issuance date.
- Consist of at least 90% first lien loans.
- Include tranches with ratings of AAA, AA, A, BBB and BBB–.
- Have issued the five required tranches within the six months prior to the applicable semiannual roll dates (e.g., all deals included in the July 19, 2006 launch issued the five required tranches between January 20, 2006 and July 19, 2006).
- Have an average life at issuance (based on deal pricing speeds) of at least five years for the AAA tranche and at least four years for the other four required tranches.
- Have the 25th of each month as the scheduled interest payment date for all five required tranches.
- Bear interest at a floating rate, with the base index being one-month LIBOR for all five required tranches.

- Have ratings from Moody's and S&P for each of the five required tranches.
- Have the identity and principal economic terms of each of the five required tranches listed on Bloomberg.

Each set of semiannual ABX indices will consist of one deal from each of the "top 20" issuers so long as the issuer has deals that meet the above criteria. The "top 20" issuers consist of the 20 largest issuers, based on total issuance volume for the six month period prior to the index roll date. For example, selection of the "top 20" issuers for the set of indices launched on July 19, 2006 was based on issuance volumes for the six-month period from mid-January to mid-July 2006. The choice of which specific deal to include from an issuer is based on a poll of the 15 participating consortium dealers, but limited to the selection of the issuer's two largest deals that meet the above deal criteria. If more than four deals of the "top 20" have the same originator, or more than six of them have the same servicer, deals from the "top 20" will be replaced with deals from the next five issuers (i.e., those ranked 21 to 25 by issuance volume).

FUNDAMENTAL CONTRACTUAL DIFFERENCES— SINGLE-NAME ABCDS/ABX INDEX/CASH

There are some notable differences in features between single-name ABCDS and the ABX. For one thing, the ABX index PAUG contract does not include "distressed ratings downgrade" as a condition of default. Secondly, the ABX PAUG contract does not allow for physical settlement; all settlement is PAUG. Finally, the ABX PAUG contract stipulates initial payment, fixed cap applicable, and coupon stepup not applicable. This contrasts with the bulk of the single-name ABCDS trades which have stipulated no initial payment, fixed cap applicable and coupon stepup applicable.

Now we will explore how the cash, single-name ABCDS, and the ABX should trade *vis-à-vis* each other. We first look at how the following contractual differences affect relative spreads:

- Funding—cash bonds require funding, single-name ABCDS and the ABX do not.
- Termination option on ABCDS; no stepup provisions on the ABX.
- Differences in caps on interest shortfalls.
- Differences in up-front payment arrangements.
- Distressed ratings downgrade on ABCDS.

We explore each of these in turn, and show that some of these effects should make cash tighter than ABCDS and the ABX index, while some effects work in the opposite direction. Our results are summarized in Exhibit 4.5. After we discuss each of these factors, we look at the supply/demand considerations that have come to dominate these markets and cause spread relationships to be what they are.

Funding

The most important differential is that the cash bonds require funding, but single-name ABCDS and the ABX do not. This feature, taken in isolation, suggests that the synthetic should trade tighter than the cash. How do we value this? A few possibilities are detailed in Exhibit 4.6.

If the marginal buyer is a real money account, with a choice of (1) buying the cash bond or (2) buying the synthetic, and investing the money at LIBOR, there is no reason for any spread differential. However, marginal buyers are rarely real money accounts; they are more typically hedge funds, basing their analysis on a risk-adjusted return on equity. Many analysts look at the value of the funding by equating the return on equity for a cash and synthetic position. In Exhibit 4.6, we show cash spread, repo rate, and haircut (hc) for a financed cash position, and the margin applicable on synthetic trades. We assume the haircut for financing a BBB cash position is 20%, and the margin applicable to synthetic trades is 7%. As shown in Exhibit 4.6, BBB cash trades at [LIBOR+130]. Investors can finance up to 80% of the position (20% haircut) at [LIBOR + 20], thus, the return on the 20% equity investment on this position = 11.02%. Intuitively, the investor:

- *Earns* [LIBOR+130] spread on the *entire* BBB position.

EXHIBIT 4.5 Summary of Differences Affecting Cash, ABX, and CDS Basis

Feature	Effect		
	Pushes ABX Wider/Tighter vs. Cash	Pushes ABCDS Wider/Tighter vs. Cash	Pushes ABCDS Wider/Tighter vs. ABX
Funding	Tighter	Tighter	0
Coupon stepup	Wider	Wider	Wider
Cap treatment	Tighter	Tighter	0
Intial cash flow exchange	0	Tighter (minor)	Tighter (minor)
Distressed rating downgrade	0	Wider (minor)	Wider (minor)

Source: UBS CDO Research.

EXHIBIT 4.6 Value of Funded and Synthetic Positions

Rating Level	Cash Spread	Repo Rate	Haircut	Synthetic Margins	Return on Equity		Risk-Adjusted Measure		Unfunded SS
					Breakeven CDS Premium ROE Method	FV (Cash – CDS) ROE Method	Breakeven CDS Premium RA Method	FV (Cash – CDS) RA Method	FV (Cash – CDS) w/ Unfunded Super Senior
AAA	23	3	4	2	10.1	12.9	20.1	2.9	12.0
AA	30	6	6	4	16.2	13.8	24.4	5.6	12.0
A	42	10	10	5	16.5	25.5	33.0	9.0	12.0
BBB	130	20	20	7	39.9	90.1	114.0	16.0	12.0
BBB–	240	25	20	9	99.0	141.0	220.0	20.0	12.0

Source: UBS CDO Research.

■ *Pays* [LIBOR+20 bps] on *80%* of the BBB position.

With LIBOR = 5.32, we have

$$ROE = [(((L + 1.30) - ((1 - hc) \times (L + 0.20)))/hc)] = 11.02\%$$

This produces a 11.02% ROE.

To earn the same return on equity on a 7% synthetic margin, the spread on the synthetic need only be 40 bps ("Return on Equity, Breakeven CDS Premium" column and the BBB row). The difference between the +130 cash spread and the +40 breakeven synthetic spread is 90 bps (Return on Equity, FV (Cash-CDS) column and the BBB row). The problem with this analysis is that risk on the two positions is not nearly equivalent; the cash position has 20% equity, the synthetic 7% equity. This suggests that investors are willing to use a very aggressive 14.3× leverage on the CDS position.

The more rational way to look at this is via a risk-adjusted position. We formulate this by asking, if you were required to hold the same equity for a synthetic position as for a cash position, *what is the required synthetic spread?* For the BBBs, the answer is 130 bps cash spread minus the 16 bps differential to cash (Risk-Adjusted Measure, FV (Cash-CDS) column, BBB row) for a value of 114 bps (Risk-Adjusted Measure, Breakeven CDS premium column, BBB row). Intuitively, the differential arises because a cash investor bears the financing penalty, which is the [repo spread × the maximum amount you can finance] (thus 16 bps financing penalty = 20 bps on the 80% of the deal that can be financed). We see this risk-adjusted return comparison as a far better way than ROE to look at the value of funded versus unfunded positions.

Is the marginal buyer a CDO? In that case, the synthetic portion can be sold as an unfunded super senior. The unfunded super senior trades at a spread of 18 to 20 bps, which is 12 bps better than spreads on the funded bond. Thus, using synthetic collateral for part of the deal allows 12 bps better funding. This is shown in the last column of Exhibit 4.6. At the BBB and BBB− level, this is the binding constraint, because these CDOs have gobbled up close to 100% of this collateral.

We argue that synthetic spreads will be the determined by CDO buying at the BBB and BBB− rating levels. Thus for the BBB and BBB−s, the value of the unfunded super senior determines the fair value between cash and synthetic versions of the asset. This suggests that cash should trade 12 bps wider than synthetics. For higher-rated tranches, we use the risk-adjusted methodology to determine that AA cash paper should be 6 bps wider than the synthetic, and A-rated cash paper should be 9 bps wider than the synthetic.

Treatment at the Call

As mentioned earlier, there are two ways to treat the coupon stepup: "applicable" and "nonapplicable." Single-name ABCDS contracts usually contain a "coupon stepup applicable" clause. This gives the ABCDS protection buyer a one time right to terminate the contract within five days of the contract hitting its coupon stepup trigger. If exercised, there is no termination payment in either direction. If the protection buyer does not terminate the contract within five days, then the contract continues, but with the protection buyer paying a stepped up CDS premium for the rest of the contract's life.

Let's briefly consider this option. If the deal is performing well, it is likely to be called. If the deal is performing poorly, the buyer of protection will want to remain in the deal, as writedowns will likely be much higher than the stepup coupon. There are some "in between" cases where the protection buyer may opt to terminate (i.e., the deal is not called, but losses will be low enough that continued protection payments will be higher than expected writedowns). This option is valuable to the protection buyer, therefore single-name CDS should trade wider than the cash or the ABX.

Partially offsetting this, the ABX Index stipulates that the coupon stepup is "not applicable." This means the protection buyer of the ABX index does not have to pay the stepup coupon after the call date if the deal is not called and he will get protection at the original premium. Again, if the deal is performing well, it is likely to be called; if performing poorly, the bond could be completely written down by the call date. However, there will be scenarios in which collateral losses are high enough that the deal is not called, but low enough that the bond has not been written completely down. In such cases, the buyer of BBB protection does not have to pay the stepup coupon. All else being equal—this should suggest the ABX trades wider than the cash.

This feature, taken in isolation, suggests that both single-name ABCDS and the ABX should be wider than the cash (which is reflected in Exhibit 4.5). Moreover, the termination option in a single-name ABCDS should be worth slightly more than the ABX without the termination feature, pushing the ABCDS wider to the ABX.

Cap Treatment

There are also minor basis differences caused by the differential cap treatment. Both single-name ABCDS and the ABX specify a "fixed cap" arrangement. This means that if there is an interest shortfall, the protection seller's payment to the protection buyer is limited to the CDS premium. The net payment amount, then, can never be a payment from the protection seller to the protection buyer. An interest shortfall simply reduces the premium the protection buyer pays the production seller. As noted earlier, in a cash bond, if there is an interest shortfall, the investor (protection seller) bears the full cost of both the premium above LIBOR and the LIBOR component of the coupon. In CDS documentation, the "interest shortfall cap not applicable" would have the same economic consequences as owning the bond directly (i.e., the protection seller pays the protection buyer the full amount of the cash interest shortfall). Consequently, sellers of CDS protection do a bit better in the "fixed cap" arrangement. This suggests that CDS protection sellers should collect less of a premium than cash spreads, hence, as reflected in Exhibit 4.5, ABCDS and the ABX should trade tighter than cash.

Initial Cash Exchange

Both the ABX indices and cash securities have their coupons set at inception, and the price on these securities will fluctuate. In the single-name ABCDS market, there is no initial cash flow exchange; the coupon is set to then current market conditions. Single-name ABCDS are much easier to use in a CDO deal, as there is no markup or markdown from par. Since CDOs are primarily sellers of single-name protection, these provisions will, at the margin, drive spreads marginally tighter in the single-name ABCDS versus cash and the ABX.

Distressed Ratings Downgrade

Distressed ratings downgrade is a credit event allowing physical settlement in the single-name ABCDS market, but not in the ABX market. A distressed ratings downgrade occurs if any rating agency downgrades the ABS tranche to CCC/Caa2 or below, or withdraws its rating. This credit event gives the buyer of protection the option of delivering the security, and getting paid out at par on the ABCDS. The existence of this additional option suggests that the single-name ABCDS should sell wider than cash or ABX. But it is important to realize that unless there are huge cash market dislocations, the distressed downgrade option has limited value. If the bond has performed poorly enough to experience a downgrade to a distressed level (CCC), writedowns are likely and just a matter of time. The net result will be very similar if the exposure is held in CDS or in physical form. Since this is an option, the buyer of protection is under no obligation to deliver the bond; if the bond is not delivered, writedowns occur in the normal course of events. Since we think distressed ratings downgrade is a minor benefit to protection buyers, we put it as a minor spread widening factor for single-name ABCDS and ABX in Exhibit 4.5.

We have shown that there are a number of contractual differences between cash, single-name ABCDS, and ABX, which deliver mixed results as to where these three instruments should trade vis-à-vis each other. On one hand, the fact that the cash needs to be financed suggests that it should be wider than either the ABX or single-name ABCDS. However, both the ABX and single-name ABCDS grant advantages to the seller (buyer of protection) to either terminate the contract or avoid paying the stepup amount. That should make the cash tighter than the synthetic. Other differences—in cap treatment, initial payment, distressed ratings downgrade—are minor.

SUPPLY/DEMAND TECHNICALS

The contractual differences mentioned above should result in a very stable spread relationship between cash, the single-name ABCDS market, and the ABX index. However, there has been a tremendous variation in relative spreads over time. We now focus on the supply and demand technicals that can overwhelm the contractual differences. We show that the current imbalance is caused by a tug-of-war between macro-hedge funds buying protection on the ABX and mezzanine ABS CDOs selling protection in single-name ABCDS.

Exhibit 4.7 shows the historical relationship between BBB– cash, ABCDS, and ABX spreads. Note that the representative cash and ABCDS spreads in the exhibit capture the "average" credit at each rating level. The major rea-

EXHIBIT 4.7 BBB– Spreads for ABX, CDS, Cash

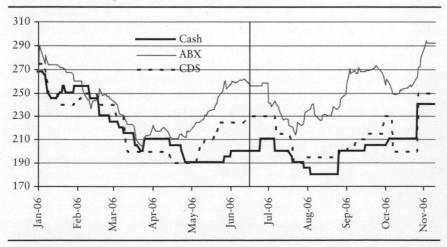

Source: UBS CDO Research.

son the ABX.HE.BBB– is much wider than the cash and ABCDS markets is that ABX clientele consists primarily of macro-hedge funds. These funds are looking to sell the ABX index (buy protection) as a way of playing a housing slowdown. In fact, for a macro-hedge fund, there are only a limited number of ways to bet on a fall in home prices. They can short the equities of sub-prime mortgage originators, home builders, or REITs; or they can buy pro-tection on subordinate tranches of subprime mortgage deals. From the point of view of these participants, it is better to buy protection when the stocks of subprime originators and home builders are considerably off their highs (so shorting has already had some of its potential steam taken out of it), and when spreads on Baa2 and Baa3 bonds are near historic tights.

Macro-hedge fund participation in the ABX market was high in the second half of 2006. Economic data paints the picture that a housing cor-rection is under way. Studies have shown that in a flat home price apprecia-tion (HPA) environment, losses on subprime deals are likely to be in the 8% to 9% range. If HPA is negative, losses will be around 12%. Most subprime BBB– bonds begin to take losses in the 8% to 10% range. Thus, macro-hedge funds view the BBB– ABX as a cheap option—they pay 250 bps/annum for a potentially large upside. And even if the ABX BBB– index does *not* experience a writedown, spreads should *widen* from current levels as the housing market contracts.

Macro-hedge funds like the idea of playing the BBB– ABX index, as they are less interested in the characteristics of its individual credits. In fact, Exhibit 4.8 shows that one of the widest point for the ABX index in Septem-ber, 2006 occurred a few months after the decline in homebuilders' equity prices. Macro-hedge fund investors were reluctant to short homebuilders at distressed levels, and looked for alternative ways to play a housing slow-down. In fact, at that time, a number of macro-hedge fund investors pur-chased the home builders index and sold the ABX.

By contrast, the clientele for the cash and single-name ABCDS markets are primarily CDOs. These investors are buyers of mortgage credit (i.e., sellers of protection). They do their homework on the characteristics of individual deals, then opt to buy (sell protection on) deals in which they are comfortable with the collateral, originator, and servicer. CDO manag-ers do extensive stress testing on individual deals, and select portfolios that will withstand housing market downturns. In their view, current spreads on these deals are sufficient to pay all CDO liabilities and generate an attractive equity yield.

Therefore, the basis at the BBB and BBB– level is primarily a story of the tug-of-war between macro-hedge fund protection buyers of the ABX index and CDO protection sellers of cash and single-name ABCDS. When the basis gets too wide, CDO begin using the ABX as a substitute for single-

EXHIBIT 4.8 Home Builder Stock Index versus ABX

Source: S&P, UBS CDO Research.

EXHIBIT 4.9 ABS Market Basis Relationship as of 11/28/2006

	Cash	ABX	Basis	CDS	Basis
AAA	23	9			
Credit spread	7	5			
AA	30	14			
Credit spread	12	40			
A	42	54	14	40	–2
Credit spread	88	133		85	
BBB	130	187	62	125	–5
Credit spread	110	109		125	
BBB–	240	296	46	250	10

Source: UBS CDO Research.

name assets, buying back protection on credits in the ABX that they do not want to position. Given current dynamics, with the participation of the macro-hedge funds as protection buyers on the ABX, and CDOs as protection sellers in the single-name ABCDS sellers—it is unlikely that the single-name ABCDS-ABX relationship will converge.

Exhibit 4.9 shows spreads between cash, ABX, and ABCDS at ratings from AAA to BBB–. Note that for AAA and AA ratings, cash is much wider than the ABX. We argue below that this primarily reflects funding differences, although trading volume in the ABX's AAA- and AA-rated tranches is low (~5% of total ABX volume). However the A, BBB, and BBB– ABX tranches trade more actively (A tranches ~15% of trading volume; BBB flat 30%, and BBB– 50% of total trading volume) and for these cash is tighter than the ABX. Volume in the BBB and BBB– reflects the trading activity of both macro-hedge funds and CDOs.

WHAT KEEPS THE ARBITRAGE FROM GOING AWAY?

Clearly, the primary reason the ABX is wider than the single-name ABCDS market or the cash market is that macro-hedge funds are primarily sellers of the ABX, while CDOs are primarily buyers of cash and single-name ABCDS. But why is this differential not arbitraged away? There are three reasons:

1. Not all credits in the ABX are actively traded. Exhibit 4.10 shows individual midmarket CDS spreads at the BBB– level on credits that are actively traded, and UBS estimates for those less actively traded.
2. The single-name CDS market has a bid/ask spread of approximately 25 basis points at the BBB– level. The ABX market has a bid-ask spread of 4 to 5 bps at the BBB– level. The sizeable bid/ask spreads in the single-name market inhibits investors from trading back and forth.
3. Cash cannot be shorted; the market is very thin, and volumes are limited. ABCDS volumes are a multiple of cash volumes.

We expand on these three reasons below.

First, in the cash market, there is little differentiation between issuers. In the single-name ABCDS market, we have captured the "average" spread on the actively traded issues. In reality, there is really quite a dispersion of credits in the ABX index. The index is formed from one deal from each of the "top 20" issuers. With 20 diverse issuers in the index, it is not surprising that a few credits in the index sell at much wider levels and oftentimes do not trade actively on a single-name basis. For example, Exhibit 4.10 shows BBB– single-name ABCDS midmarket spreads ranging from 175 to 475 bps, averaging 275 bps, and with median of 260 bps. If we eliminate the bottom five bonds with the widest spreads and which trade less actively and have bid/ask spreads of 40 bps or more, the average midmarket spread then falls to 244 bps.[2]

---

[2] Note that these values are slightly different than the generic bid side numbers in Exhibit 4.7 which is exactly the point.

EXHIBIT 4.10 ABX.HE 06-2 BBB– Index

Bonds	Full Deal Name	Intex Name	Tranche	Cusip	Orig. Rating Moody	Orig. Rating S&P	Midmarket Spread
1	FFML 2006-FF4 B1	FFML06F4	B1	362334GJ7	Baa3	BBB+	175
2	SASC 2006-WF2 M9	SAS06WF2	M9	86360LAN6	Baa3	BBB–	190
3	CARR 2006-NC1 M9	CMLT06N1	M9	144531FG0	Baa3	BBB+	200
4	MLMI 2006-HE1 B3A	MLHE06H1	B3A	59020U3Q6	Baa3	BBB+	200
5	SABR 2006-OP1 B3	SABR06O1	B3	81375WJP2	Baa3	BBB	200
6	GSAMP 2006-HE3 M9	GSA06HE3	M9	36244KAP0	Baa3	BBB+	225
7	ACE 2006-NC1 M9	ACE06NC1	M9	004421VC4	Baa3	BBB+	250
8	MABS 2006-NC1 M9	MAB06NC1	M9	57643LNQ5	Baa3	BBB	250
9	RASC 2006-KS3 M9	RFC06KS3	M9	76113ABU4	Baa3	BBB+	250
10	SVHE 2006-OPT5 M9	SVHE06O5	M9	83612CAP4	Baa3	BBB–	260
11	LBMLT 2006-1 M9	LBML0601	M9	542514RW6	Baa3	BBB+	260
12	MSC 2006-HE2 B3	MSAB06H2	B3	617451FE4	Baa3	BBB	270
13	MSAC 2006-WMC2 B3	MSAB06W2	B3	61749KAQ6	Baa3	BBB–	275
14	JPMAC 2006-FRE1 M9	JPA06FR1	M9	46626LFW5	Baa3	BBB–	350
15	RAMP 2006-NC2 M9	RFC06NC2	M9	75156TAM2	Baa3	BBB–	300
16	CWL 2006-8 M9	CWHE0608	M9	045427AN1	Baa3	BBB–	300
17	BSABS 2006-HE3 M9	BSHE06H3	M9	07387UJA0	Baa3	BBB–	325
18	ARSI 2006-W1 M9	ARS06W01	M9	040104RR4	Baa3	BBB+	350
19	HEAT 2006-4 B1	HEAT0604	B1	437084VZ6	Baa3	BBB	400
20	SAIL 2006-4 M8	SAIL0604	M8	86360WAN2	Baa3	BBB–	475
	Average						275

Source: UBS CDO Research.

Second, even though the average spread in the single-name market is somewhat tighter than the ABX, the bid-ask spread in the single-name market is quite wide, about 25 bps. Most single-name ABCDS trades with a 20 to 30 bps bid/ask spread. It is important to realize that there are more protection sellers on the four or five bonds in the index with the tightest spreads. Moreover, on bonds with the widest spreads, there are many more protection buyers than protection sellers, and the Street has a very limited appetite to take the other side. As a result, bid/ask spreads on the bottom four or five bonds in the index are 40 to 50 bps wide. The bid/ask spread in the BBB and BBB– ABX is about 5 bps.

Finally, cash can stay rich to CDS for a long time. Cash cannot be sold short, so there is no way to alleviate richness of cash other than increased supply. And on a representative subprime deal, only 3% to 4% of the deal is rated within the BBB range. With a thin cash market, ABCDS volumes are a multiple of cash.

BOTTOM LINE—BUYERS VERSUS SELLERS

In this chapter, we found that the main driver of the basis between cash, single-name ABCDS, and the ABX is that the macro-hedge funds are primarily sellers of the ABX, while CDOs are buyers in the cash and single-name ABCDS markets. Moreover, the "arbitrage" between the sectors is much less than perfect. It is impossible to short cash; single-name ABCDS trading volumes for the bottom bonds in the ABX are limited; and bid/ask spreads in single-name ABCDS are very wide.

THE CASH/ABCDS BASIS AND THE CDO ARBITRAGE

The development of the ABCDS market has revolutionized mezzanine ABS CDOs. Volumes are up, deals ramp faster, and managers have more flexibility and are happier with the collateral in their CDOs. We saw earlier in this chapter that prior to the development of ABCDS, the amount of mezzanine ABS CDOs that could be done was limited by the amount of cash collateral. And deals took eight to nine months to ramp, as CDO deal managers waited for deals to come to market. Even so, mezzanine ABS CDOs absorbed close to 100% of the BBB cash collateral issued in 2005. With subprime issuance flat for 2006, there would have been no scope for increased issuance. The very sharp increase in issuance is due to the development of a synthetic market in ABS.

The development of ABCDS has also allowed the CDO managers to ramp up more quickly and to sell protection on the BBB and BBB– names of their choice, without regard to cash issuance. Thus, they are able to place more Resi B&C paper in their deals on which they have done their homework and are comfortable with the credit. It also means less barbelling with A and BB tranches, as BBB and BBB– tranches are readily available in synthetic form.

Not only has the ABCDS market provided the raw material for greater deal volume, it has also improved the CDO arbitrage. Exhibit 4.11 shows a hypothetical hybrid deal (cash plus ABCDS) and a hypothetical cash deal. In both cases, the rating splits are identical: 65% senior AAA, 12% junior AAA, 9% AA, 7% A, 1% BBB, 2% BBB, 1% BBB–, and 4% equity. In the cash of the hybrid deal, the use of ABCDS allows the use of an unfunded super senior tranche. We assume that the unfunded super senior trades

EXHIBIT 4.11   Hybrid and Cash Mezzanine ABS CDO Arbitrage

	Percent	Hybrid Spread	Cash Spread
Senior AAA	65%	0.18%	0.30%
Junior AAA	12%	0.44%	0.44%
AA	9%	0.53%	0.53%
A	7%	1.40%	1.40%
BBB+	1%	2.65%	2.65%
BBB	2%	3.30%	3.30%
BBB–	1%	3.70%	3.70%
Equity	4%		
Total	100%		
Average debt spread		0.46%	0.54%
Upfront and running fees		0.78%	0.78%
Total debt and fee spread		1.24%	1.32%
Average asset spread		1.88%	1.65%
Excess spread		0.64%	0.33%
Times 25 leverage		16.06%	8.28%
Plus swap rate		5.00%	5.00%
Targeted equity return		21.06%	13.28%

Source: UBS CDO Research.

about 12 bps tighter than cash. We also assume that the bonds purchased in the single-name ABCDS market are about 23 (1.88 to 1.65) bps wider than the cash. This is consistent with the names we see chosen in the single-name ABCDS market.

The result of these changes is very dramatic for the CDO arbitrage. Note that the equity on the hybrid CDO is able to achieve an attractive 21% internal rate of return. By contrast, the cash deal is only able to achieve a 13% internal rate of return.

This analysis would suggest that, if the levels shown above were reasonably close to the actual market levels, there should be no pure cash deals, and many hybrid and pure synthetic deals. In fact, this statement does capture the state of the mezzanine ABS CDO issuance in 2006.

SINGLE-NAME ABCDS VERSUS ABX IN CDOs

As was pointed our earlier, most CDOs use the single-name ABCDS market, while macro-hedge funds are much more involved in the ABX market. We are, however, seeing increased participation by CDOs in the ABX market. We estimate that about 20% of hybrid and pure synthetic mezzanine ABS CDOs have used the ABX. This has included static deals in which, as the bonds or CDS runoff, reinvestment is in the ABX. This allows for reinvestment within the context of a static deal. This has also included several managed deals where the ABX is used to help ramp the deal, and single-name ABCDS is substituted later. The ABX has been used when (1) the ABX-ABCDS basis is very wide or (2) when synthetic spreads are very wide. The manager wants to be opportunistic, and either single-name liquidity is insufficient or the manager has not yet had a chance to do their homework on individual deals.

Most importantly, a number of CDOs have sold protection on the ABX, and bought protection on several of the better names in the index. That is, they thought the better names were trading too tight; and by buying protection just on these entities, the CDO manager is essentially eliminating them from the index. Why don't they just sell protection on the remaining single-names individually? It comes back to the bid/ask spreads in the single-name ABCDS market. If, out of the 20 names in the index, a CDO manager wants to sell protection on 15, it is more economic to sell protection on the ABX and buy protection on the unwanted names.

The ability of CDO managers to sell protection on the ABX rather than on individual names will keep the ABX from getting "too far" out of line with the single-names that comprise it.

SUMMARY

In this chapter, we looked at how the three different forms of subprime mortgage risk, cash, ABCDS, and the ABX differ and what drives their relative spreads. We explained what spread differences should be from a credit and cash flow perspective, and what credit spreads are from a supply and demand technicals perspective. We showed how ABCDS has revolutionized mezzanine ABS CDOs, allowing for larger deals, shorter ramp-ups, providing CDO managers with greater flexibility to choose the credits on which to sell protection. Finally, we showed the difference in mezzanine ABS CDO equity arbitrage returns with cash and synthetic assets and addressed the role of the ABX in ABS CDOs.

CHAPTER 5

Hybrid Assets in an ABS CDO

The term *hybrid* refers to CDO *assets* being comprised of both ABS credit default swaps (CDS) and asset-backed securities (ABS) cash bonds.[1] So far, almost all hybrid asset CDOs have been mezzanine ABS CDOs, focused on ABS backed by home equity loans rated BB through A. These CDOs obtain 60% to 80% of their exposure by selling protection on ABS credit default swaps (ABCDS) and the remainder of their exposure by purchasing cash ABS bonds.

The development of hybrid ABS CDOs was spurred by the standardization of ABCDS documentation and the codification of "Pay As You Go" settlement in June 2005.[2] The popularity of ABCDS allowed, for the first time, the shorting of mortgage credit without the shorting of mortgage ABS bonds. Dealers are using the new market to buy credit protection to hedge

---

[1] What is an asset and what is a liability? It is common to call a super-senior tranche a CDO liability, but economically, that depends on the instrument's mark. The mark would be in favor of the CDO, and the super-senior tranche would be a CDO economic asset, if the CDO was paying a below-market rate for protection. For sure, the super-senior tranche replaces a cash-funded CDO debt, which can only be a liability. The CDO transfers credit risk to its investors via super-senior tranches or cash-funded debt.

When the CDO sells protection on ABCDS, the mark could be in favor of the CDO's counterparty and therefore a CDO economic liability. But selling protection on ABCDS replaces cash ABS bonds, which can only be assets. Thus, the CDO assumes credit risk via either selling protection on ABCDS or buying mortgage ABS cash bonds.

In this chapter, we follow market convention and refer to super-senior tranches as a CDO liability and ABCDS as CDO assets. But do not expect assets and liabilities, defined this way, to equal one another.

[2] At least $10 billion of hybrid mezzanine ABS CDOs have been issued, and Fitch reports that 75% of its 2006 mezzanine ABS CDO pipeline is comprised of hybrid CDOs. Fitch also reports that the hybrid structure is also being used for portfolios consisting of commercial mortgage-backed securities and expects it to be used for high-yield loans before the end of 2006.

their mortgage warehouses. Macroeconomic hedge funds are using the market to buy protection and create short mortgage credit positions. Mortgage hedge funds are participating on both sides of the ABCDS market to create relative value positions based around perceived differences in originators, vintages, and structures. The demand for protection from these participants gives CDO managers opportunities to sell credit protection on residential mortgage ABS via their CDOs.

In this chapter, we identify the advantages of the hybrid CDO structure. Then we devote the balance of the chapter to showing how CDO structurers overcome the challenges posed by incorporating both cash and CDS assets in the same CDO structure.

CORPORATE CDS AND ABCDS

To understand the hurdles for ABCDS and the various attempts made in the ABCDS market to overcome these obstacles, we begin with a review of the differences between corporate credit and ABS credit that drive the structure of their respective credit default swaps.

The first difference is the *generality* of corporate credit risk versus the *specificity* of ABS credit risk. In the corporate market, the focus is on the corporate entity (e.g., GM) with less emphasis placed on the credit's individual obligations (e.g., the 4-3/8% of 2008). In the ABS market, the focus is very specific: a particular tranche from a particular securitization of a particular originator (e.g., the Class M7 of Home Equity Loan Trust 2005–AB4 originated by Countrywide).

In corporate CDS, the usual practice is for all senior unsecured obligations to be the reference obligations. So corporate obligations may be retired and new ones created, but the corporate CDS overarches them all and has its own maturity. The corporate CDS market runs on the assumption that it does not much matter which senior unsecured obligation is tendered for physical settlement or marked to market for cash settlement. The model here is bankruptcy, where all senior unsecured debts are supposed to be treated the same in that their eventual recovery (in cash or new securities) is the same regardless of maturity or coupon. Credit events that allow for differences in the value of reference obligations, such as restructuring, are the source of concern, controversy, and remediation.

Things could not be more different with ABCDS. This is because each tranche in an ABS transaction intentionally has its own distinct credit quality from that of other tranches. This is reflected in the different ratings on tranches. For example, it is not uncommon for a home equity loan-backed securitization to issue tranches in every investment-grade rating category from AAA down to BBB–; and each securitization is backed by its own unique pool of assets. ABCDS follow credit reality and focus on a specific tranche as a reference obligation. ABCDS maturity and amortization follow the maturity and amortization of the tranche reference obligation.

The second difference between corporate credit and ABS credit is the *clarity* of a corporate credit problem versus the *ambiguity* of an ABS credit problem. The model in the corporate market is that a corporation fails to pay interest or principal on an obligation, cross defaults with its other obligations occurs, and pretty soon the corporation is filed into bankruptcy (if the corporate does not file for bankruptcy first). These events are dramatic, easily discernable, and severe. In contrast, a credit problem at an ABS transaction can be subtle. For example, an ABS transaction should never go into bankruptcy. In essence, the expense, delay, and uncertainty of bankruptcy are unnecessary evils as securitization documentation already encompasses the possibility that cash flows from the collateral may not be enough to pay liabilities. In essence, an ABS transaction comes with a prepackaged insolvency plan that eliminates the need for judicial interference. Furthermore, the flexibility of an ABS tranche's cash flows is such that the existence or extent of a credit problem is ambiguous. Problems may be minor, they may resolve themselves, or they may not rise to the same level of distress as a defined credit event in a corporate CDS. Here are five examples:

1. Many ABS tranches are structured to defer interest payments if collateral cash flow is insufficient due to delinquencies and defaults. Later, if collateral cash flow recovers, deferred interest is made up.
2. Many mortgage ABS tranches are structured to defer interest payments if collateral cash flow is insufficient due to interest rate caps on underlying collateral. Many mortgages have restrictions on how fast homeowner interest rate and payments can rise. These restrictions might cause an interest rate mismatch with the securitization's tranches. If so, the *available funds cap* causes tranches to defer interest, as they would if the shortfall in collateral cash flow had been caused by defaults. Later, if collateral cash flow recovers, deferred interest is made up.
3. Many ABS transactions call for the writedown of tranche principal in the case of collateral losses. From that point forward, interest and principal payments are based on the lower written-down amount. However, some of these writedowns are reversible and in practice are reversed as collateral performance stabilizes or improves. (Moody's calculates that 19% of such structured finance impairments have been cured.)
4. Some ABS transactions do not use the writedown process. Tranche principal is not considered defaulted until some far off legal final maturity. So there is no official early acknowledgment of a principal default.

5. Each ABS tranche has an expected maturity based on underlying collateral maturities and prepayments. However, this expected maturity could be violated due to either slower than expected collateral prepayments or higher than expected collateral losses.

The differences between corporate and ABS credit generally work against the creation of ABCDS. Or more accurately, the differences work against creating ABCDS in the image of corporate CDS.

Two consensuses drive the corporate CDS market. First, a credit event triggering a payment from the protection seller to the protection buyer should be the result of a significant credit problem. Second, the settlement process should address credit losses rather than market value risks. The ideal corporate CDS combination is therefore a bankruptcy credit event and a physical settlement. Bankruptcy is ideal because it indicates a severe credit problem. Physical settlement is ideal because the process avoids dealer polling and the difficulty of valuing a defaulted obligation. In physical settlement, the protection seller pays the protection buyer par in exchange for the reference obligation. The protection seller can then decide to hold the reference obligation or sell it whenever advantageous.[3]

ABS credits lack anything as clear cut as bankruptcy. Interruptions in interest payments are incremental and reversible. So are principal writedowns and some ABS transactions do not even have principal writedowns. It violates CDS market consensus to trigger a credit event because of an interest deferral or principal writedown that is small and could very well be reversed later. On the other hand, it seems unfair to force a protection buyer to wait for a far-off legal final maturity before calling a credit event.

The small size of underlying ABS tranches presents settlement problems. Typically, ABCDS are written on tranches in the BBB to A range of the securitization. For a subprime MBS securitization, these tranches make up only 5% to 10% of the deal's total capital structure. In a $1.6 billion securitization, these tranches are in the range of $10 to $20 million each. These small sizes would make it very difficult for a protection buyer (other than someone who already owned the tranche) to make physical settlement. Contrast this to the corporate CDS market where any unsecured debt of the reference obligor is deliverable. The small sizes of ABS tranches (not to mention the difficulty of analyzing ABS credit) would also make dealer polling in cash settlement especially arbitrary.

There have been three attempts to create ABCDS documentation to overcome these problems: (1) traditional SF CDS circa 1998 to 2004 based

---

[3] In the alternative, cash settlement, bids for the reference obligation are obtained from security firms and averaged. The protection seller then pays the protection buyer par minus this average price.

on corporate CDS; (2) the dealer-mixed pay-as-you-go and physical settlement template; and (3) the end-user pure pay-as-you-go template. We discuss next the second template. The development of the second template in June 2005 has spurred the growth of the hybrid asset CDO. The innovation of pay-as-you-go CDS (PayGo CDS) is softer and reversible credit events (called *floating amount events*) and partial reversing settlements (Pay As You Go Settlement). Also, the CDS template eliminates cash settlement and the risks of dealer polling.

ADVANTAGES OF HYBRID ASSETS IN AN ABS CDO

The ABCDS market has been a liberating experience for ABS CDO managers. For two to three years before the advent of ABCDS in 2005, the ABS CDO market was hampered by a relative scarcity of mezzanine mortgage ABS. Simply put, the demand for CDO liabilities was greater than the supply of cash CDO assets. This was extremely frustrating to ABS CDO managers, who would do a considerable amount of credit work on a bond and sometimes get an insultingly small allocation. It was not unheard of for a manager to receive $1 million of a $5 million order. Small asset allocations also made it impossible for good managers to scale up the size and frequency of their CDO offerings.

ABCDS has multiplied the supply of credit risk to ABS CDOs, thereby decoupling asset selection from the new issue cash market. This allows ABS CDO managers to be more selective about credits and focus more intently on collateral attributes and originator and servicer quality. Asset supply has broadened along two dimensions. First, ABS CDO managers can do credit work on new issues, perhaps get only a small allocation in the new issue cash market, but obtain the same credit risk exposure by selling protection via ABCDS in a size that is a multiple of their cash allocation. Second, ABS CDO managers can select credits from older vintages as seasoned issues are much more readily accessed through CDS than in the secondary cash market. And for CDO structural reasons, ABCDS is an advantageous way for the manager of an ABS CDO to access bonds from earlier vintages trading at a premium.[4]

---

[4] CDO issuance is simplified if collateral par is equal or nearly equal to liability par, and paying a bond premium puts the CDO further away from that goal. When a cash instrument is traded, the buyer and seller naturally cannot change the instrument's coupon spread. The bond must be traded at a premium or a discount to equalize the instrument's coupon spread to current market spreads. But in an ABCDS, counterparties can adjust the protection premium to current market rates and avoid an upfront exchange. With a great deal of ABS collateral trading at a premium, this means that the CDO can access credit risk via an ABCDS and avoid paying a premium for a cash bond or making an upfront payment on a CDS.

Selling protection via ABCDS is arguably a better credit risk for the CDO than purchasing an equivalent cash bond. Market practice is for the ABS CDO to sell protection under the fixed cap or "premium squeeze-to-zero" CDS option.[5] As such, the CDO's loss due to available funds cap risk is limited to the CDS premium. In a cash ABS investment, the CDO could lose not just the bond's spread above LIBOR, but also the LIBOR component of the coupon. It is important to note that the rating agencies do not take this benefit into consideration when they rate a hybrid ABS CDO. Therefore, there is no offsetting compensation in the CDO structure and the effect is an increase in CDO debt credit quality.

Another result of ABCDS is that CDOs now take considerably less than the six to nine months they previously took to ramp up and have been accomplished in as few as three weeks. The ease of ramp-up allows for a larger deal size and for fixed issuance costs to be spread out over a larger issuance base.

The ability of hybrid ABS CDOs to accommodate both cash and synthetic assets allows the CDO manager to create more diversified portfolios than would be the case with only one asset type. During the first period of hybrid ABS CDO issuance, ABCDS often traded at a positive basis to cash bonds, that is, the CDS premium was greater than the cash bond's spread to LIBOR. Negative basis is more common now. However, the premium on the large super-senior tranche that the hybrid ABS CDO issues has consistently been lower than the coupon spread the CDO would have to pay on an equivalent cash bond. So lower issuance cost on the super-senior tranche is a positive for the economics of the CDO, even if CDS premiums are tighter than cash bond spreads.

Moreover, the CDO manager has an important option with respect to the mix of cash and synthetic assets in a hybrid CDO. The CDO manager can sell cash ABS and enter into ABCDS. The manager can also exit ABCDS and buy cash ABS. This flexibility allows the CDO manager to take advantage of positive or negative basis between the synthetic and cash markets as opportunities arise. To buy cash ABS, the CDO manager can call for funding from super-senior counterparties. This turns some of the super-senior into a funded bond. This is a completely different use of the super-senior

---

[5] For a PayGo ABCDS, there are three options presented for sizing the protection seller's payments under an interest shortfall: no cap applicable, variable cap, and fixed cap. The market convention is to elect fixed cap. With this option, the protection seller's payment to the protection buyer is limited to the CDS premium. The net amount, then, can never be a payment from the protection seller to the protection buyer. For a discussion of these three options, see Chapter 15 in Douglas J. Lucas, Laurie S. Goodman, and Frank J. Fabozzi, *Collateralized Debt Obligations: Structures and Analysis, Second Edition* (Hoboken, NJ: John Wiley & Sons, 2006).

tranche than in fully synthetic asset CDOs, where the super senior's only cash obligation is to provide protection payments if CDS losses exceed subordination.

A final advantage of the hybrid structure is its ability to incorporate short positions in ABCDS, where the CDO purchases protection on underlying reference ABS. This is generally limited to around 10% of the CDO's long portfolio and protection premiums are paid out of excess spread from ABCDS premiums and cash ABS interest. The accommodation of short positions allows the CDO manager to take relative value views on credits. Credit judgment can be applied not only to the question of which credits to buy, but also to which credits to short.

ILLUSTRATIVE HYBRID ABS CDO STRUCTURE

Exhibit 5.1 illustrates the structure of a hybrid ABS CDO. At the far left of the exhibit, a number of counterparties have purchased protection on single-name ABCDS. These counterparties could be dealers, macro-hedge funds, or mortgage hedge funds. But these protection-buying counterparties do not enter into swaps directly with the CDO. Instead, a highly rated intermediary (sometimes the bank structuring and underwriting the hybrid CDO) stands between the counterparties and the CDO. As the CDO faces the intermediary on its swaps, the CDO is protected from the credit risk of the counterparties. The intermediary also cleanses the counterparty swaps of any break clauses they might contain. Break clauses allow the counterparties and the intermediary the mutual option to terminate the swap at market value after, say, 10 years. As the CDO is not set up to handle the potential market value loss of making break clause payments, the swaps between the intermediary and the CDO do not contain break clauses.

At the far right of Exhibit 5.1, the CDO has issued an unfunded super-senior swap and various classes of cash bonds and preferred shares. These classes are illustrated in order of declining seniority, from top to bottom. It is important to keep in mind that there is no compartmentalization between the CDO's cash and synthetic assets and the CDO's cash and synthetic liabilities. Cash bondholders are responsible for losses on both the cash and synthetic parts of the CDO portfolio in accordance with the seniority of their bonds. Likewise, super-senior swap counterparties are responsible for losses on both the cash and synthetic parts of the CDO portfolio in accordance with their seniority above the cash bondholders.

Proceeds from the issuance of the cash bonds are put to two uses: to purchase cash ABS bonds and to create a reserve fund.

EXHIBIT 5.1 Illustrative Hybrid CDO Structure

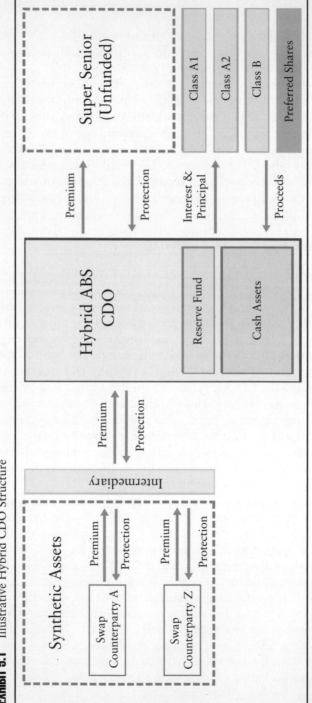

Source: UBS CDO Research.

CASH FLOW CHALLENGES

Given this quick summary of the hybrid ABS CDO structure, we now address the four major challenges a hybrid CDO structure has to handle: (1) CDS protection payments; (2) CDS and CDO liability amortization; (3) cash asset and CDO liability amortization; and (4) trading CDS.

CDS Protection Payments

The hybrid CDO may be required to make protection payments under the ABCDS. Protection payments might be for a portion of the swap amount following a writedown under pay-as-you-go settlement. Or the protection payment might be for the entire swap notional under a physical settlement, where the CDO must take delivery of the underlying ABS bond at par.

The reserve fund is the CDO's first source for making protection payments under credit default swaps. The reserve fund is usually funded at the beginning of the deal with proceeds from cash liability issuance. Less frequently, it is funded over time with excess spread from cash asset interest and CDS premium.

To preserve the ability of the CDO to make protection payments, the reserve fund must invest in liquid assets with minimal market risk. One common means is a guaranteed investment contract (GIC) from a highly-rated counterparty. The GIC pays the CDO, for example, LIBOR + 8 to LIBOR – 6 basis points, depending on the flexibility of cash withdrawals. GICs are typically set to be freely drawable on the 30th of each month. This aligns the liquidity of the GIC with pay-as-you-go settlements, which occur five business days after trustee remittances report writedowns on underlying mortgage ABS instruments. Interperiod draws at other times are subject to a breakage fee.

Exhibit 5.2 shows a draw from the reserve fund to make a protection payment under the ABCDS. The reserve fund and the outstanding notional of the ABCDS are both reduced. There is also an implicit loss to the most subordinated CDO obligation outstanding.

If the reserve fund is insufficient to make the protection payment, the super-senior tranche must advance funds. These draws essentially turn a portion of the unfunded super-senior tranche into a cash bond. Again, this is a different use of the super-senior tranche than in a fully synthetic asset CDO. Even though the super-senior tranche is funding the CDS protection payment, it can reasonably expect to be repaid. In a fully synthetic asset CDO, super-senior cash payments are almost always permanent losses. Exhibit 5.3 illustrates the CDS loss payment along with the implicit loss that a subordinate tranche incurs. When the super senior is drawn, payments to the super seniors

EXHIBIT 5.2 CDS Protection Payment from Reserve Fund

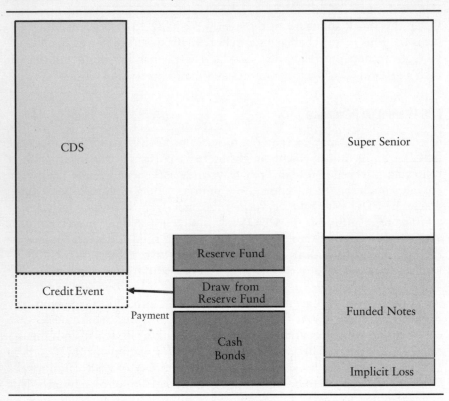

Source: UBS CDO Research.

increase, for example, from 15 to 20 basis points to LIBOR + 29 to 30 basis points. This later amount is similar to what the CDO would have to pay to issue a cash-funded senior AAA bond. The additional payment to super seniors increases the CDO's interest costs and obviously reduces equity returns even beyond the implicit loss associated with the protection payment.

An important inequality ties together three important quantities of the hybrid CDO:

$$\text{Reserve fund} + \text{Unfunded super senior} > \text{ABCDS notional}$$

This inequality ensures that the CDO has available funds to pay the full notional amount on all its CDS obligations, either from the reserve fund or from draws on the super-senior tranche. We will refer to this formula again and again.

EXHIBIT 5.3   CDS Protection Payment from Super-Senior Tranche

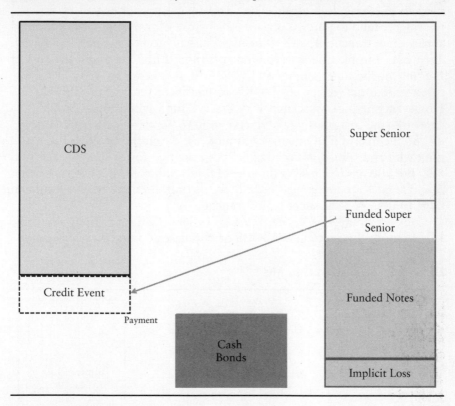

CDS

Credit Event

Payment

Cash
Bonds

Super Senior

Funded Super
Senior

Funded Notes

Implicit Loss

Source: UBS CDO Research.

CDS and CDO Liability Amortization

The notional amount of the CDO's ABCDS portfolio amortizes as the underlying reference instruments experience scheduled amortizations and prepayments. The most obvious thing for the CDO manager to do is replace amortizing ABCDS notional by selling additional protection through ABCDS. In terms of the inequality, we introduced, amounts are both subtracted and added to the right side of the inequality:

$$\text{Reserve fund + Unfunded super senior}$$
$$> \text{ABCDS notional} - \text{CDS amortizations} + \text{New CDS}$$

When ABCDS notional decreases and is not replaced with new ABCDS, the excess on the left side of the equation increases. This means that the reserve fund or the unfunded super-senior tranche is freed up and could be used to purchase cash assets. The CDO manager is obligated to first use the reserve fund to purchase cash assets before drawing upon the unfunded super-senior tranche. The CDO manager has an incentive to do this anyway; as in our example, the reserve fund is earning LIBOR – 6 and the cost of funding via the super seniors is LIBOR + 30. It is better for the CDO structure to forgo the receipt of LIBOR – 6 than incur the cost of LIBOR + 30. However, penalties associated with reserve fund withdrawals would also enter into the cost of using the reserve fund to purchase cash collateral.

So the hybrid CDO manager cannot just weigh the CDS premium and the cash bond spread in deciding between the two forms of mortgage ABS risk, but also has to consider the cost of funds to buy the cash asset. Exhibit 5.4 illustrates the investment in cash bonds from both the reserve fund and from draws upon the super-senior tranche.

But what happens during the CDO's amortization period, when the CDO cannot enter into new ABCDS or purchase additional cash assets and

EXHIBIT 5.4   Investing in Cash ABS

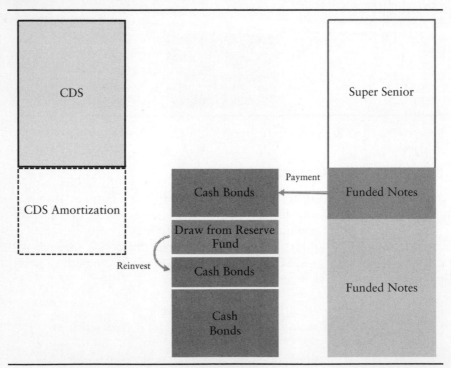

Source: UBS CDO Research.

must instead amortize its liabilities? The issue is complicated by the fact that hybrid CDO structures usually have a period of pro rata amortization before switching to sequential amortization. We now show an example to make things clear.

In the column labeled "$0" of Exhibit 5.5, comes the hybrid ABS CDO before any ABCDS amortization. The CDO has raised $300 through the issuance of funded debt, purchased $250 of cash ABS, and deposited $50 into a reserve fund. It has issued a $700 super-senior tranche and sold protection on $750 of ABCDS. In the next period, shown in the "−$100" column of Exhibit 5.5, $100 of ABCDS amortizes. Working from top to bottom of the column, the new notional of ABCDS is $650 and cash ABS remains the same.

Since the CDO is in its pro rata amortization phase, we want to amortize the super-senior tranche by $70 and the cash liabilities by $30 to maintain the 70/30 split between synthetic and cash liabilities. In order to pay down the CDO's cash liabilities, $30 is taken from the reserve fund. The super-senior tranche is amortized $70 and the cash liabilities are amortized $30. Afterwards, we check and make sure that the sum of the unfunded super-senior tranche and reserve fund at least equals the ABCDS notional. Everything is correct, as both sides of the equation equal $650.

Amortization of ABCDS does not generate cash. Therefore, amortization of the CDO's cash liabilities is only possible to the extent there are monies in the reserve account. In the column labeled "−$200," the CDO can only amortize its cash liabilities by the $20 available in the reserve account.

EXHIBIT 5.5   Effects of Successive $100 ABS CDS Amortization

ABS CDS amortization	$0	−$100	−$200	−$300
ABS CDS notional	$750	$650	$550	$450
Cash ABS	$250	$250	$250	$250
Assets	$1,000	$900	$800	$700
Reserve account	$50	$20	$0	$0
Unfunded super senior	$700	$630	$550	$450
Cash liabilities	$300	$270	$250	$250
Liabilities	$1,000	$900	$800	$700
Equation check:				
Unfunded super senior + Reserve account	$750	$650	$550	$450
ABS CDS notional	$750	$650	$550	$450

Source: UBS CDO Research.

The super-senior tranche is therefore amortized an extra $10. In the column labeled "–$300," the CDO cannot amortize its cash liabilities at all and the super seniors are amortized the full $100 of ABCDS amortization.

Typically, the hybrid CDO is allowed to pay half of its liabilities down pro rata before it must switch to sequential pay down. However, if a coverage test is violated, the CDO goes into sequential paydown immediately. If the CDO is in its sequential amortization phase, or in its pro rata amortization period, but failing a coverage test, the $100 of ABCDS amortization would be applied solely to the super-senior tranche as in the "–$300" column of Exhibit 5.5, even if there are monies in the reserve fund.

Cash Asset and CDO Liability Amortization

The first claim to principal proceeds from the amortization of cash ABS assets is to pay unpaid expenses, deferred liability interest, and cure coverage tests. Next, during the CDO's reinvestment period, the CDO manager can either invest in new cash ABS or sell protection on new ABCDS.

If the hybrid CDO does not reinvest cash ABS amortization in new cash ABS, it usually must pay down any funded super-senior tranche outstanding. Any remaining cash is deposited into the reserve fund.[6] Both the paydown of funded super-senior tranche and the deposit into the reserve fund increases the left side of the hybrid CDO inequality. This allows the CDO to enter into additional ABCDS.

$$\text{Reserve fund + Unfunded super senior} > \text{ABCDS notional}$$

Exhibit 5.6 shows cash disbursement if the CDO is in its pro rata amortization phase and not violating any coverage tests. In the column labeled "$0," we show the hybrid ABS CDO before any cash ABS amortization. At this point, the hybrid CDO has $600 of ABCDS and $400 of cash ABS. It has $600 of an unfunded super-senior tranche, $100 of a funded super-senior tranche, and $300 of cash liabilities. In the next period, shown in the next column of Exhibit 5.6 labeled "–100," $100 of cash ABS amortizes. Working from top to bottom of the column, the notional of ABCDS remains the same and cash ABS declines $100.

Since the CDO is in its pro rata amortization phase, we want to amortize the super-senior tranche by $70 and the cash liabilities by $30 to maintain the 70/30 split between synthetic and cash liabilities. The CDO applies

---

[6] But if the CDO manager has a choice, the manager would probably apply cash principal proceeds in this order anyway, because, by our example, the CDO is paying LIBOR + 30 for the funded super-senior debt and would only receive LIBOR – 6 for deposits in the reserve fund.

EXHIBIT 5.6   Effects of Successive $100 Cash ABS Amortization

Cash ABS amortization	0	−100	−200	−300
ABS CDS	$600	$600	$600	$600
Cash ABS	$400	$300	$200	$100
Assets	$1,000	$900	$800	$700
Reserve fund	$0	$0	$40	$110
Unfunded super senior	$600	$600	$560	$490
Funded super senior	$100	$30	$0	$0
Cash liabilities	$300	$270	$240	$210
Liabilities	$1,000	$900	$800	$700
Equation check:				
Unfunded super senior + Reserve account	$600	$600	$600	$600
ABS CDS notional	$600	$600	$600	$600

Source: UBS CDO Research.

the $70 allocated to super seniors to funded super-senior liabilities. In the next column, another $100 of cash ABS amortizes. Again we want to amortize $70 of the super-senior liabilities. But since there is only $30 of funded super-senior liabilities remaining, the CDO pays that amount off and deposits $40 in the reserve account. The deposit into the reserve account allows the unfunded super-senior notional to be reduced $40. Meanwhile, we amortize the CDO's cash liabilities by another $30. In the last column, the entire $70 of the super senior's share of cash ABS amortization is deposited into the reserve fund and the unfunded super-senior notional is reduced by the same amount. The CDO's cash liabilities are reduced by $30.

There may be times during the CDO's pro rata amortization period when amortization of the CDO's cash liabilities lags behind amortization of the super-senior liability. This would occur if ABCDS amortization outpaces cash ABS amortization. In that case, cash ABS principal payments would be allocated to the hybrid CDO's cash liabilities until pro rata amortization is achieved.

Typically, the hybrid CDO is allowed to pay off half of its liabilities pro rata before it must switch to sequential paydown. However, if a coverage test is violated, the CDO goes into sequential paydown immediately. If the CDO is in its sequential amortization phase, or in its pro rata amortization period, but failing a coverage test, the $100 of cash ABS amortization would be deposited into the reserve fund and the super-senior liability would be reduced by $100. Note that deposits into the reserve fund amortize unfunded super-senior notional dollar for dollar. This is because amounts in the reserve fund are available to make CDS protection payments.

The hybrid CDO's principal waterfall, coverage tests, and the switch to sequential liability paydown ensure that cash liabilities do not pay down too soon and leave the super-senior tranche without subordinate protection. Rating agencies stress the hybrid CDO's cash and synthetic portfolios with different patterns of amortization and default. For example, hybrid CDOs are tested in scenarios in which cash ABS assets amortize quickly, ABCDS amortize slowly, and ABCDS require protection payments late in their life.

Trading CDS

Cash assets can be sold, but CDS are terminated, assigned, or offset. The method used by a CDO manager to dispose of an ABCDS position affects hybrid CDO cash flows.

In termination, the two counterparties to an ABCDS tear up the swap and it exists no more. This generally requires a termination payment from one party to another. For example, say that the protection premium on an ABCDS contracted three years ago is 200 basis points, but the going market rate for such protection is now only 150 basis points. If the CDS is terminated, the protection seller cannot resell the protection for 200 basis points. Instead, the protection seller must make due with 150 basis points. Therefore, the existing ABCDS has value to the protection seller who will want to be compensated for terminating it early. The termination fee will be the present value of 50 basis points over the remaining life of the underlying mortgage ABS, taking into account the ABS' potential rate of amortization. A good analogy is to cash bonds trading at either a premium or a discount because the coupon on the bond is different from the borrower's current market interest rate.

In assignment, another party is found to take over one's place in the CDS. But if the market price of protection on a mortgage ABS is 150 basis points, the replacement party will need an enticement to take over the CDS and pay 200 basis points for protection. Again, the enticement, or assignment fee, will be the present value of 50 basis points over the remaining life of the underlying mortgage ABS, taking into account its potential rate of amortization.

Termination and assignment are like selling a cash bond. The CDO either receives a fee or pays a fee analogous to the profit or loss from selling a cash bond. Like the sale of a cash bond, the CDO is also completely out of the position. There is no further monitoring or accounting of CDS cash flows.

In actual market practice, there is a more liquid market for offsetting ABCDS trades than for terminating or assigning them. The CDO manager would reverse out of an ABCDS he had sold protection on by buying protection on the same underlying with a new counterparty at the going market rate. The CDO therefore has two positions. The original ABCDS they sold protection on and the new ABCDS they have just purchased protection on. In our example, the CDO had sold protection for 200 basis points and now buys protection for 150 basis points. This leaves the CDO with a 50 basis points interest income stream. But if the price of protection had risen rather than decreased, the CDO would have an interest expense stream.

Offsetting a CDS, which is the most common execution, gives the hybrid ABS CDO prepayment and extension risk. The underlying reference mortgage ABS might prepay faster or slower than expected. Faster than expected prepayments reduce the value of an interest income stream. Slower than expected prepayments increase the cost of an interest expense stream. Additionally, offsetting means that the hybrid CDO must perform the operational duties of monitoring and accounting for two separate trades.

CONCLUSIONS

In this chapter, we reviewed the advantages of the hybrid ABS CDO structure: increased access to collateral, more diversified portfolios, shorter collateral ramp-up periods, diminishment of available-funds cap risk, flexibility to switch from cash to synthetic assets to take advantage of negative or positive basis, and cheap super-senior credit protection. These advantages lead to the issuance of $45 billion of hybrid ABS CDOs in 2006 and the continued dominance of this structure in the foreseeable future. The hybrid structure also seems poised to be used for CDOs of commercial MBS and high-yield loans.

We then reviewed four cash flow challenges structurers of hybrid ABS CDOs face. First, hybrid CDOs make CDS protection payments by drawing upon their reserve funds and super-senior tranches. Second, during the reinvestment phase of a CDO, CDS amortization can be reinvested in new CDS or used to free up the reserve fund or the unfunded super-senior tranche to allow the purchase of cash ABS. During the CDO's amortization period, ABCDS amortization can be used to amortize the unfunded super-senior tranche or free up the reserve fund to amortize the CDO's cash liabilities. Third, cash asset amortization is first available for unpaid expenses and deferred interest on CDO liabilities. During the reinvestment period, if cash amortization is not used to purchase new cash assets, it must first be used to pay down the funded super-senior tranche and then to increase the reserve fund. Either use allows the CDO to sell additional CDS protection. During the CDO's amortization period, cash asset amortization can used to catch up on principal payments to cash liabilities and deposited into the reserve fund to amortize the unfunded super senior. Finally, in trading CDS, the CDO manager has to choose among termination, assignment, and offset. Offset is more commonly available, but carries with it operational burdens and prepayment or extension risk.

CHAPTER 6

Synthetic CDO Ratings

A CDO is rated by a single rating agency when that is all that is necessary to sell its tranches. In fancier language, CDO bankers stop buying ratings when the cost of the marginal rating exceeds the benefit. Oftentimes, the efficient number of ratings for a synthetic CDO referencing corporate credits is one. On the cost side of the equation, rating fees can eat into a significant part of tranche spread. On the benefit side, an investor who relies on his own credit judgment and only needs one rating for internal or external regulatory requirements may not find much value in a second rating.

But given that a synthetic CDO only has one rating, which rating agency will be selected? The answer is obvious: The CDO banker will select the rating agency that provides the highest rating. It turns out that that depends on two separate factors: (1) the rating agency's CDO rating methodology and (2) the rating agency's ratings on underlying credits.

In this chapter, we compare S&P's and Moody's synthetic CDO ratings. We find that given equally-rated reference portfolios, Moody's rates AAA synthetic CDO tranches the same or lower as S&P, AA tranches lower, and A, BBB, and BB tranches higher. However, Moody's lower reference ratings cause it to rate almost every tranche we looked at lower than S&P.

TESTS OF INDEX PORTFOLIOS

To compare S&P's and Moody's synthetic CDO ratings, we first compare ratings assuming CDO portfolios comprised of credits in the major credit default swap indices: the CDX investment grade, the iTraxx Europe, and the CDX high yield. For example, in the top panel of Exhibit 6.1, we use the names in the CDX NA IG as a 5-year synthetic CDO's reference portfolio. However, rather than use the standard index tranches of 0% to 3%, 3% to 7%, and so on, we select attachment and detachment points in such a way as to achieve S&P ratings of AAA, AA, A, BBB, and BB. The first two

EXHIBIT 6.1 S&P Ratings versus Difference in Moody's Ratings on Different Credit Default Swap Index Portfolios

CDX NA IG 5 Portfolio, 5-Year Maturity

Attach	Detach	S&P Rating	Difference in Moody's Ratings	Difference in Moody's Ratings Using S&P's Reference Credit Ratings
5.9%	100.0%	AAA		
5.0%	5.9%	AA	−1	
4.5%	5.0%	A		+1
3.4%	4.5%	BBB	+1	+2
2.3%	3.4%	BB		+1
WARF		279	316	279

iTraxx Europe 4 Portfolio, 5-Year Maturity

Attach	Detach	S&P Rating	Difference in Moody's Ratings	Difference in Moody's Ratings Using S&P's Reference Credit Ratings
5.0%	100.0%	AAA		
4.2%	5.0%	AA	−1	−1
3.8%	4.2%	A		
2.8%	3.8%	BBB		
1.8%	2.8%	BB		
WARF		236	249	236

CDX NA HY 5v3 Portfolio, 5-Year Maturity

Attach	Detach	S&P Rating	Difference in Moody's Ratings	Difference in Moody's Ratings Using S&P's Reference Credit Ratings
30.2%	100.0%	AAA		
28.0%	30.2%	AA	−4	−1
26.6%	28.0%	A	−2	+1
23.4%	26.6%	BBB		+2
19.4%	23.4%	BB	−1	+1
WARF		2,423	2,852	2,423

columns show tranche attachment and detachment points and the third column shows the tranche's S&P rating.

In the fourth column, we use negative and positive numbers to show how Moody's ratings would differ from S&P's ratings. For example, the −1 for the 5.0% to 5.9% tranche indicates that Moody's would rate this tranche one rating notch lower, at Aa3 instead of Aa2 (which is equivalent to S&P's AA rating). The +1 in the same column for the 3.4% to 4.5% tranche indicates that Moody's would rate this tranche one rating notch higher, at Baa1 instead of Baa2 (which is equivalent to S&P's BBB rating).

There are two reasons why Moody's synthetic ratings differ from S&P's:

1. Moody's obviously has a different synthetic CDO rating methodology than S&P.
2. Moody's rates the CDX IG reference portfolio lower than S&P.

Note that at the bottom of the third and fourth columns of the panel, we calculate the portfolio's weighted average rating factor (WARF) two different ways. In the third column we use S&P's ratings on the collateral and calculate a WARF of 279. In the fourth column we use Moody's ratings on the collateral and calculate a WARF of 316. The higher Moody's WARF indicates that, on average, Moody's rates the CDX NA IG portfolio slightly lower than S&P.

We are interested in separating out these effects and determining how Moody's would rate the CDO tranches if the agency rated the CDO's reference credits the same as S&P. So in the fifth and final column of Exhibit 6.1 we calculate Moody's synthetic CDO ratings using S&P's reference ratings. That is why the 279 WARF in the fifth column is the same as the S&P WARF in the third column. The +1, +2, and +1 in the fifth column indicate that Moody's would rate the associated tranches A1, A3, and Ba1, respectively. Comparing the two Moody's columns, one can see that below the AAA tranche, Moody's would rate tranches one rating notch higher if it rated the underlying portfolio as high as S&P.

In the second and third panels of Exhibit 6.1, we perform the same analysis on iTraxx Europe and CDX NA HY reference credits in a 5-year synthetic CDO. There is not much difference in S&P's and Moody's rating of the iTraxx Europe-based CDO. Nor is there much difference in S&P's and Moody's reference ratings. And there is no difference between Moody's ratings with its own reference ratings or Moody's ratings with S&P's reference ratings.

Moody's ratings of the CDX high-yield index have the greatest disparity from S&P's, ranging from the same to four rating notches lower. The difference in reference ratings is particularly great in this portfolio. Without the difference in underlying ratings, Moody's would tend to rate the tranche the same or higher than S&P.

AAA RATINGS AND EXPECTED LOSS VERSUS DEFAULT PROBABILITY

Note that so far we have not discussed differences in S&P and Moody's rating methodologies. Our excuse is that since a large number of assumptions go into a rating model, it is useless to focus on particulars. A rating agency's conservatism with regards to one input might be offset by their anticonservatism with two others. It seems more practical to us to compare rating agency results, as we did in Exhibit 6.1.

However, there is one important difference between Moody's and S&P's CDO rating methodologies that drives their results, particularly at the AAA/Aaa rating level: the *measurement* of credit quality. S&P measures a CDO tranche's credit quality by *default probability*; that is, how likely is the tranche to incur a default. Moody's, in contrast, measures a CDO tranche's credit quality by its *expected loss*: the combination of default probability and default severity.

S&P is essentially saying that credit quality is like death, pregnancy, or being in Chicago. To them, it's an either/or proposition and the question of severity is irrelevant. In contrast, Moody's says that credit quality is like wealth, health, or good looks. They see it as a question of degree, where it does matter whether default is accompanied by a 1% loss of principal or a 100% loss of principal.

Ratings of AAA/Aaa CDO tranches nicely illustrate the difference. Using the CDX NA IG 5 portfolio as an example, S&P collateral assumptions come to the conclusion that there is a very small probability ("a AAA probability") that losses on the portfolio will exceed 5.9% of notional. Therefore, any tranche with an attachment point of 5.9% or greater deserves an S&P AAA rating, as shown in the first three rows of the Exhibit 6.2. Meanwhile, the probability of the CDX NA IG experiencing more than 3.8% losses is a little greater ("a BBB+ probability") and a tranche with an attachment point of 3.8% gets an S&P BBB+ rating, as shown in the bottom row of the exhibit.

For Moody's expected loss methodology, the width of the tranche matters. This is because the larger the width of the tranche, the less any default loss is *as a percentage of the tranche*. So, as shown in the top row of Exhibit 6.2, a tranche with an attachment point of 5.9% must have a detachment point of at least 10.9% and a width of at least 5.0% to receive a Aaa from

EXHIBIT 6.2 S&P AAA and Moody's Aaa Synthetic CDO Ratings CDX NA IG 5 Portfolio, 5-Year Maturity

Attach	Detach	Width	S&P Rating	Moody's Rating
5.9%	10.9%	5.0%	AAA	Aaa
5.9%	6.9%	1.0%	AAA	Aa1
5.9%	6.0%	0.1%	AAA	Aa2
3.8%	100.0%	96.2%	BBB+	Aaa

Moody's. Moving down the exhibit, a tranche with an attachment point of 5.9% must have a detachment point of at least 6.9% and a width of at least 1.0% to get a Moody's Aa1. Finally, just about any width tranche with an attachment point of 5.9% can get a Moody's Aa2. The last row in the exhibit shows that a truly huge tranche, with a detachment point of 100%, could stretch all the way down to 3.8% and receive a Aaa from Moody's.

BARBELL PORTFOLIOS

Next we look at portfolio barbelling, and how the two rating agencies address homogeneous portfolios and barbell portfolios. Using CDX investment grade and high yield credits, we create three different portfolios: a *homogenous portfolio*, a *modest barbell portfolio*, and an *extreme barbell portfolio*. The rating distributions of these three portfolios are shown in Exhibit 6.3.

The exhibit shows for each portfolio, the percent of credits in each rating category. So for the homogeneous portfolio, 11% of the portfolio is rated BBB+. Each portfolio has approximately the same average rating, as indicated by the WARFs in the last row of the exhibit, which range from 1,038 to 1,200. But collateral in the homogenous portfolio ranges in rating from BBB+ to B– while collateral in the extreme barbell portfolio ranges from AAA to CCC–.

Exhibit 6.4 shows our results in the same format as Exhibit 6.1, again assuming a 5-year synthetic CDO. We see that the greater the discrepancy in rating agencies' reference ratings, the greater the difference in their synthetic CDO tranche ratings. For instance, the S&P WARF for the extreme barbell portfolio is 1,186, while Moody's WARF is 1,561. Moody's rates the CDO tranches from this portfolio one to six rating notches lower. If Moody's rated the reference credits the same as S&P, Moody's would rate some tranches higher than S&P.

EXHIBIT 6.3   Portfolio Rating Distributions

	Portfolios		
S&P Rating	**Homogenous**	**Modest Barbell**	**Extreme Barbell**
AAA	—	—	4%
AA+	—	—	—
AA	—	—	2%
AA–	—	—	2%
A+	—	—	6%
A	—	14%	18%
A–	—	16%	18%
BBB+	11%	18%	16%
BBB	29%	10%	7%
BBB–	12%	1%	—
BB+	13%	—	—
BB	11%	1%	—
BB–	8%	4%	2%
B+	10%	13%	3%
B	—	16%	6%
B–	6%	6%	8%
CCC+	—	1%	3%
CCC	—	—	2%
CCC–	—	—	3%
WARF	1,038	1,200	1,186

SUMMARY

Our empirical analysis finds that when the synthetic CDO's reference portfolio is rated the same by both rating agencies, Moody's ratings tend to be:

- Usually lower than S&P at the AAA level.
- The same or one notch lower at the AA level.
- The same to two notches higher at the A, BBB, and BB level.

However, Moody's usually rates underlying reference portfolios lower than S&P. This creates downward pressure on Moody's synthetic CDO rat-

EXHIBIT 6.4 S&P Ratings versus Difference in Moody's Ratings Homogenous and Barbell Portfolios

Homogenous Portfolio, 5-Year Maturity

Attach	Detach	S&P Rating	Difference in Moody's Ratings	Difference in Moody's Ratings Using S&P's Reference Credit Ratings
15.8%	100.0%	AAA		
14.2%	15.8%	AA	−1	−1
13.1%	14.2%	A		+1
10.9%	13.1%	BBB		+1
8.3%	10.9%	BB		+1
WARF		1,038	1,105	1,038

Modest Barbell Portfolio, 5-Year Maturity

Attach	Detach	S&P Rating	Difference in Moody's Ratings	Difference in Moody's Ratings Using S&P's Reference Credit Ratings
16.5%	100.0%	AAA		
15.2%	16.5%	AA	−3	−2
14.2%	15.2%	A	−2	
12.2%	14.2%	BBB	−1	
9.7%	12.2%	BB	−1	
WARF		1,200	1,297	1,200

Extreme Barbell Portfolio, 5-Year Maturity

Attach	Detach	S&P Rating	Difference in Moody's Ratings	Difference in Moody's Ratings Using S&P's Reference Credit Ratings
15.3%	100.0%	AAA	−1	
14.2%	15.3%	AA	−6	−1
13.5%	14.2%	A	−4	
12.0%	13.5%	BBB	−3	+1
10.1%	12.0%	BB	−4	+1
WARF		1,186	1,561	1,186

ings relative to S&P. Given the difference in underlying reference ratings, Moody's synthetic CDO ratings tend to be:

- The same as or one notch lower than S&P for investment-grade reference portfolios.
- The same to four notches lower for speculative grade reference portfolios.
- One to six notches lower for an extreme barbell portfolio where 6% of the portfolio is in CCC names.

CHAPTER **7**

Credit Default Swaps on CDOs

In June 2006, the International Swap & Derivatives Association (ISDA) released a template that sellers and buyers of credit protection can use to negotiate the terms of credit default swaps (CDS) on securitized products (ABS, RMBS, and CMBS). There are four reasons why CDO investors need to understand CDO CDS documentation and trading.

First, selling protection on a CDO CDS provides a new way to access CDO risk and opens up investment opportunities to a broader range of CDOs than those available in the cash market. Second, CDO CDS allows one to efficiently short CDOs for the first time. Applications range from simply providing another way to get out of long-cash CDO positions to the execution of various long-short strategies. These long-short strategies could involve tranches within the same CDO, tranches from different CDOs, or CDO tranches and underlying CDO assets. Third, supply and demand technicals across cash and synthetic CDO markets almost guarantee price misalignments and therefore profitable trading opportunities. Finally, trading levels of CDO CDS will enlighten one's view of the cash CDO market. Price distinctions among vintages and managers may be more apparent, or apparent sooner, in the synthetic market than in the cash market. And even if CDO CDS levels do not affect one's view of the quality and value of cash CDOs, CDS levels will impact the views of other cash market participants. And one needs to understand what others are thinking to trade optimally.

In this chapter, we explain the documentation for trades of credit defaults swaps (CDS) on CDOs. In a simple, straightforward way, we explain the CDO credit problems the documentation recognizes, the consequences for which CDO CDS documentation provides, and the choices of interest rate cap. We also address miscellaneous CDO CDS terms, the differences between selling protection on a CDS and owning a cash CDO, how one exits a CDO CDS, and rating agency concerns when a CDO enters into a CDO CDS.

Note that in this chapter, capitalized terms are ISDA-defined terms that one will find in CDO CDS documentation. Lower-case terms are widely-understood colloquialisms not found in CDO CDS documents.

CDO CDS NOMENCLATURE

It takes two parties to make a CDO CDS: a *credit protection buyer* and a *credit protection seller*. Naturally, it also takes a CDO tranche to be the subject of the CDO CDS between the two parties. Formally, the CDO tranche is the *Reference Obligation* and the CDO it is part of is the *Reference Entity*. The protection buyer buys credit protection from the protection seller on a specific CDO tranche in a dollar-amount size called the "notional amount." As shown in Exhibit 7.1, the protection buyer pays the protection seller a fee based on a number of basis points per annum times the notional amount times the appropriate day count fraction of a year. These payments are paid by the protection buyer quarterly for the life of the CDO CDS, assuming certain CDO credit problems (defined below) do not occur.

As shown in Exhibit 7.2, the protection buyer is known as the *Fixed Rate Payer* while the protection seller is known as the *Floating Rate Payer*, in ISDA swap documentation. This is holdover from ISDA interest rate swap terminology in which one party pays a fixed interest rate and the other party pays a floating interest rate. The buyer of protection is said to be long the CDS, but since he has a similar risk to someone who has shorted the referenced CDO tranche (he loves defaults!), he is said to be short the CDO. The seller of protection is short the CDS, but since he has a similar risk to someone who owns the referenced CDO tranche (he hates defaults!), he is long the CDO.

In a CDO CDS, the notional amount of the CDS amortizes in step with the CDO tranche. For example, if 50% of the CDO tranche amortizes, 50% of the CDS notional is considered to have amortized. Therefore, the life span of a CDO CDS mirrors the life span of the CDO tranche. The amortization of CDO CDS is in contrast to corporate CDS. While a corporate CDS has a *single* Refer-

EXHIBIT 7.1   Initial Cash Flows of a Credit Default Swap

Credit Protection Buyer	Periodic Payments — Basis points × Notional amount →	Credit Protection Seller

EXHIBIT 7.2   Equivalent Buyer and Seller Designations

Credit Protection Buyer Fixed rate payer is long, the CDS is short the underlying CDO	Periodic Payments — Basis points × Notional amount →	**Credit Protection Seller** Floating rate payer is short, the CDS is long the underlying CDO

ence Entity (e.g., IBM), it usually encompasses a class of Reference Obligations (e.g., all senior unsecured debt of IBM). The *term* of the corporate CDS overarches specific Reference Obligations. In other words, Reference Obligations may be issued or retired over the life of the corporate CDS; but as long as some issue of the Reference Entity fits the Reference Obligation definition, the corporate CDS can continue. In contrast, the specificity of CDO CDS to a particular CDO tranche drives CDO CDS amortization and restricts CDO CDS tenor.

CDO CREDIT PROBLEMS AND THEIR CONSEQUENCES

As we all know, a CDO can experience credit problems. ISDA CDO CDS documentation specifically defines five CDO credit problems with respect to a CDO tranche. As shown in the left column of Exhibit 7.2, these are: *Interest Shortfall*, *Failure to Pay Interest*, *Writedown and Implied Writedown*, *Failure to Pay Principal*, and *Distressed Ratings Downgrade*.

Now note that shown across the top of Exhibit 7.2 are two consequences of a CDO credit problem: *Floating Amount Events* and *Credit Events*. As shown in the exhibit, Floating Amount Events are subject to Floating Payments, which is known colloquially as *pay as you go settlement*. Credit Events are subject to *Physical Settlement*. ISDA documentation also has specific definitions of these terms.

Different CDO credit problems have different consequences. For now, just note that Exhibit 7.3 shows that the consequence of some CDO credit problems is a Floating Amount Event, the consequence of other CDO credit problems is a Credit Event, and some CDO credit problems can have either a Floating Amount Event or a Credit Event consequence.

EXHIBIT 7.3 CDO Credit Problems and Their Consequences

	Two Consequences	
	Floating Amount Events	Credit Events
Five CDO Credit Problems	Subject to Floating Payments (Pay as you go settlement)	Subject to Physical Settlement
Interest Shortfall	X	
Failure to Pay Interest		X
Writedown and Implied Writedown	X	X
Failure to Pay Principal	X	X
Distressed Ratings Downgrade		X

In the next section, we discuss the five CDO credit problems that ISDA CDO CDS documentation recognizes and defines. Then we discuss the two consequences for which the documentation provides. Afterwards, the CDO CDS system of CDO credit problems and consequences will gel.

CDO Credit Problems

Interest Shortfall is the failure of the CDO to pay all interest due on the Reference Obligation. Note that interest due includes interest that is PIKable[1] under the terms of the CDO tranche.

Failure to Pay Interest has a more stringent definition than Interest Shortfall. Skipping a PIKable interest coupon does not trigger Failure to Pay Interest unless the CDO has been PIKing for one year. Furthermore, for both non-PIK and PIKable CDO tranches, the amount of unpaid interest involved must be at least $10,000. The more stringent requirement of Failure to Pay Interest over Interest Shortfall has to do with their differing consequences. Interest Shortfall is Floating Amount Event subject to a Floating Payment (pay as you go settlement) while the Failure to Pay Interest is a Credit Event subject to Physical Settlement.[2]

CDOs rarely have mechanisms that formally realize principal losses due to credit losses in the underlying collateral portfolio. But if a CDO did have this feature, those events would be captured by the *Writedown* definition. In the absence of a Writedown mechanism in the CDO, the parties to a CDO CDS can elect to use *Implied Writedown*. Simplified, a CDO tranche is implicitly written down if its par overcollateralization ratio falls below 100%. For purposes of Implied Writedown, overcollateralization is calculated by the terms of the indenture, including its treatment of par haircuts for downgraded or defaulted collateral.[3]

Failure to Pay Principal is the failure of the reference CDO to pay the reference tranche's principal by the *effective* maturity of the CDO, which is the earlier of (1) the time the CDO's assets have all been amortized or liquidated or by (2) the legal final maturity of the Reference Obligation.

Distressed Ratings Downgrade occurs if any rating agency downgrades the CDO tranche to CCC/Caa2 or below or withdraws its rating.

---

[1] A *pay-in-kind* (PIK) *bond* or *PIK feature* is one where instead of paying current copon, the par value of bond is increased by the appropriate amount.

[2] For those interested in the differences between CDO CDS and ABS CDS standard documentation, Failure to Pay Interest is not a Credit Event in ABS CDS.

[3] Regarding the differences between CDO CDS and ABS CDS standard documentation, Implied Writedown is mandatory for ABS CDS, but optional for CDO CDS.

Consequences

As we said, ISDA documentation also defines two "consequences" of a "CDO credit problem": Floating Payments (pay as you go settlement) or Physical Settlement. Note again that Implied Writedown and Failure to Pay Principal can be either a Floating Amount Event or a Credit Event. The choice is up to the protection buyer.

Floating Amount Events cause Floating Payments, or pay as you go settlement. Interest Shortfall, Implied Writedown, and Failure to Pay Principal are Floating Amount Events. The protection seller must pay the amount of the Interest Shortfall or Implied Writedown to the protection buyer. Note that the amounts involved in an Interest Shortfall or an Implied Writedown might be small relative to the notional amount of the swap. Any payment period's Interest Shortfall can be no more than the amount of interest due in that payment period. The amount of an Implied Writedown could be a small fraction of CDS notional.

A unique aspect of Interest Shortfall and Implied Writedown is that they are reversible. If a CDO pays previously PIKed interest on the reference tranche, or if a CDO tranche's par overcollateralization ratio climbs back above its trigger amount, the credit protection buyer must make a reversing payment to the protection seller called an *Additional Fixed Payment*. These reversing payments can take place up to one year and five days after the effective maturity of the CDO.

Because unpaid PIKable interest is included in Interest Shortfall, and paid by the Protection Seller at the time of the shortfall, interest on capitalized PIK interest is *excluded* from future calculations of Interest Shortfall. This is only fair: the protection buyer has received the interest payment from the protection seller, thus should not be entitled to interest on interest.

Failure to Pay Principal is a Floating Amount Event so that at the end of the CDO, the protection buyer can receive a payment even if he does not own the CDO. In this case, the protection seller pays the remaining notional amount of the CDO CDS to the protection buyer. Note that the protection buyer does not get to double count Implied Writedowns and Failure to Pay Principal. When an Implied Writedown amount is paid, the notional amount of the CDO CDS is reduced. That is, to the extent that Implied Writedowns have been taken, CDO CDS notional is reduced. The protection buyer can't subsequently claim the written down amount again as a Failure to Pay Principal.

Credit Events cause Physical Settlement. At the protection buyer's option, the protection buyer delivers the CDO tranche and the protection seller pays par. Failure to Pay Principal, Implied Writedown, Failure to Pay Interest, and Distressed Ratings Downgrade are Credit Events causing

Physical Settlement. Once done, Physical Settlement cannot be reversed. The protection buyer can deliver less than the full notional amount of the CDS and the remainder of the CDS notional will continue in force.

Note that there is no cash flow effect to the CDO from a ratings downgrade and no dollar amount of impairment can be specified. Therefore, Distressed Ratings Downgrade is only a Credit Event causing Physical Settlement, and can not be a Floating Payment Event causing pay as you go settlement.

An advantage of Floating Payments over Physical Settlement is that the protection buyer does not have to own the CDO tranche to collect a protection payment. Both Floating Payment and Physical Settlement have an advantage over Cash Settlement, in that they eliminate the need to poll dealers for the market price of what may be an extremely illiquid instrument by the time it is in severe distress. Cash Settlement is not a standard choice under CDO CDS documentation, as it is in corporate CDS because of the difficulty of determining a market price for a failing CDO tranche. Pay as you go settlement was, in fact, developed to provide a practical alternative to cash settlement.

ALTERNATIVE INTEREST CAP OPTIONS

Standard CDO CDS documentation provides for three ways to size the protection seller's responsibility for Interest Shortfalls under Floating Payment or pay as you go settlement. Two of them, Interest Shortfall Cap Not Applicable and Variable Cap, are similar, while Fixed Cap greatly limits the protection seller's obligation.[4]

Interest Shortfall Cap Not Applicable

The protection seller pays the protection buyer the full amount of the cash CDO's Interest Shortfall. If no interest whatsoever is paid on the reference obligation, the protection seller would pay the obligation's LIBOR index plus coupon spread. But this payment, like all Interest Shortfall payments to the protection buyer, is netted against the CDS premium payment the protection buyer pays the protection seller. So the protection seller's maximum obligation to the protection buyer for an Interest Shortfall is

LIBOR + The cash CDO coupon spread − The CDS premium

---

[4] For those interested in the differences between CDO CDS and ABS CDS standard documentation, note that these interest cap options are the same as those for ABS CDS.

Variable Cap

The protection seller's obligation depends on the relationship of the CDS premium to the cash CDO coupon spread. If the CDS premium is *less* than the cash CDO coupon spread, the protection seller's gross payment is limited to the reference obligation's LIBOR index plus the CDS premium. If the CDS premium is *greater* than the cash CDO's coupon, the protection seller's gross payment is limited to the reference obligation's LIBOR index and coupon spread. Again, Interest Shortfall payments to the protection buyer are netted against the CDS premium payment the protection buyer pays the protection seller. So the maximum obligation of the protection seller to the protection buyer for an Interest Shortfall is:

LIBOR + (The lesser of the CDS premium or cash CDO coupon spread) – The CDS premium

Fixed Cap or "Premium Squeeze to Zero"

The protection seller's payment to the protection buyer is limited to the CDS premium, that is, the protection seller is not responsible for the LIBOR component of the cash CDO coupon. The net payment amount, then, can never be a payment from the protection seller to the protection buyer. An Interest Shortfall amount only reduces the premium the protection buyer pays the protection seller. It never reverses the direction of the payment. Note that the withholding of the CDS premium fully extinguishes the protection seller's obligation in that period, which is to say that the amount of interest lost on the cash CDO but not covered by withholding the CDS premium is not carried forward into future interest periods.

Under any of the three interest cap options, if the CDO tranche catches up on an Interest Shortfall, the protection buyer must repay the Interest Shortfall amount to the protection seller. Compounding this reimbursement at LIBOR plus the CDS premium is optional, decided by mutual agreement of the protection seller and buyer at the inception of the CDO CDS.

Exhibit 7.4 illustrates these interest cap options using the example of a cash CDO tranche with a coupon of LIBOR + 300 bps, a CDO CDS with a premium of 280 bps, and where LIBOR equals 4%. In the exhibit, the maximum the protection seller can pay under No Cap Applicable is the coupon on the CDO (LIBOR + 300 bps) netted against the CDO CDS premium (280 bps) or LIBOR + 20 bps. Assuming LIBOR equals 4%, this comes to 420 bps. The maximum the protection seller can pay under Variable Cap is LIBOR plus the CDO CDS premium (LIBOR + 280 bps) netted against the

EXHIBIT 7.4 Example of CDO CDS Interest Rate Caps

Assumptions

CDO Coupon = LIBOR + 300 bps
CDO CDS Premium = 280 bps
LIBOR = 4%

Cash Bond Pays LIBOR + 300	Protection Seller's Gross Payment	Protection Seller's Net Receipt/(Payment)
Cap not applicable	0 bps	280 bps
Variable cap	0 bps	280 bps
Fixed cap	0 bps	280 bps

Cash Bond Pays LIBOR + 280	Protection Seller's Gross Payment	Protection Seller's Net Receipt/(Payment)
Cap not applicable	20 bps	260 bps
Variable cap	20 bps	260 bps
Fixed cap	20 bps	260 bps

Cash Bond Pays LIBOR + 100	Protection Seller's Gross Payment	Protection Seller's Net Receipt/(Payment)
Cap not applicable	200 bps	80 bps
Variable cap	200 bps	80 bps
Fixed cap	200 bps	80 bps

Cash Bond Pays LIBOR + 0	Protection Seller's Gross Payment	Protection Seller's Net Receipt/(Payment)
Cap not applicable	300 bps	(20 bps)
Variable cap	300 bps	(20 bps)
Fixed cap	300 bps	0 bps

Cash Bond Pays LIBOR − 200	Protection Seller's Gross Payment	Protection Seller's Net Receipt/(Payment)
Cap not applicable	500 bps	(220 bps)
Variable cap	500 bps	(220 bps)
Fixed cap	280 bps	0 bps

Cash Bond Pays LIBOR − 400	Protection Seller's Gross Payment	Protection Seller's Net Receipt/(Payment)
Cap not applicable	700 bps	(420 bps)
Variable cap	680 bps	(400 bps)
Fixed cap	280 bps	0 bps

EXHIBIT 7.5 Protection Seller Receipt (Payment)

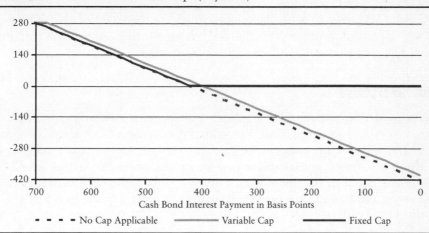

CDO CDS premium (280 bps) or LIBOR flat. As we assume LIBOR equal 4%, this comes to 400 bps. Finally, the maximum the protection seller has to pay under Fixed Cap is the premium on the CDO CDS (280 bps) netted against the CDO CDS premium (280 bps) or 0 bps. We graph these results in Exhibit 7.5.

Exhibits 7.4 and 7.5 make clear which interest cap terms a protection seller or protection buyer would like to have. All other things equal, including CDO CDS premium, a protection buyer wants No Cap or Variable Cap; a protection seller wants Fixed Cap.

MISCELLANEOUS TERMS

There are a few other points to make about the standard CDO CDS contract.

CDO Tranche Events of Default

Some circumstances constituting Events of Default on the underlying cash CDO tranche may not be Floating Payment Events or Credit Events under the CDO CDS. These cash CDO Events of Default have no effect on the CDO CDS. Examples include: low overcollateralization results, manager bankruptcy or fraud, and the CDO being required to register as an investment company.

Voting Right and Control

A cash CDO debt tranche might gain control of the CDO as classes below it are wiped out. A protection seller doesn't gain voting rights or control unless delivered the cash bond via Physical Settlement.

Upfront Exchange

Instead of adjusting the CDS premium to reflect current market spreads, an upfront exchange can be made. For example, suppose a CDO with a coupon of LIBOR + 200 bps trades at 102% of par, providing a discount margin of LIBOR + 150 bps, given expected amortization. Instead of setting the CDS premium equal to the discount margin of 150 bps, the CDS premium can be set at 200 bps and the protection seller can pay the protection buyer $2 upfront.

Documents and Calculations

The protection buyer is responsible for providing trustee reports to the protection seller. In trades between two dealers, the protection seller is the Calculation Agent. In trades between a dealer and an end user, the dealer is the Calculation Agent.

CASH CDO VERSUS CDO CDS

Some investors are concerned about the fidelity of CDO CDS to a cash position in the referenced CDO. From the protection seller's point of view, how well do the Floating Amount Events and Credit Events replicate the economic experience of owning the underlying reference CDO?

The too easy answer is that Credit Events and Physical Settlement provide the closest fit to owning a cash CDO. Obviously, the protection seller will get the cash instrument's cash flows if he buys the cash instrument, as one essentially does in Physical Settlement. But if that's what the protection seller really wants, he should buy the cash CDO to begin with. What one is probably looking for in a CDO CDS is the economic equivalence of a cash CDO in *synthetic* form. Without the uncertainties of the mark-to-market process in a total return swap, the protection seller wants to monetize the pluses and minuses, due to credit experience, of owning the cash CDO.

By this logic, Credit Events and Physical Settlement, except for Failure to Pay Principal which occurs at the end of the CDO's life, do not do a good job of replicating the credit pluses and minuses of owning the cash CDO.

On the other hand, Implied Writedown attempts to quantify credit deterioration of the cash CDO as it occurs. No Cap Applicable and Variable Cap do the best job of capturing the effect of lost interest payments. The reversible nature of Floating Amount Events compensates the protection seller if the initial loss measurement is too sensitive.

Current documentation trends, however, tend to split the difference between the cash replication of Implied Writedown on one hand and the cash replication of No Cap or Variable Cap on the other. The two most popular combinations of CDO CDS are Variable Cap with no Implied Writedown and Fixed Cap with Implied Writedown. Obviously, the protection seller likes Fixed Cap, as the responsibility for Interest Shortfalls is limited to loss of the incoming CDS premium. Likewise, no Implied Writedown delays payment of CDS notional to the protection buyer. No Implied Writedown also maintains the CDS premium at a higher amount, as it is calculated off a higher notional amount. On the other hand, not writing down the CDO may mean that the protection seller has to protect the interest due on that unwritten-down amount.

EXITING A CDO CDS

Investors considering getting into a CDO CDS should also consider how they would get *out* of the trade. Naturally, the CDO CDS can be held to maturity, but there are three routes for exiting the trade before that time.

Termination

By mutual agreement, the two counterparties to the CDO CDS tear up the swap and it exists no more. This usually involves a termination payment from one party to another. The direction of the termination payment is determined by the relationship of the contracted premium protection and the current market price of protection on the referenced CDO tranche. For example, suppose the CDO CDS premium is 20 bps lower than the current cost of protection on the CDO tranche. The protection buyer will have to pay 20 bps more to enter into a replacement CDO CDS with a new counterparty. In this case, the protection seller needs to compensate the protection buyer to terminate (also known as unwind) the CDO CDS. The payment will be based on the present value of the 20 bps times the notional amount of the CDS over the expected amortization of the CDO tranche.

Assignment

The party wishing to exit the CDO CDS finds another to take its place in the transaction. The replacement must be agreeable to the party who wishes to continue in the CDO CDS. The exiting party pays (receives) an assignment fee to (from) the new party to the CDO CDS. Analogous to a termination fee, the assignment fee compensates the new counterparty for entering into an off-market transaction, that is, a CDO CDS done at a premium other than the current market premium.

Offsetting

The party wishing to exit the CDO CDS does an offsetting trade. A party reverses out of a CDO CDS it has sold protection on, for example, by buying protection on the same underlying CDO with a new counterparty at the going market rate. Now the party has two trades whose terms might not be completely identical and whose premiums might be different. To equalize cash flows as much as possible, the party should match their actions on the CDO CDS that they have bought protection on to those of the protection buyer of the CDO CDS they sold protection on. That is, they should call Floating Payment Events and Credit Events when the protection buyer does. Alternatively, if they feel the protection buyer has suboptimally called an Event, they can refrain from calling an Event on the offsetting position and take a position on the cash flow differences between the two CDO CDS. Offsetting is the most common way to exit ABS CDS; it may also become the most common exit for CDO CDS.

RATING AGENCY CONCERNS ON CDOS THAT SELL PROTECTION VIA CDO CDS

When a CDO^2 (*CDO squared*) or any CDO sells protection via CDO CDS, rating agencies are concerned that the CDO take on no more risk than it would if it purchased cash CDO tranches outright. Rating agencies rely on their default studies and sometimes have a hard time sizing risks not incorporated in those default studies or otherwise reflected in the modeling and stress testing they put CDO tranches through. One such concern is market value risks. For example, rating agencies do not want to see a CDO manager forced to sell cash collateral upon a default. Instead, they want the manager to time any liquidation optimally. When analyzing a CDO, the rating agencies don't want the manager to be forced to sell CDO tranches received via Physical Settlement. If the CDO structure requires the quick sale of such a

CDO, the rating agencies will assume a lower recovery value than if the timing of the sale is up to the CDO manager.

A CDO selling protection via CDO CDS might also have to make payments under pay as you go settlement. To the extent these reflect risks not incorporated in rating agency default studies, the CDO must have additional protections and liquidity. To limit this risk, CDOs usually choose to not include Implied Writedown as a Floating Amount Event or Credit Event.

SUMMARY

Investors who already owns cash CDOs and anyone who wants to get long, or get short, CDOs in the future must understand the ISDA CDO CDS documentation. We broke the document into its working parts and explained each. We think Exhibit 7.3 nicely sorts out the five credit problems the documentation recognizes can happen to a CDO and the two consequences for which the documentation provides. We also addressed the *three* choices of interest rate cap, miscellaneous CDO CDS terms, the differences between selling protection on a CDS and owning a cash CDO, how one exits a CDO CDS, and rating agency concerns when a CDO enters into a CDO CDS.

PART Three

Emerging CDO Products

CHAPTER 8

Trust-Preferred CDOs

Trust-preferred security-collateralized debt obligations or TruPS CDOs, are unusual in many respects. Other CDOs are comprised of senior-secured obligations (e.g., collateralized loan obligations (CLOs)) or investment-grade collateral (e.g., ABS CDOs). TruPS CDOs, however, are comprised of the deeply subordinate and unrated debt of banks, insurance companies, and REITs.

Other CDOs are either arbitrage transactions, in which a collateral manager assembles a portfolio from securities available in the market; or balance sheet transactions, in which a seller sheds its own assets and places them in a CDO. TruPS CDOs fit neither case. Instead, the collateral of a TruPS CDO is specifically issued to be purchased by a CDO and the CDO is the sole purchaser of the entire issue.

Additionally, TruPS CDOs exist in a niche, with issuance only a small portion of U.S. CDO issuance. They thus provide diversity from the usual asset classes represented in CDOs.

In this chapter we (1) we define trust-preferred securities and other assets that are regularly included in TruPS CDOs; (2) describe the issuance trends and structural features of TruPS CDOs; (3) discuss how the falling coupon on bank TruPS will affect TruPS CDO prepayments; (4) show how rating agencies use historical data in determining their trust-preferred default, recovery, and diversification assumptions; and (5) show how trust-preferred collateral has performed within seasoned CDOs.

TRUST-PREFERRED SECURITIES

Trust-preferred securities (TruPS) combine the best of both worlds for a bank, insurance company, or REIT issuer. TruPS dividends are a tax-deductible interest expense, yet they are treated as equity by regulators and rating agencies. The trick is that TruPS are long-term securities subordinate to all other debts of the issuer and the issuer is contractually allowed to defer interest payments for up to five years.

EXHIBIT 8.1   TruPS Issuance Diagram

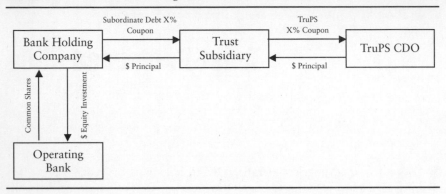

Mechanically, a bank or thrift holding company issues a 30-year non-amortizing junior subordinated loan or note to a wholly-owned grantor trust subsidiary, as shown in the left of Exhibit 8.1. The trust, in turn, issues TruPS directly to a TruPS CDO. The trust uses proceeds from the sale of TruPS to pay for the subordinate debt of the bank holding company.

The coupon and 30-year maturity of the junior subordinated obligation from the bank holding company to the trust match those of the TruPS from the trust to investors or a TruPS CDO. The trust uses cash flow from the subordinate debt to make payments on its TruPS. Dividends on TruPS are cumulative, meaning that if a TruPS misses its coupon one period, it has the obligation to make up the missed interest payment and pay interest on interest. However, interest payments can be deferred for five years. In fact, interest payments can be repeatedly deferred over the TruPS 30-year life, so long as no single continuous deferral period lasts more than five years. That is, the TruPS can defer interest payments for five years, catch up on interest payments, and then defer for another five years. The subordinate note from the bank holding company to the trust has these same deferral features. TruPS have a call option, but the pertinent state or federal bank regulator must approve any prepayment.

The Federal Reserve formally recognized TruPS as Tier 1 capital at the bank holding company level in 1996 and reaffirmed their opinion in 2004.[1]

---

[1] The tax deduction on TruPS arises from the *deconsolidation* of the trust from the bank holding company. The trust and the TruPS are ignored for tax purposes and the bank simply has the junior subordinated obligation to the trust and the accompanying interest expense deduction. Prior to 2003, the trust was consolidated onto the bank's generally accepted accounting principles (GAAP) financials and the bank recorded the TruPS as a minority ownership interest. However, the same accounting crusade that fueled Financial Accounting Standards Board (FASB) attempts to *consolidate* CDOs on their manager's balance sheet also called for

If the proceeds of the issuance are downstreamed to operating banks in the form of a holding company equity investment in the operating bank, the TruPS issuance provides Tier 1 capital to the operating bank.

Insurance company TruPS mirror bank TruPS. As insurance holding companies are not regulated, the regulatory benefit of an insurance TruPS issuance comes about when proceeds are downstreamed to operating insurance companies. If contributed as an equity investment in the operating insurance company, the operating insurance company receives 100% capital credit in regulatory capital ratios. TruPS are typically rated four to five rating notches lower than the claims paying ability of the operating insurance company. There are two reasons for this.

First, insurance holding company debt is structurally subordinate to insurance operating company insurance claims because the holding company claim upon the operating insurance company is only that of an equity holder. In other words, the insurance holding company only receives cash from the insurance operating company in the form of common stock dividends after insurance claims and other debt holders at the insurance operating company are satisfied. Second, the TruPS are subordinate to the insurance holding company's more senior debt.

REITs are investment vehicles that own real estate or debt collateralized by real estate. They are not subject to entity level taxation as long as they (1) have at least 75% of their assets in real estate; (2) derive at least 75% of their income from real estate; and (3) distribute at least 90% of each year's income to their shareholders. Equity REITs own and operate real estate assets while mortgage REITs own real estate related debt. The mechanics and terms of REIT TruPS are similar to bank and insurance TruPS.

Before their incorporation into CDOs, TruPS were issued by large institutions that had the name recognition, and capital appetite, to issue in quantities of $100 million or more. The innovation of the TruPS CDO allowed smaller entities to pool their TruPS issuance, share underwriting and issuance costs, and gain access to the broader capital markets.

---

banks to *unconsolidate* these trusts from bank balance sheets. Thus, bank balance sheet presentation switched from carrying the TruPS as minority interest to recognizing it instead as junior subordinated debt. This change in GAAP treatment caused the Federal Reserve to rethink the applicability of TruPS as Tier 1 capital. But in 2004, the Fed formally recognized that the economics of the TruPS had not changed, regardless of the GAAP treatment. However, the Fed ruled that TruPS can comprise no more than 25% of a bank's Tier 1 capital and only 15% if the bank is "internationally active."

OTHER TruPS CDO ASSETS

More senior obligations from banks, insurance companies, and REITs are sometimes included in TruPS CDO portfolios. Typically, bank debt is incorporated in CDOs that invest in bank TruPS, insurance company debt is incorporated in CDOs that invest in insurance TruPS, and REIT debt is incorporated in CDOs that invest in REIT TruPS.

Bank subordinated notes are issued from either the holding company or operating bank. Because interest on subordinated debt is not deferrable, this debt has a superior claim upon the issuing entity over the deferrable subordinated debt issued in the TruPS scheme. Because of this, the Fed only allows Tier 2 regulatory capital treatment for bank subordinated debt. Maturities are usually 10 years with a 5-year noncall period.

Insurance company senior and subordinated debt is usually issued out of insurance holding companies. It generally has 10-year maturities and 5-year noncall periods. Insurance company surplus notes are usually issued by operating insurance companies and usually by mutual insurance companies that do not have a holding company structure. Therefore, surplus notes avoid the structural subordination of insurance holding company debt. However, interest and principal payments are subject to regulatory approval. Rating agencies generally rate surplus notes two notches below the insurance company's claims paying rating. Insurance company surplus notes generally have a 30-year maturity and a 5-year noncall period.

Unsecured REIT debt and commercial mortgage-backed securities (CMBS) are incorporated in some TruPS CDOs. They usually have maturities of 10 years.

TruPS CDO ISSUANCE

TruPS CDO issuance has been on an upward trajectory since the first CDO was issued in 2000. As shown in Exhibit 8.2, yearly issuance rose from $0.8 billion in 2000 to $9.8 billion in 2005 to $6.5 billion in the first half of 2006.[2] The exhibit also shows the mixture of TruPS CDO collateral between bank, insurance company, REIT, and other bank TruPS CDOs. It can be seen from the exhibit that bank-collateral-fueled volume increases from 2001 through 2004. Insurance collateral actually peaked in 2003. Volume was essentially static in 2004 and issuance would have decreased in 2005 were it not for the advent of REIT obligations in TruPS CDOs. TruPS CDOs also began including older vintages of TruPS CDOs in their collateral port-

---

[2] Statistics on TruPS CDO issuance were complied from data on *www.FitchRating. com* and the rating agency's research reports on individual issuers.

EXHIBIT 8.2 TruPS CDO Issuance by Collateral Type

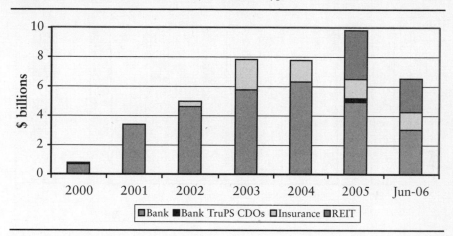

Source: FitchRatings, UBS Calculations.

EXHIBIT 8.3 Number and Average Size of TruPS CDOs by Vintage

Year	Number	Average Size ($ million)
2000	3	252
2001	6	562
2002	10	49.5
2003	18	433
2004	19	408
2005	16	612
Jun-06	9	673

Source: FitchRatings, UBS Calculations.

folios in 2005. Exhibit 8.3 shows the number of TruPS CDOs issued each year and the average size of TruPS CDOs, which rose significantly in 2005.

Exhibits 8.4 provides another picture of the share of bank, insurance company, REIT, and TruPS CDO obligations in TruPS CDOs. Bank collateral has ranged between 46% and 100% and was at the lower point of that range in the first six months of 2006. Insurance company collateral has ranged between 0% and 27% and is at 19% as of the first six months in 2006. REIT collateral debuted in 2005 at 34% and is at 35% as of the first six months of 2006. As of the first six months of 2006, the percent of col-

EXHIBIT 8.4   Percent of Collateral Type in TruPS CDOs by Vintage

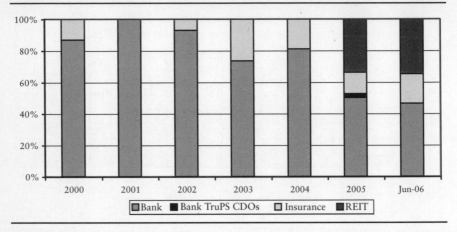

Source: FitchRatings, UBS Calculations.

EXHIBIT 8.5   Collateral Type Combinations in TruPS CDOs

Year	Bank	Bank & Insurance	Insurance	REITs	Bank, REITs & Insurance	Total
2000	2	1				3
2001	6					6
2002	9		1			10
2003	12	1	5			18
2004	12	5	2			19
2005	3	8		4	1	16
Jun-06		3		3	3	9
Total	44	18	8	7	4	81

Source: FitchRatings, UBS Calculations.

lateral type in TruPS is as follows: bank (46%), REIT (35%), and insurance (19%).[3]

Although one of the first TruPS CDOs issued in 2000 contained both bank and insurance company collateral, mixed portfolios were rare until 2004. But as shown in Exhibit 8.5, hybrid TruPS CDOs became the norm in 2005. In the first half of 2006, REIT TruPS were included in hybrid CDOs as often as they were in 100% REIT TruPS CDOs. In 2005, bank and insur-

---

[3] The source is FitchRatings and UBS calculations.

ance company collateral were almost always included in mixed collateral TruPS CDOs. As bank TruPS spreads declined (see the discussion in the next section), CDO structurers had to include other higher yielding assets in TruPS CDO portfolios so as to create an attractive arbitrage for equity holders. The next thing we expect to see is middle-market loans and small and medium enterprise loans included with bank TruPS in CDOs.

BANK TruPS PREPAYMENTS AND NEW CDO ISSUANCE

The weighted average spread (WAS) of bank TruPS in CDOs has declined pretty consistently since the first TruPS CDO in 2001. Exhibit 8.6 shows the WAS of bank TruPS in 43 CDOs issued between 2001 and 2005. The spread of Bank TruPS in these CDOs fell 242 basis points, from LIBOR + 410 to LIBOR + 168. This was partly due to the general tightening of credit spreads in these years and partly due to the increased demand from TruPS CDOs for bank TruPS.

Most of the $4 billion of bank TruPS issued into TruPS CDOs in 2000 and 2001 emerged from their noncall periods in 2006. Obviously, any bank that can take advantage of lower spreads will want to do so. It is possible that bank TruPS CDOs from 2000 and 2001 will see massive collateral prepayments, causing TruPS CDO tranches to amortize. How will the TruPS CDO market react to such an increase in bank TruPS supply? Will the influx of so many bank issuers refinancing their TruPS at the same time reverse the tightening trend? We already saw some of that as spreads of the best bank TruPS issuers widened from LIBOR + 135 to 140 in December 2005

EXHIBIT 8.6   Bank TruPS Weighted Average Spreads

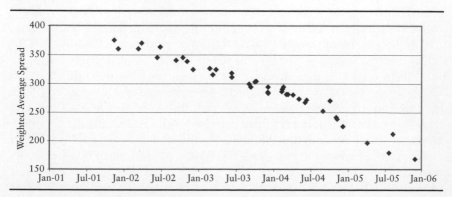

Source: FitchRatings, Trustee Reports.

to LIBOR + 155 to 170 by mid-2006. Note that these are still attractive spreads for banks that sold TruPS into CDOs in 2000 and 2001.

We expect demand for bank TruPS by CDOs to keep TruPS spreads fairly tight. Since prepaying TruPS amortize CDO liabilities dollar for dollar, they create their own demand, as long as TruPS CDO liability holders want to replace their amortizing assets. As the TruPS CDO market is almost an afterthought in terms of the volume of the entire CDO market, new demand from other CDO investors should not be so hard to find. Finally, the street's capacity to underwrite TruPS CDOs has expanded, thanks to the proliferation of banks interested in the product.

TruPS CDO STRUCTURE

TruPS CDOs have traditional overcollateralization (OC) tests or optimal principal distribution amount (OPDA) tests. Some TruPS CDOs begin with OC tests, then switch to OPDA tests. The other relevant variable is the amount of excess spread allocated to cure a failure of the applicable test, which can vary from 50% to 100% of available excess spread.

OC tests in TruPS CDOs operate as in most cash flow CDOs. At the point of the OC test failure in the CDO waterfall, excess spread is diverted from subordinate tranches and used to pay down the CDO's senior-most tranche until the CDO is back in compliance with the OC test. Deferring TruPS are considered to be in default and are significantly haircut in the numerator of the CDO's overcollateralization ratios. For example, Moody's guidelines call for deferring TruPS to be counted in the CDO's overcollateralization ratios at 10% of par. In practice, some CDOs give deferring TruPS zero credit in their OC tests.

OPDA tests require the CDO to divert cash flow to pay down its senior-most tranche by the aggregate amount of all deferring TruPS in the CDO collateral portfolio. Thus, if $10 million of TruPS collateral is deferring, $10 million of senior tranche principal must be paid down. Usually, 50% to 70% of excess spread is allocated to senior tranche amortization.

OPDA tests are more advantageous to debt tranches than are OC tests. OC tests are set below the initial OC level for each CDO tranche. They then operate to get the tranche's OC back up to the test level. Thus, OC tests allow a certain amount of par deterioration. OPDA tests do not allow any deterioration before they become effective and push the CDO to higher levels of OC. Suppose that a CDO has $100 of assets and $90 of debt. Its overall OC is $100/$90 or 111%. If $10 of TruPS defers, the OPDA test immediately begins paying down $10 of CDO debt. When complete, the CDO has $90 of assets and $80 of debt for an OC of $90/$80 or 113%.

Whether OC or OPDA tests are used, deferring TruPS often emerge from deferral and catch up on their skipped interest payments. Fitch's upgrades of three TruPS CDOs were occasioned when deferring TruPS resumed interest payments. These CDOs significantly amortized their tranches while some of their collateral was in deferral. When the collateral became current, the pool of performing collateral grew significantly relative to the CDO's outstanding debt.

Furthermore, REIT TruPS CDOs include collateral haircuts that are applied to TruPS from struggling issuers. These haircuts reduce the par value of TruPS for purposes of overcollateralization tests. Haircuts might range from 20% to 50% based on the REIT's interest coverage ratio, leverage ratio, fixed charge ratio, and whether or not common dividends have been paid. So if a REIT is doing particularly poorly, its securities will only be counted at half their par amount in the numerator the CDO's OC test. The rationale for singling out REITs for collateral haircuts is that they do not have regulators who would step in early and cause the entity to defer interest on their TruPS. REITs might be in bad financial shape for a while before they defer on their TruPS. For this reason, the rating agencies want REIT TruPS CDO cash diversion mechanisms to begin sooner rather than later.

TruPS CDOs often dedicate a portion of excess spread to retiring debt even before the violation of an OC or OPDA test. Usually this amortization occurs pro rata across the CDO debt tranches or in reverse order of seniority.

Almost all TruPS CDO divert a portion of excess cash flow (cash flow after CDO expenses and interest expense) toward the building of a reserve fund until the fund reaches a certain amount. Any draws made from the reserve fund to pay expenses and note interest are replaced with a portion of excess cash flow.

TruPS have 30-year final maturities, but TruPS CDO liabilities are expected to have average lives of 9 to 10 years based on prepayments of underlying assets. But there is risk of extension if underlying assets do not, in fact, prepay. At some point in the life of the CDO, usually at 10 years, an auction of CDO assets is held. If proceeds from an auction of TruPS CDO assets would raise enough to retire the CDO's debt, the auction sale is consummated. Sometimes it is a further requirement of the auction call that it raise enough cash to create a minimum internal rate of return (IRR) for the CDO's equity.

If the auction would not raise the required amount, the auction sale is not completed. The auction is attempted every CDO payment period or every six months until it is successful or until the collateral completely amortizes. After a failed auction, a portion of excess cash flow (50% to 75%) is used to pay down the CDO's notes sequentially.

The first TruPS CDOs had static portfolios. In some new structures, a manager is now allowed to sell defaulted or credit risky assets. Within certain limitations, the manager may reinvestment proceeds from such sales in new collateral. Sometimes reinvestment depends on a vote of senior investors, but usually reinvestment is just a matter of the usual rating agency requirements concerning collateral and portfolio quality. But the amount of actual trading in TruPS CDOs has been very little.

ASSUMPTIONS USED BY RATING AGENCIES

We will now look at the assumptions used by the rating agencies in evaluating TruPS CDOs. Normally, we think rating agency criteria is as interesting as watching paint dry; and about as enlightening. The reason is that because the rating agencies must make so many collateral and modeling assumptions in rating a CDO, focusing on individual assumptions does not make much sense. A conservative assumption here might be out weighed by an anticonservative assumption there. Yet, we thought it worthwhile to discuss how the agencies derive the default and recovery assumptions they use in rating CDOs backed by bank, insurance, and REIT TruPS. But note that we do not attempt to explain every rating agency assumption for every type of TruPS CDO.

Historical Bank Interventions and Fitch Collateral Default Assumptions

Fitch studied FDIC bank interventions since 1970 to determine a 30-year benchmark default rate for bank TruPS.[4] FDIC interventions *over*estimate bank defaults because interventions include cases where banks were allowed to remain in operation and cases where banks did not default on any of their obligations. Fitch did not factor in bank intervention data before 1970 because the rating agency thought changes in bank regulations made that earlier experience irrelevant. Fitch excluded data on thrifts, which historically have had higher failure rates than banks. However, going forward, Fitch believes that regulatory changes made to align thrift and bank regulation will cause thrift intervention rates to be similar to bank intervention rates.

The rating agency notes that their study years include the savings and loan crisis, 1984 to 1994, and that bank intervention rates in those years were actually worse than bank interventions rates during the Great Depression. Looking at banks with assets between $200 million and $10 billion (in 1999 U.S. dollars), Fitch calculated a 30-year cumulative intervention rate of 9.83%.

---

[4] John Schiavetta, Marion Silverman, James E. Moss, Julie A. Burke, and James B. Auden, *Rating Criteria for U.S. Bank and Insurance Trust Preferred CDO*, FitchRatings, February 2, 2005.

EXHIBIT 8.7 Fitch 30-Year Default Assumptions for Financial Institutions

Fitch's Adjusted Bank Score	Desired Rating of CDO Tranche (%)														
	B	B+	BB–	BB	BB+	BBB–	BBB	BBB+	A–	A	A+	AA–	AA	AA+	AAA
1	0	0.25	0.5	0.75	1	1.3	1.6	2	2.5	3	3.75	4.5	5.35	6.25	7.25
1.5	2.5	2.75	3	3.5	4	4.75	5.5	6	7	7.5	8.25	9.5	10.5	11.5	13
2	3.25	3.75	4.75	6.25	7.5	8.75	10	11.5	13	15	17	19	21.5	23	25
2.5	6	7	8.25	10	11.35	13.25	15	16.75	19	21.5	24.5	28	31.5	35	38
3	10	11.25	12.65	14.25	15.5	17.25	19.75	22.5	25.5	28.75	32.25	36	40	45	52
3.5	13	14	15	16.5	18.5	21	23.75	27.25	31.25	35.75	40.5	46	51.5	58	65
4	16.5	17.5	18.5	20	22.5	25.25	28.75	32.65	37.25	42.25	48	54.25	61	68.5	76
4.5	24	25	26.25	27.75	30	34	38.5	43.5	49	55.5	61	66.5	73	81	88
5	34	35	36.25	38	41.5	45	48	53	59	65	71.5	78	85	93	100

Source: FitchRatings.

Fitch used this information in developing the default stress tests for Bank TruPS that we replicate in Exhibit 8.7. The matrix shows the percentage of collateral defaults Fitch requires a bank TruPS CDO tranche to be able to withstand and still be able to pay its principal and interest. Moreover, the tranche must be able to perform whether the defaults occur at the beginning, middle, or end of the CDO's life.

Fitch's "required collateral defaults" depend on two inputs in the matrix. First, the higher the desired rating of the tranche, the higher the default rate the CDO tranche must be able to withstand. Thus required default rates increase to the right of the exhibit. Second, Fitch's methodology also demands higher required default rates for lower quality banks. In Exhibit 8.7, Fitch's "Adjusted Bank Score" measures bank credit quality on a scale of 1 to 5, with higher scores indicating lower credit quality. Thus, required default rates increase down the exhibit.

Looking at the row of required default rates for banks rated "3" in the exhibit, one sees that to achieve a B rating, the CDO tranche must be able to sustain 10% collateral defaults without suffering a loss of principal or interest. This is a little more than the 9.83% default rate that Fitch identifies as its benchmark. But to obtain a AAA rating, the CDO tranche must be able to sustain 52% collateral defaults, over five times Fitch's benchmark. Furthermore, moving up and down the exhibit, for any desired tranche rating, there is a great difference in required default rate over the bank credit quality measure. For example, to obtain a BBB rating, a tranche backed by banks with a credit score of 1 must be able to withstand 1.6% collateral defaults. But a tranche backed by a portfolio of banks with a credit score of 5 must withstand 48% collateral defaults.

Distinctions in bank credit quality are important because as the bank TruPS CDO market evolves, collateral appears to be getting more risky. Banks represented in 2002 TruPS CDOs had an adjusted Fitch bank score of 2.85. By 2004, that figure was 3.11.

What makes a bank a "1" versus a "5"? Fitch starts with a quantitative model of bank credit quality that uses financial ratios encompassing earnings, liquidity, asset quality, and capital. In creating their model, Fitch benefited from the complete record of audited financials and bank interventions collected by the FDIC over many years. In addition to the quantitative model, Fitch makes qualitative downward adjustments to their bank scores if the bank has less than five years operating history, or less than $70 million in assets, or if it is operating under any formal or informal regulatory agreement. Additionally, Fitch will penalize a bank score if the bank engages in activities that are outside industry norms or if the bank obtains more than 60% of its Tier 1 capital from TruPS. Finally, Fitch will penalize a bank score if the bank's TruPS or debt make up more than 3% of the TruPS portfolio.

EXHIBIT 8.8   Fitch Recovery Assumptions for Bank and Insurance TruPS

Desired Rating of CDO Tranche	Fitch Recovery Assumption
AAA	5%
AA	10%
A	15%
BBB	20%
BB	25%

Source: FitchRatings.

Fitch recognizes that the historical bank intervention rate they calculate from FDIC data includes cases where there was never a loss. Thus, in those situations, the default recovery rate was 100%. Yet, "for purposes of conservatism," Fitch assumes the low recoveries shown in Exhibit 8.8. Assumed recoveries depend upon the desired rating of the tranche: the higher the desired rating, the lower the assumed recovery.

Moody's Bank TruPS Collateral Default Assumptions

Interestingly, Moody's looked at the same FDIC data as Fitch, and determined a 17.5%, 30-year bank default rate, much higher than Fitch's 9.83% rate.[5] Obviously, Moody's included in their analysis of FDIC data some of the time period or thrift history that Fitch excluded. Another difference in Moody's collateral assumptions is that the rating agency uses a constant 10% recovery rate rather than Fitch's tiered default rates we showed in Exhibit 8.8. But these differences in default and recovery rates are less significant than one would think, because Moody's cash flow modeling methodology is also different from Fitch's.

In Moody's methodology, the CDO is modeled in many different default scenarios ranging from none of the collateral defaulting to all of the collateral defaulting. The significance of Moody's 17.5% default benchmark is that it influences the probabilities Moody's assigns to each default scenario. Simplifying Moody's rating approach, Moody's rating depends upon the loss a CDO tranche experiences averaged over all default scenarios. In the Fitch approach, the tranche must survive a prescribed level of defaults and recoveries without any loss at all.

The final result of the differences in collateral assumptions and modeling procedures between Fitch and Moody's depends on the rating of the CDO tranches. For tranches that Fitch rates A and above, the Moody's rat-

---

[5] Phillip Mack and Jim Leahy, *Moody's Approach To Rating U.S. Bank Trust Preferred Security CDOs*, Moody's Investors Service, April 14, 2006.

EXHIBIT 8.9   Fitch and Moody's Ratings of I-Preferred Term Securities IV

Tranche	Fitch	Moody's
A	AAA	Aaa
B	A	Aa3
C	BBB	Baa2
D	BBB–	Ba2

Source: FitchRatings, Moody's.

ing is generally the same, but in a few instances Moody's rating is higher. For BBB and BB tranches, Moody's is usually lower than Fitch, which explains why Moody's ratings are not always sought all the way down the capital structure of TruPS CDOs. An example that shows the greatest difference between Fitch and Moody's ratings is a bank-insurance hybrid TruPS CDO, I-Preferred Term Securities IV, whose ratings we show in Exhibit 8.9. Note that Moody's rating is two notches higher than Fitch's in the B tranche and two notches lower than Fitch's in the D tranche.

Historical Insurance Impairments and Fitch Collateral Default Assumptions

A. M. Best conducted a study of insurance company impairments.[6] Best defined "impairment" as the first action by insurance regulators that restricts an insurance company's business activity. This includes everything from the involuntary liquidation of the insurance company to a "cease and desist" order to an administrative order. Best notes that their definition of insurance company impairment is broader than the definition of default, as regulators often take action before an insurance company defaults on any obligation. Moreover, issues that lead to regulatory action may be resolved without the insurance company defaulting on any obligation.

Best calculated impairment rates across property/casualty and life/health insurance companies using standard rating agency cohort methodology. We reproduce some of Best's average cumulative impairment rates in Exhibit 8.10.

As with bank TruPS, Fitch's default stresses for insurance TruPS CDOs depend upon the credit quality of the insurance company and the desired rating of the CDO tranche. Therefore, the defaults rates in Exhibit 8.11 increase to the right as desired tranche rating increases and increase down the exhibit as the credit quality of the insurance company decreases. Fitch's quantitative insurance scoring model takes into account the company's capital, earnings, asset quality, and leverage. In addition, other variables

---

[6] Emmanuel Modu, *Best's Impairment Rate and Rating Transition Study–1977 to 2005*, A. M. Best, March 31, 2006.

EXHIBIT 8.10 Insurance Company Impairment Rates, 1977–2005

A. M. Best Rating	1-Year	5-Year	10-Year	15-Year
A++/A+	0.06%	0.73%	2.23%	4.24%
A/A-	0.21%	2.21%	5.42%	8.13%
B++/B+	0.66%	5.55%	10.90%	15.51%
B/B-	1.98%	9.96%	19.33%	26.98%
C++/C+	3.39%	13.51%	24.78%	30.26%
C/C-	5.95%	16.91%	31.38%	39.81%
D	7.44%	25.66%	41.00%	49.78%
Secure: B+ and above	0.24%	2.25%	5.10%	7.78%
Vulnerable: B and below	3.63%	14.38%	25.96%	33.63%
All insurance companies	0.71%	3.90%	7.97%	11.41%

Source: A. M. Best Co.

such as size, operating history, and amount of TruPS issuance are explicitly addressed in the quantitative scoring model, eliminating the need to make qualitative adjustments to the model's output.

While there are differences in the two agency's rating scales, and differences in their opinions of insurance company credit quality, a company that Fitch assigns a "3" to in Exhibit 8.11 would probably be rated BB+ or A– by A. M. Best in Exhibit 8.10. If so, one can compare the 8% to 16%, 15-year historical default rate that A. M. Best calculates to the 14% to 50%, 30-year default rate assumption Fitch uses in rating insurance TruPS CDOs.

REIT Credit Quality and Moody's Collateral Default Assumptions

If a REIT is rated, Moody's relies on its senior unsecured rating to indicate its default probability.[7] But for unrated mortgage REITs, Moody's uses a scoring system based on four accounting variables: the REIT's asset size, return on equity, leverage, and volatility of profitability. Each attribute is scored on a one-to-four scale which depends on whether the mortgage REIT invests in prime residential, subprime residential, or commercial assets. For example, leverage of 14 times would earn a prime mortgage REIT a score of 4, a subprime mortgage REIT a score of 3, and a commercial mortgage REIT a score of 2. The four scores are averaged for a score which is still

---

[7] James Brennan and Jim Leahy, *Moody's Approach to Rating U.S. REIT CDOs,* Moody's Investors Service, April 4, 2006.

EXHIBIT 8.11 Fitch 30-Year Default Assumptions for Insurance Companies

Fitch's Adjusted Insurance Co. Score	Desired Rating of CDO Tranche (%)														
	B	B+	BB-	BB	BB+	BBB-	BBB	BBB+	A-	A	A+	AA-	AA	AA+	AAA
1	0	0.25	0.5	0.75	1	1.3	1.6	2	2.5	3	3.75	4.5	5.35	6.25	7.25
1.5	2.5	2.75	3	3.5	4	4.5	5.25	5.75	6.5	7.25	8.1	9.25	10.25	11.15	12
2	6.5	7	7.75	8.5	9.35	10.25	11.25	12.35	13.5	14.5	15.75	17.25	18.75	20.5	22.5
2.5	12	12.75	13.75	15	16.25	18	19.5	22	24	25.5	27	29	30.75	32.5	35
3	14	15	16.5	18	19.5	22.25	24.5	26.5	30	33	36.25	39.75	42.5	45.5	50
3.5	16.5	18	20	22	24.25	27.5	30	33	37	40.5	44.5	49	53	57	62
4	23	25	27.5	30	33.25	37	40.5	44	48	51.5	55	60	64	68.5	74
4.5	30	32.5	35	38	41	46	50.5	55	61	64.5	67.5	72	76.5	82	88
5	41	42	44	46	50	52	59	63	67	73	77	83	89	95	100

Source: FitchRatings.

EXHIBIT 8.12 Moody's Default Probability Assumptions for Unrated Mortgage REITs

Mortgage REIT Score	Assumed 10-Year Default Probability
3.5 to 4.0	9.71%
2.5 to 3.4	12.21%
1.5 to 2.4	14.96%
1.4 to 1	19.20%

Source: Moody's.

EXHIBIT 8.13 Moody's Default Probability Assumptions for Unrated Equity REITs

Equity REIT Score	Assumed 10-Year Default Probability
4.5 to 5.0	7.43%
3.5 to 4.4	9.71%
2.5 to 3.4	12.21%
1.5 to 2.4	14.96%
1.4 to 1	19.20%

Source: Moody's.

open for adjustment by Moody's REIT fundamental analysts. The final score is translated into the default probabilities shown in Exhibit 8.12.

For unrated equity REITs, Moody's looks at the same four accounting variables on a scale of one-to-five. The four scores are averaged for a final score and translated into the default probabilities shown in Exhibit 8.13.

To determine an assumed recovery rate for rated REITs, Moody's compares the rating of the particular REIT obligation in the TruPS CDO with the REIT's senior unsecured rating. For example, if a REIT TruPS is rated three notches lower than the REIT's senior unsecured debt, Moody's would assume 15% recovery on the TruPS. If a REIT's secured debt is rated two notches greater than the REIT's senior unsecured debt, Moody's would assume 60% recovery on the secured debt.

Diversification

Diversification is a particularly important issue for TruPS CDOs because TruPS CDOs include issues from one, or at most three, industries: banks, insurance companies, and REITs. But the small banks represented in the typical TruPS CDO operate in local economies rather than in the greater U.S. economy. FDIC data shows that the defaults of smaller banks are more regionally correlated than nationally correlated. In fact, across different re-

EXHIBIT 8.14 Fitch TruPS Regions for Diversification

Region	States Making Up Region
1	CT, DE, ME, MA, NH, NJ, NY, PA, RI, VT
2	AL, IL, IN, KY, MI, MS, OH, TN, WI
3	AZ, CO, ID, IA, KS, MN, MO, MT, NE, NV, ND, SD, UT, WY
4	AK, LA, NM, OK, TX
5	AK, CA, HI, OR, WA
6	FL, GA, NC, SC, VA, DC, WV, MD
7	U.S. related territories and commonwealths, multiregional institutions, and nontraditional financial institutions.

Source: FitchRatings.

gions, the defaults of small banks are no more correlated than the defaults of industrial firms across different industries.

Based on this research, Moody's and Fitch divide the U.S. into five or seven regions and basically treat each region as they would separate industries for diversification purposes. Exhibit 8.14 shows the seven regions that Fitch recognizes as distinct "industries." Moody's makes a distinction between banks and thrifts, as they believe the latter are more correlated across regions because of their concentration in mortgage-related assets.

For insurance companies, the rating agencies look at the insurance company's business line as well as the geographical scope of their business. Distinctions are made between life and health companies and different types of property and casualty companies, such as auto, home, commercial, workers compensation, and diversified companies. Interestingly, the rating agencies view it better to have insurance companies in a variety of specific lines of business than for all the insurance companies to be diversified.

Moody's divides REITs into eight categories to assess diversity: hotel, multifamily, office, retail, industrial, healthcare, self-storage, and diversified.

TruPS Deferrals Within CDOs

A Fitch study quantifies deferrals of bank and insurance TruPS within TruPS CDOs.[8] The ability of banks and insurance companies to defer interest payments on their TruPS is part of what allows those institutions to count TruPS as equity in their capital structure. Obviously, the rate of deferral is important to TruPS CDO investors as deferrals reduce current collateral interest

---

[8] Marion Silverman, Russ Thomas, and James E. Moss, *Trust Preferred CDO Performance Update*, FitchRatings, as updated December 1, 2005. Fitch shared an unpublished update of this data as of May 2006, for which we are grateful.

and presage the loss of principal. Fitch also quantified the rate of deferral on insurance company TruPS in CDOs. Since Fitch has rated every TruPS CDO but one, their study of CDO experience with these assets is definitive.

Bank TruPS Deferrals

Fitch has identified 10 banks in CDO portfolios that through May 2006 had at some point deferred interest payments on their TruPS. These banks are coded A through J in Exhibit 8.15. As can be seen in the exhibit, six of the deferring banks appear in more than one TruPS CDO. One bank appears in six CDOs. Altogether, the 10 banks appear 20 times across the 11 affected CDOs. Also shown in Exhibit 8.15 are the beginning and (if appropriate) end dates of the TruPS interest deferrals. Note that of the ten banks that have deferred interest, all but two have emerged from deferral. Two CDOs sold deferring TruPS.

The fact that one bank deferring on its TruPS obligation appears in six TruPS CDOs begs a question on the degree of collateral overlap among TruPS CDOs.[9] TruPS CDO managers view their ability to source TruPS from small banks as a proprietary competitive advantage and are unwilling to publicize the names of issuers. But Fitch examined a sample of nine bank TruPS CDOs issued between 2002 and 2004 and reported on the degree of collateral overlap.[10] The rating agency found that 67% of the 400 TruPS issuers appeared once throughout the nine CDOs, 17% appeared twice, 6% appeared three times, 4% appeared four times, 4% appeared five times, and 1% appeared six times.

The banks that have deferred interest on their TruPS in Exhibit 8.15 come from the universe of banks whose TruPS are included in CDOs, which Fitch estimates at 1,500. So, by number of banks, 0.7% (10/1,500) have deferred on TruPS interest payments. The two banks that continue to defer interest on their TruPS are 0.13% (2/1,500) of the 1,500 banks. These are very small rates, but they do not take into account the increased issuance of TruPS CDOs over time and the effect of seasoning on the rates.

Typically, financial problems do not occur until a while after an entity has issued securities. There are two reasons for this. The first reason is that the entity usually must pass an underwriting process associated with the security issuance. It takes a while for the financial condition of the entity to deteriorate after passing that review. The second reason is that the security issuance provides cash, which helps the entity deal with any financial prob-

---

[9] Unfortunately, we cannot apply the systemic study we did on CLO collateral portfolios in Chapter 13 because detailed data on TruPS CDO collateral are not available in trustee reports or on INTEX.

[10] Again, Marion Silverman, Russ Thomas, and James E. Moss, *Trust Preferred CDO Performance Update*, FitchRatings, as updated December 1, 2005.

EXHIBIT 8.15   Deferring Bank TruPS in TruPS CDOs

Deferring Security Code	Amount of Deferral ($ millions)	Begin Date of Deferral	End Date of Deferral	Length of Deferral in Years
Regional Diversified Funding I				
A	10	3/8/02	9/10/04	2.5
B	6.1	9/9/02	9/10/03	1.0
C	10	3/8/04	Deferring	2.4
MM CAPS Funding I				
D	11	6/16/03	12/10/03	0.5
E	3.7	12/31/04	7/29/05	0.6
MM Community Funding I				
F	15	1/27/03	1/26/06	3.0
G	23	1/26/04	1/26/05	1.0
MM Community Funding II				
F	8	12/9/02	12/9/05	3.0
D	20	6/9/03	12/9/03	0.5
TPREF Funding I				
F	10	1/7/03	10/11/05	2.8
H	3	3/7/05	1/10/06	0.8
Preferred Term Securities I				
I	10	9/9/02	12/31/02	0.3
I	10	3/7/03	9/30/04	1.6
D	15	9/8/03	3/30/04	0.6
C	15	3/8/04	Deferring	>2.4
J	6	9/7/05	Deferring	>0.9
Preferred Term Securities II				
D	12	8/22/03	2/28/04	0.5
E	15.67	1/13/05	8/24/05	0.6
C	15	2/23/04	Deferring	>2.4
Preferred Term Securities III				
D	6	7/30/03	2/27/04	0.6
G	12	10/31/03	5/31/05	1.6
ALESCO Preferred Funding V				
H	6	3/4/05	1/10/06	0.9
Trapeza CDO I				
C	11	Credit risk sale		
Trapeza CDO II				
C	9	Credit risk sale		

Source: FitchRatings.

lems that do occur. The TruPS that have deferred have done so an average of two years and five months after the TruPS CDO was formed.

TruPS CDOs have experienced bludgeoning issuance, with about half of outstanding TruPS CDOs being less than two years old. The large number of recently issued CDOs, with collateral that has not had time to defer, artificially lowers deferral rates. To account for this problem, default researchers perform vintage analysis.

Exhibit 8.16 explores the deferral rate by dollar amount and vintage. The exhibit shows that both of the two bank TruPS CDOs from 2000 have had collateral deferrals. In total, $82 million of bank TruPS have deferred out of $556 million issued and incorporated in CDOs in 2000. This gives a 14.8% rate of bank TruPS deferral from the 2000 vintage. $31 million, or 5.6% of bank TruPS in the 2000 vintage, continue to defer interest. Deferral rates and continue-to-defer rates drop to 4.2% and 0.4% in the 2001 vintage. Two 2002 TruPS CDOs suffered asset deferrals leading to 0.5% and 0.2% deferral and continue-to-defer rates, respectively. One CDO in each of the 2003 and 2004 vintages suffered deferrals in their collateral portfolios. The 2005 vintage is too new to have had any deferrals.

Naturally, the applicability of these historic deferral rates in predicting the future depends on a number of factors that must be carefully assessed. These factors include underwriting trends, mergers and acquisitions among obligors, and changing economic conditions.

Insurance TruPS Defferals

Two insurance TruPS included in CDOs have deferred interest. As shown in Exhibit 8.17, one affected two CDOs and the other affected seven CDOs. The deferral rates in Exhibit 8.18 are calculated as a percentage of insurance assets in TruPS CDOs including TruPS, subordinated debt, and surplus notes. Again, the applicability of these default rates in predicting future performance must be carefully assessed.

TruPS CDO PERFORMANCE

As of 2006, none of the major rating agencies have never downgraded a TruPS CDO. Fitch has, however, upgraded a tranche from each of three TruPS CDOs (MM Community Funding II, Preferred Term Securities I, and TPREF I). These CDO all suffered multiple deferrals in their collateral portfolios, which caused excess spread to be diverted from the equity tranche and instead used to pay down senior debt tranche principal. Later, these TruPS deferrals were cured. Having already delevered by paying down their

EXHIBIT 8.16 Performance of Bank TruPS in TruPS CDOs

Vintage Analysis	Amount of Bank TruPS in TruPS CDOs ($ million)	Bank TruPS to Ever Defer ($ million)	Bank TruPS to Ever Defer (%)	Bank TruPS Continuing to Defer ($ million)	Bank TruPS Continuing to Defer (%)
2000 Vintage					
Preferred Term Securities I	314	56	17.8%	21	6.7%
Regional Diversified Funding I	242	26	10.8%	10	4.1%
Total/Average	556	82	14.8%	31	5.6%
2001 Vintage					
MM CAPS Funding	294	15	5.0%	0	0.0%
MM Community Funding I	523	38	7.3%	0	0.0%
MM Community Funding II	766	28	3.7%	0	0.0%
Preferred Term Securities II	347	43	12.3%	15	4.3%
Preferred Term Securities III	516	18	3.5%	0	0.0%
Preferred Term Securities IV	927	0	0.0%	0	0.0%
Total / Average	3,373	141	4.2%	15	0.4%
2002 Vintage					
8 TruPS CDOs with no deferrals	3,675				
TPREF Funding I	582	13	2.2%	0	0.0%
Trapeza CDO I	337	11	3.3%	11	3.3%
Total / Average	4,594	24	0.5%	11	0.2%
2003 Vintage					
12 TruPS CDOs with no deferrals	5,314				
Trapeza CDO II	412	9	2.2%	9	2.2%
Total / Average	5,726	9	0.2%	9	0.2%
2004 Vintage					
16 TruPS CDOs with no deferrals	5,982				
Alesco Preferred Funding V	365	6	1.6%	0	0.0%
Total / Average	6,347	6	0.1%	0	0.0%
2005 Vintage					
12 TruPS CDOs with no deferrals	4,899				
Total / Average	4,899	0	0.0%	0	0.0%

Source: FitchRatings, UBS Calculations.

EXHIBIT 8.17 Deferring Insurance TruPS in TruPS CDOs

Deferring Security Code	Amount of Deferral ($ millions)	Begin Date of Deferral	End Date of Deferral	Length of Deferral in Years
I-Preferred Term Securities II				
L	15	8/23/04	Sold 11/22/05	
I-Preferred Term Securities III				
K	20	3/31/06	Deferring	>0.3
InCapS Funding I, Ltd.				
L	15	5/23/05	Deferring	>1.2
K	20	2/23/06	Deferring	>0.4
InCapS Funding II, Ltd.				
K	12	1/9/06	Deferring	>0.5
Alesco VII				
K	20	12/15/05	Deferring	>0.6
Alesco VIII				
K	1	12/15/05	Deferring	>0.6
Dekania CDO I				
K	10	12/15/05	Deferring	>0.6
Dekania CDO II				
K	15	2/15/06	Deferring	>0.4

Source: FitchRatings.

debt, the CDOs now had more performing assets relative to their remaining debt and upgrades were appropriate.

TruPS ISSUERS AND ISSUES

Exhibit 8.19 shows the largest issuers of U.S. TruPS CDOs as of mid-2006. FTN Financial and Keefe, Bruyette and Woods dominate TruPS CDO issuance, having issued 26 CDOs amounting to $16 billion and equaling 38% of the total TruPS CDO issuance. They were also one of the first TruPS CDO issuers, having issued their first Preferred Term Securities series in 2000. The series began as all-bank collateral CDOs and added a minority of insurance collateral in 2004. Later issues have had about 65% bank collateral, 25% insurance collateral, and 10% REIT collateral. Between 2002 and 2004,

EXHIBIT 8.18   Performance of Insurance Assets in Fitch-Rated TruPS CDOs

Vintage Analysis	Amount of Insurance Assets in TruPS CDOs ($ million)	Insurance TruPS Continuing to Defer ($ million)	Insurance TruPS Continuing to Defer (%)
2002 Vintage			
1 TruPS CDO with no insurance defaults	359	0	0.0%
2003 Vintage			
1 TruPS CDOs with no insurance defaults	19	0	0.0%
InCaps Funding I	386	15	3.9%
InCaps Funding II	313	12	3.8%
I-Preferred Term Securities II	523	15	2.9%
I-Preferred Term Securities III	521	20	3.8%
Dekania CDO I	307	10	3.3%
Total/Average	2,068	72	3.5%
2004 Vintage			
7 TruPS CDOs with no insurance defaults	1,059	0	0.0%
Dekania CDO II	415	15	3.6%
Total/Average	1,474	15	1.0%
2005 Vintage			
11 TruPS CDOs with no insurance defaults	1,322	0	0.0%

Source: FitchRatings, UBS Calculations.

FTN Financial and Keefe Bruyette issued four all-insurance backed CDOs under the I-Preferred Term Securities series.

Another major TruPS CDO issuer is Cohen Brothers, which has issued 19 CDOs under its Alesco, Taberna, and Dekania series. Combined, the firm has issued $12 billion of TruPS CDOs in 19 issues and obtained a 28% market share. Alesco began with all-bank collateral CDOs in 2003, but since 2004 it has adopted a formula of about two-thirds bank collateral and one-third insurance collateral. The Taberna series, named after a subsidiary of Cohen Brothers, issues pure REIT collateral CDOs. Dekania, named after

EXHIBIT 8.19 Largest Issuers of TruPS CDOs as of Mid-2006

Issuer	CDO Series Name	CDOs in Series	Issued ($ million)	Share	Recent Collateral Composition	Vintages
FTN Financial and Keefe Bruyette	Preferred Term Securities I-Preferred Term Securities	26	15,738	38%	Bank, insurance, and REIT	2000-06
Cohen Brothers	Alesco	11	6,136	15%	Bank & Insurance	2003-06
Taberna Capital (Cohen Bros)	Taberna	6	4,682	11%	REIT	2005-06
Dekania (Cohen Bros)	Dekania	2	722	2%	Insurance	2003-04
Sandler O'Neill	InCaps, MM Community, MMCAP, TRPEF	11	5,403	13%	Bank	2001-05
Trapeza Capital	Trapeza	10	3,654	9%	Bank, insurance, and REIT	2002-06
StoneCastle	U.S. Capital Funding	4	1,147	3%	Bank	2004-05
All others	All others	8	3,430	8%	Bank, insurance, and REIT	2000-06

Source: FitchRatings, Moody's.

another Cohen Brothers subsidiary, issued two all-insurance TruPS CDOs from 2003 to 2004.

The last issuer in Exhibit 8.19 we will discuss is Sandler O'Neill, which we credit in the exhibit with $5 billion of TruPS CDO issuance and a 12% market share. We hedge ourselves by using the word "credit" because the case of Sandler reveals flaws in Exhibit 8.19. There is a lot of work in the production of a TruPS CDO. Someone has to source the bank, insurance company, and REIT borrowers. Someone has to vet them for credit quality. In newer TruPS CDOs, assets are purchased before the TruPS CDOs are issued and stored in a warehouse facility. This allows TruPS issuers flexibility as to when they can raise funds, but it also means that someone must fund the warehouse facility. Someone must sell the CDO obligations. And in nonstatic deals, someone must buy and sell the CDO's assets. Often these roles are performed by several different entities.

So the "issuer" in Exhibit 8.19 is a bit nebulous and would be so even if we had perfect information about the roles of various parties in a deal, which we do not. In the exhibit, we have tried to focus on originators and underwriters of CDO assets. Further confusion exists here, because sometimes a number of parties perform these functions. For example, besides the MM Community and MMCAP series, Sandler O'Niell also contributed CDO assets to the first three Alesco CDOs, the second and third Regional Diversified Funding CDOs, and the first three U.S. Capital series. The bottom line is that credit for TruPS CDO is probably more diffuse than we make it seem in Exhibit 8.19.

SUMMARY

With 30-year maturities and the ability to defer interest for five years, regulators and rating agencies treat trust preferred securities like equity in capital calculations. CDOs pool TruPS from smaller institutions together and attract the interest of capital markets participants. While TruPS CDOs have grown rapidly, from $1 billion of issuance in 2000 to about $12 billion in 2006, issuance pales in comparison to CLOs and SF CDOs.

The collateral mixture in TruPS CDOs has changed since 2000. Formerly comprised solely of bank TruPS, recent vintages have included the obligations of insurance companies, REITs, and even other TruPS CDOs. More senior obligations of banks, insurance companies, and REITs are also included in TruPS CDOs.

TruPS CDOs have normal overcollateralization tests like other CDOs and/or more restrictive optimal principal distribution amount tests. TruPS

CDOs usually have reserve funds and auction calls of collateral after 10 years. Recent TruPS CDOs allow limited trading.

Rating agencies look at historical default studies to determine their assumptions regarding TruPS CDO collateral defaults, recoveries, and diversification. There is enough history on TruPS CDO collateral portfolios to calculate deferral rates. These must be carefully assessed to judge their applicability in predicting future performance and compared to the protective mechanisms of TruPS CDOs. So far, no TruPS CDO has been downgraded and tranches of three CDOs have been upgraded.

TruPS CDOs will appeal to CDO investors seeking wider spreads and looking for diversification away from traditional CDO assets.

CHAPTER 9

Commercial Real Estate Primer

In the next chapter, we discuss collateralized debt obligations backed by commercial real estate—a pool of individual commercial real estate loans or securities backed by commercial real estate loans. A commercial real estate loan is secured by a commercial real estate property, such as an office building or by an interest in the entity that owns the property. The principal and interest on the loan are generally paid from cash flows generated by the property. Real estate borrowers, or sponsors, will take out loans to purchase properties, refinance existing debt, or add-on to an existing loan.

Over the years, commercial real estate finance has evolved from simple first lien mortgage loans on commercial real estate properties to a variety of different types of loans and real-estate-related securities. The most common real estate loans and securities in the market today include:

- Commercial real estate loans
  - Whole loans and A-notes
  - B-notes
  - Mezzanine loans
  - Preferred equity
- Commercial mortgage-backed securities
- REIT securities

While all of these investments are on some level supported by real estate properties, their risks are considerably different, depending not only on the type of loan or security, but also on the underlying property type, geographic location, and tenant concentration, to name a few differences.

In this chapter, we explain different types of commercial real estate (CRE) loans and securities, analyzing the structures, investment considerations, and the risks of CRE loans and CMBS and REIT securities.

LOAN ORIGINATION

To obtain a loan on a commercial property, a sponsor typically turns to a commercial loan originator. Originators include commercial banks, insurance companies, real estate investment trusts (REITs), commercial mortgage-backed securities (CMBS) conduits, and CRE collateralized debt obligations (CDOs). Originators may keep the loans for their own portfolios, or sell the loans in the secondary market. Others, particularly CMBS conduits, may also serve as warehouses, collecting a pool of loans, often referred to as "conduit loans," to later be securitized as CMBS.

Loan originators underwrite loans and determine the appropriate loan structure and terms based on the results of their due diligence. The performance of the loan is often related to the quality of the underwriting done by the originator. In fact, rating agencies will look at the performance history of the loans underwritten by the originator when assigning a rating to a new loan.

Many of the loans originated today are pooled to create CMBS. CMBS issuers perform their own due diligence on each loan in the pool. In addition, they look at the pool on an aggregate basis, assessing portfolio risks such as concentrations of property type, geography, and loans. The pool of loans is then tranched into individual securities and sold to third-party investors. We discuss CMBS later in this chapter.

Underwriting a Loan

An originator's due diligence includes verifying a property's value, cash flow, and credit quality. Originators typically require and review:

- Current property appraisals.
- Current leases and rent rolls.
- Tax filings and bank statements.
- Tenant credit quality.
- Site inspections.
- Environmental and engineering reports from reputable firms.
- Title insurance and other legal property documents.
- Lockbox provisions requiring that all revenues generated by the property be collected by a trustee, who first pays all operating expenses, debt service, and any other expenses. Excess cash flow is then distributed to the sponsor.
- Escrow accounts holding cash reserves to meet unexpected cash shortfalls. The amount typically equals one-month's debt service, real estate taxes, property insurance, and sometimes re-leasing costs.

■ Reserve accounts holding cash reserves for property maintenance and pending repairs.

A lender, particularly the most senior lender in the property's capital structure, often requires cash management provisions, such as lockboxes and escrow/reserve accounts on highly leveraged properties. Higher leverage increases the stress on a property's cash flows, ultimately increasing the risk and severity of losses. Cash management provisions are important controls to ensure that the sponsor and property managers operate and maintain the property efficiently.

Most CRE loans are nonrecourse. That is, in the event of default, the lender's claim is to the property only; the sponsor is not personally responsible to cover any losses. However, originators usually require nonrecourse carveouts, holding sponsors personally liable for fraud, misrepresentation, misappropriation, and environmental issues. Most loans also require environmental indemnifications protecting lenders from third party claims related to property environmental conditions.

Typically, a good originator has expertise not only in real estate, but also in the particular type of property (office, industrial, etc.), the local real estate market, and the type of financing desired. Good originators also perform thorough due diligence on every property underwritten. The performance of loans previously underwritten by an originator can provide insight into the quality of that originator's underwriting practices.

The continued strength of the real estate market and the resulting demand for CRE loans have made the loan origination business much more competitive. As a result, some originators have relaxed their underwriting standards, for example, taking on loans with higher leverage, making more aggressive property performance assumptions, or waiving reserve requirements. Given this trend, the quality and motivation of the originator are increasingly important. For instance, originators looking for market share may be more willing to relax their underwriting. While relaxed standards alone may not spell disaster, the terms of the loan, that is, the interest rate and covenants, should be appropriate for the higher levels of risk.

The Master and Special Servicers

At origination, a *master servicer* and a *special servicer* are appointed. In the event of a short-term cash shortfall, the master servicer advances principal and interest payments to the lender and pays real estate taxes and insurance premiums up to the amount the servicer is likely to recover. The master servicer also monitors documents required by the loan, such as annual property performance reports. For performing these ongoing services, the master servicer earns a fee based on a percentage of the outstanding principal balance of the loan.

The special servicer is appointed to resolve issues relating to a delinquent or defaulted loan. Usually the master servicer hands over a loan to the special servicer when the loan is more than 60 days delinquent. The special servicer's role is to maximize the amount recovered from a defaulted loan and minimize loan losses. The special servicer is compensated by a fee on the principal balance of the assets it is monitoring (often twice the master servicer's fee), an additional workout fee for loans in default, as well as a percentage of the loan's principal and interest recovered through workout. Typically, the special servicer also has an equity interest in the property, increasing the motivation for successfully working out and remedying the defaulted loan.

PROPERTY-LEVEL LOANS

The most basic commercial real estate loan is a first-lien mortgage loan. The first-lien mortgage loan (also known as the "mortgage" or "whole loan") is the senior-most loan secured by the property. At origination, a mortgage's principal balance is typically 65% to 80% of a property's appraised value, commonly referred to as the LTV, or loan-to-value. The mortgage can be split into a senior and a subordinate piece, the A-note and the B-note.

The remaining 20% to 35% is the sponsor's equity interest in the property. However, a sponsor typically targets a 0% to 15% equity interest, depending on the sponsor's motivation. To increase the leverage on a property, a sponsor can take out a mezzanine loan. A mezzanine loan is a senior participation in the equity in the property. The loan is not secured by the property itself, but by an interest in the entity that owns the property (the sponsor). A mezzanine loan essentially reduces the sponsor's equity interest in the property. The loan can raise total leverage on the property to 85% to 100% LTV. In other words, the sum of the mortgage(s) plus the mezzanine loan can equal 85% to 100% of the property's appraised value. As a result, the sponsor's equity interest in the property can be reduced to 0% to 15% of the property's value.

A sponsor may also take out a second lien mortgage on a property to reduce the equity contribution. Similar to a mezzanine loan, a second lien mortgage is junior to the first lien mortgage. However, unlike a mezzanine loan, a second lien mortgage is secured by the property directly, rather than by an interest in the property's equity. As such, a second lien mortgage increases the senior debt's risk of default and loss more so than a mezzanine loan. Therefore, first lien mortgage lenders rarely allow sponsors to take out second lien mortgages.

EXHIBIT 9.1 Typical Property Capital Structure

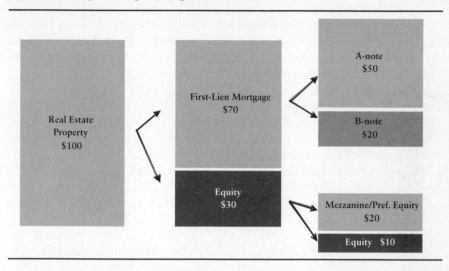

Some mortgages also prevent a sponsor from taking out a mezzanine loan. In such cases, the sponsor can instead issue preferred equity. Preferred equity in a property is essentially the same as an equity interest, but has a senior claim on the excess cash flow available after servicing the loans on the property.

Exhibit 9.1 illustrates a single property's capital structure. Each type of property loan, from A-note through mezzanine, has distinct terms, structure, and risks that we will discuss in the next few sections.

First-Lien Commercial Mortgage Loans

First-lien commercial mortgage loans range from $300,000 to $1 billion. They are typically 10-year balloon loans with 30-year amortization schedules, although there is an increasing number of interest-only loans. Most commercial mortgage loans are fixed rate. Generally, interest rates are 75–150 bps above the 10-year Treasury, but they vary depending on leverage and other property-specific factors.

Prepayment Risk and Extension Risk

Unlike residential mortgages, commercial mortgages have low prepayment risk, thanks to the numerous call protection mechanisms built into the loan terms. Call protection mechanisms include the following:

- *Lockout*—prepayments are prohibited during a 2- to 5-year lockout period.
- *Yield Maintenance*—equivalent to a "make-whole" premium in corporate bonds. To prepay a loan, the sponsor must make the lender whole. The yield maintenance cost is equivalent to the present value of all the future cash flows due on the loan, discounted at the then-prevailing yield of a comparable maturity U.S. Treasury.
- *Defeasance*—to defease a loan, the sponsor must pledge to the lender U.S. Treasury securities that generate cash flows equal to the cash flows due to the lender under the terms of the loan. From the lender's viewpoint, cash flows are the same, but the underlying collateral will be upgraded to U.S. Treasury securities.
- *Prepayment Penalty Points*—in prepaying a loan, a sponsor pays the lender a fee equal to a set percentage of 1% to 5% of the outstanding loan balance. Penalty points usually decrease as the remaining life of the loan decreases, e.g., 5% in Year 6, 4% in Year 7, 3% in Year 8, and so on.

The most common call protection mechanism is a combination of lockout for the first five years, followed by defeasance, which remains in effect until approximately six months before maturity. The sponsor then has a six-month window to refinance the loan without penalty.

Call protection mechanisms lessen the economic incentive to refinance a commercial mortgage. Essentially, a sponsor is only likely to prepay a commercial mortgage if the property is being sold, and the gain on the property exceeds the cost of prepaying the mortgage.

Although there is little prepayment risk in commercial mortgages, there is *refinancing risk*. The 10-year balloon structure of mortgage loans makes extending the loan past the 10-year maturity unlikely, which is a plus for many investors. If the mortgage is not paid off or refinanced at maturity, the loan is in default.

The ability to refinance at maturity, however, depends on several factors that are often out of the sponsor's and the lender's control, such as prevailing interest rates, the strictness of current underwriting requirements, credit conditions, and property occupancy at the time of refinancing. Some loan originators allow short-term extensions, but historically there are significant disincentives for extending. However, in strong markets, originators may relax these disincentives, thereby introducing greater extension risk into commercial mortgages.

Some commercial mortgages are partially or fully interest-only loans, which contribute to extension risk. An interest-only loan faces more extension risk because its principal has not amortized, therefore leaving a larger outstanding loan balance to refinance.

The A/B Structure

A mortgage is often split into a senior and junior participation, the A-note and the B-note. In the A/B structure, as it is called, the A-note has a senior claim on cash flows generated by a property, while the B-note has a subordinate claim on cash flows.[1]

Payment of principal and interest can either be pro rata or sequential. The desired rating on the A-note determines the size of each piece. Typically, the A-note is sized for a BBB or BBB– rating, while the B-note is below investment grade or unrated. The B-note provides credit enhancement and essentially reduces the leverage of the A-note. For example, while the LTV of the entire mortgage may be 80%, the LTV of the A-note would only be 65%, assuming an 80/20 split between the A-note and B-note.

The A-note is usually placed in a trust for securitization. The B-note, on the other hand, is held by a third party, often an experienced real estate investor. In the worst case scenario, the B-note holder could essentially become the equity owner of the property. Therefore, the B-note holder is usually experienced in underwriting, monitoring, and, if need be, remedying property performance. The B-note holder is compensated for that increased risk position, though returns depend on the underlying property's characteristics, most notably its leverage. Spreads on B-notes can range from as low as 75 bps to more than 1,000 bps above Treasuries.

If a sponsor defaults on a mortgage loan, the A-note holder has the right to foreclose and take possession of the property. In this case, the B-note holder loses all collateral securing the note, and is essentially left with an equity interest in the property. This process can take 6–18 months, during which time the value of the property may deteriorate, thus increasing the B-note holder's risk of losses. To avoid this scenario, the B-note holder is granted specific rights, which are outlined in the participation agreement and the pooling and servicing agreement.

For instance, in the event of a mortgage default, the B-note holder has the right to cure the default. The B-note holder would thus pay the principal and interest due to the A-note holder, plus any accrued interest, legal fees, and advances. B-note holders are likely to exercise this right if there is sufficient property value above the principal of the A-note and the B-note, or if the property is a *transitional* property.

A transitional property is a poorly performing property, where performance and value can be increased by an improvement in the overall real estate market, improving the property through capital expenditures or new leases,

[1] The first lien mortgage can also have an A/B/C structure. This is similar to the A/B structure, but the C-note becomes the most junior note in the structure. Since the concept is very similar, and less common, than the A/B structure, we focus our attention in this chapter on the A/B structure.

or by replacing the existing property manager. In such cases, the B-note holder typically has experience in turning around properties. The B-note holder has 3 to 6 months to exercise her right to cure the mortgage.

The B-note holder also has the right, if the mortgage is in default, to buy out the A-note holder. In this case, the B-note holder becomes the senior mortgage lender and gains full control over the entire debt structure of the property, and can foreclose on the property at any time. To exercise this right, the B-note holder must pay the A-note holder the value of the A-note plus accrued interest, legal fees, and advances. A B-note holder with workout experience is likely to choose this option if the economics make sense.

If the B-note holder chooses *not* to exercise either the right to cure the defaulted mortgage or the right to buy out the A-note holder, she still has the right to approve the special servicer and the terms of the workout plan for the defaulted loan. This allows the B-note holder some control over the workout process, which directly impacts the level of potential losses the B-note holder may realize.

In addition to rights in the event of default, the B-note holder has pre-default rights. For instance, the B-note holder typically has the right to approve:

- Annual property budgets.
- Key tenant leases.
- Property management and leasing agents.
- Transfer of the property by the equity holders.
- Escrow/reserve disbursements.

Approval rights over the budget, leases, property management, leasing agents, and property transfer give the B-note holder some control over the property's performance. Rights over escrow/reserve disbursements provide the B-note holder with protection over improper cash flow distributions to equity holders. B-note holders can also institute an excess cash flow trap to redirect cash flows from equity holders if the property's cash flows trip a specified trigger. The excess cash trigger is typically set at a minimum debt service coverage ratio, a measure we discuss later in this chapter.

Mezzanine Loans

Mezzanine loans are the junior-most loans in a property's capital structure. They enable a sponsor to increase a property's leverage, raising total loan-to-value ratio (LTV) to 85% to 100%. These loans typically have a minimum size of $3 million.

Mezzanine loan terms depend on the sponsor's motivation. If current rates are high, the sponsor may opt for a first lien mortgage with a low LTV, then supplement it with a short-term mezzanine loan to reduce her equity contribution. This arrangement allows the sponsor to refinance the mezzanine loan (or the entire mortgage, if the economics work) at a later date when rates are lower, or when the property is performing better. Alternatively, a sponsor may choose a mezzanine loan coterminus with the mortgage to take maximum advantage of an arbitrage opportunity. Therefore, maturities on mezzanine loans range from 18 months to 10 years; some are amortizing, some interest-only, depending on the property and the sponsor's preferences.

As mentioned earlier, a mezzanine loan is not secured by the property itself, but by an interest in the entity that owns the property. It is the first loan to absorb any losses or cash flow shortfalls. Therefore, mezzanine lenders demand a higher interest rate than A-note holders, sometimes significantly higher (upwards of 1,000 bps) depending on the property and its leverage. Historically, mezzanine loans are held by experienced third-party real estate investors.

Similar to B-note holders, a mezzanine lender has specific rights to protect her investment and minimize losses. These rights are outlined in the intercreditor agreement between the mortgage lenders and the mezzanine lender. For example, if a sponsor defaults on the mezzanine loan, while the first lien mortgage is still current, the mezzanine lender has the option of foreclosing on the sponsor and taking control of the property (subject to the terms of the property's existing mortgage).

Foreclosing on the sponsor is generally quick, taking 60 to 90 days rather than the 6 to 18 months it would take an A- or B-note holder to foreclose on the property. Therefore, the mezzanine lender can gain control of the property more quickly than a B-note holder if property performance goes south. The quicker a lender can take control of a property in default, the sooner she can take actions to remedy or turn around the property, thus minimizing potential losses.

In the event the sponsor defaults on both the mortgage and the mezzanine loan, either the A-note or B-note mortgage lender can foreclose on the property. In this case, the sponsor no longer owns the property; the foreclosing lender does. The sponsor therefore has no collateral, and since the mezzanine lender is secured by an interest in the sponsor, the value of the mezzanine loan goes to zero.

To protect the mezzanine lender in the event of default on the mortgage, the mezzanine lender has rights similar to those of a B-note holder. First, the mezzanine lender has the right to cure the mortgage. This is identical to the right of the B-note holder, but the mezzanine lender has an unlimited amount of time to exercise this right, whereas the B-note holder has to exercise within three to six months. The mezzanine lender also has the option to buy out the mortgage from the mortgage lenders and take control of the property's entire capital structure, with the right to foreclose at any time. Which right the mezzanine lender exercises depends on her real estate expertise.

A mezzanine lender also has predefault rights, similar, though junior to the B-note holder's predefault rights as outlined above. The mezzanine lender also has the right to approve any refinancing of the mortgage. Furthermore, the mortgage lender is not allowed to make any changes to the mortgage loan documents that would be detrimental to the mezzanine lender, such as raising the mortgage rate.

Other CRE Loans

The strong performance of real estate assets over the past decade has increased demand for alternative types of CRE loans. The most common include *construction* loans, *condo-* and *co-op conversion* loans, and *land* loans. Each carries distinct risks that require additional consideration over the more traditional mortgage and mezzanine loans.

Construction loans, for example, are secured by properties that are under construction. These properties are therefore noncash-flowing, or are generating very little cash. The sponsor usually sets up a reserve account at loan origination which pays the loan's interest. Loan repayment is contingent on construction completion, at which point permanent financing (or temporary bridge financing if the property is not yet leased at completion) is put in place.

These loans tend to be floating rate with maturities of 12 to 36 months and are funded in stages as construction costs are incurred. The loan amount is determined by the construction budget plus a 10% to 20% contingency. Loan performance depends on the sponsor's credit quality and her expertise in managing and monitoring the construction process.

Rating agencies generally consider alternative loans to be riskier than first lien mortgages, so more careful underwriting and monitoring is required. Inclusion of these types of loans in CRE and CMBS CDOs often results in higher subordination requirements.

COMMERCIAL MORTGAGE-BACKED SECURITIES

Commercial mortgage-backed securities (CMBS) are backed by a static pool of commercial mortgage loans, the vast majority of which are A-notes. The pool of loans is tranched into a number of rated tranches, and principal and interest payments received from the underlying loans are used to pay principal and interest to the tranches sequentially by seniority. Any losses experienced by the underlying loan pool are absorbed, in order, by the most junior tranches.

Exhibit 9.2 illustrates the typical structure of a CMBS transaction. The AAA-rated tranche makes up a large portion of the debt structure, generally around 90%, and can be time-tranched into 5- and 10-year securities. Interest-only securities are often included in the structure as well.

CMBS deals appoint a master servicer to monitor the cash flows coming from the underlying loans and going out to the tranches. In the event there is insufficient cash to make all scheduled payments, the master servicer will advance principal and interest. Advancing will continue as long as these amounts are deemed recoverable. A special servicer is also appointed to handle any loans that are more than 60-days delinquent.

Property-type diversification is one of the principal benefits of securitization, since the performance of each property type is impacted by different sets of risks. Properties securing commercial real estate loans include office buildings, industrial buildings or warehouses, apartment buildings, hotels, and retail properties such as strip malls. The concentrations of different property types vary slightly over time, depending on collateral performance. In general, office, retail, and multifamily properties tend to dominate most CMBS, historically accounting for two thirds of the collateral in CMBS deals.

CMBS investors as a whole are a diverse group, but particular types of investors are drawn to different tranches of CMBS deals. Real money investors, financial institutions, insurance companies, *etc.*, tend to buy

EXHIBIT 9.2   Typical CMBS Structure

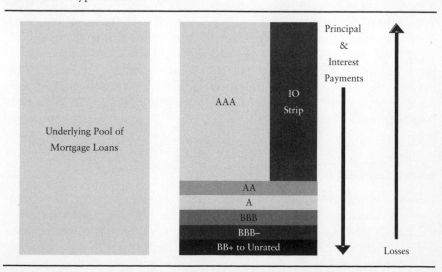

investment-grade tranches. Traditional real estate investors, hedge funds, and CRE CDOs enter the mix further down the capital structure. Buyers of tranches rated BB+ and below, collectively referred to as the "B-piece," are typically real estate investors, with expertise to underwrite the loan portfolio and accurately assess the risks of the B-piece's first loss position. Top B-piece buyers include LNR Partners, American Capital Strategies, ARCap, J.E. Roberts, and CWCapital.

Prepayment and Extension Risk

The prepayment stability offered by CMBS attracts investors looking for real estate exposure without the negative convexity found in residential mortgage-backed securities. Unless interest rates drop dramatically or property values soar, refinancing of the underlying loans is uncommon, due to the call protection mechanisms on the loans.

However, in a robust commercial real estate market, prepayments in the form of defeasance increase, as sponsors look to cash in on property price appreciation. Defeasance, however, is actually a plus for CMBS, as cash flows to the tranches remain the same, with their source becoming Treasury securities, thus raising the credit quality of the tranche's underlying collateral.

The sequential pay structure of CMBS itself provides additional prepayment protection to the junior tranches of the deal. The AA-rated tranche cannot be paid down before the AAA tranche is completely paid. And the A tranche cannot be paid down before the AA tranche, and so on. Therefore, the A tranche is guaranteed to remain outstanding in full at least until the AA tranche is completely paid down. However, principal losses from loan defaults impact the bottom of the CMBS structure upward, so the principal balance of the more junior tranches may be reduced due to principal writedowns.

Unfortunately, CMBS have extension risk, due to the 10-year balloon maturities of the underlying loans. If a loan cannot be refinanced and it defaults, the loan enters a workout period that can extend principal recovery for months, even years. The most subordinate tranches of a CMBS transaction bear the most extension risk, as they are the last to receive principal payment.

Interest Shortfalls

Interest shortfalls can be a concern to CMBS tranches, especially to the below investment grade and unrated tranches. Interest shortfalls occur when the CMBS transaction has insufficient funds to pay interest due tranches. Shortfalls are more common in CMBS transactions than other asset-backed transactions, yet they are usually less serious occurrences.

In other asset-backed securities, *basis mismatch* is the chief factor in interest shortfalls. Basis mismatch frequently occurs in rising interest rate environments when the coupons payable to the tranches reset at higher rates before the coupons on the underlying collateral reset, thus causing an interest shortfall. This type of interest shortfall is not a concern in CMBS, because CMBS have little, if any, inherent basis risk, since both the underlying loans and the coupons payable on the tranches are typically fixed rate.

Most interest shortfalls in CMBS are due to loan delinquencies and defaults. Except when the default is severe enough to cause a loss on the loan, interest will be recovered in part or in full when the sponsor cures the loan or when the property is liquidated. The CMBS master servicer advances funds to cover interest shortfalls that are likely to be recovered. Due to high collateral concentrations and long workout periods for defaulted loans, CMBS tranches can experience interest shortfalls for long periods of time, yet retain high likelihood of recovery.

Most CMBS interest shortfalls are recoverable, but some are not. For instance, the master servicer will *not* cover shortfalls resulting from delinquent loans where the underlying property has been reappraised to a negative LTV. In this case, the CMBS tranches, particularly the lowest rated, will absorb the shortfall as a loss. The master servicer does not cover shortfalls due to nonreimbursable costs such as litigation expenses or workout fees, either. Unrecoverable interest shortfalls are concerns for CMBS investors. Recent high profile interest shortfalls in a few CMBS transactions have caused tranche downgrades and principal losses, with a few tranches losing 100% of their principal, thus increasing investor concerns over interest shortfalls.

CMBS deals with interest shortfall issues include: Asset Securitization Corp. 1996-D2 due to delinquent properties being re-appraised at lower values; Morgan Stanley Capital I 1998-CF1, JP Morgan Chase Commercial Mortgage Securities Corp. 2003-FL1, LB Commercial Mortgage Trust Series 1998-C4, and Bear Stearns Commercial Mortgage Securities Series 2001-TOP2, all due to unrecoverable fees.

Types of CMBS Deals

CMBS provide investors with exposure to a diversified pool of commercial real estate loans. Variations in loan size, sponsor, property type, geographic location, leverage levels, and the like, all contribute to the diversification benefits of CMBS. These characteristics underlie the performance of the collateral and as a result impact the CMBS tranche ratings and subordination levels.

CMBS deals are often categorized into four groups, depending on the type of loans underlying the deal, as shown in Exhibit 9.3. Conduit loans are mortgage loans originated by conduit lenders for the sole purpose of

EXHIBIT 9.3 CMBS Deal Categories

Deal Categories	Description
Conduit loans	
Traditional	Pool of loans where no loan is greater than 10% of the total principal of the deal.
Fusion	Pool of loans where a few of the loans are greater than 10% of the total principal of the deal.
Large loan	Pool of loans where several loans are greater than 10% of the total principal of the deal.
Credit tenant leases	Pool of loans secured by property leases.
Single asset/ Single borrower	One loan secured by a single property or a pool of loans from the same borrower.

securitizing them. These loans tend to be small in size, generally less than $10 million, but they can be larger. Almost all conduit CMBS deals are fusion deals which consist of a diverse pool of small loans as well as a small number of larger loans. Conduit CMBS deals have historically dominated the CMBS market.

Large loans are property loans that are greater than $35 million in size. Credit tenant leases (CTLs) are often the result of sale-leaseback transactions. The tenant sells corporate-owned real estate and enters into a long-term lease on the property or properties. The leases are structured such that the default risk of the lease is tied to the credit rating of the tenant. The tenant's default risk is fundamentally different than the default risk of a traditional commercial real estate loan, and can often gain a higher credit rating. Single-asset CMBS deals contain just one, large loan on a single property, such as, a large high-rise office building. Single-borrower CMBS deals contain a pool of loans on properties with the same borrower or sponsor. Often pool loans are cross-collateralized, so that if one loan defaults, the lender has recourse to any or all of the pool's properties.

REIT SECURITIES

Real estate investment trusts (REITs) are entities that buy, develop, manage, and sell real estate assets. A special feature of REITs is that they qualify as pass-through entities which are exempt from corporate level taxes. To qualify as a REIT, the entity must pay out dividends equal to 90% of its taxable income and more than 75% of its total assets must be in real estate. A REIT generates income through the operation and management of real estate assets. Sales of asset held less than four years cannot exceed 30% of the REIT's net income. Therefore, a REIT is clearly a "buy and hold" entity, not an asset flipper or a trader.

REITs fall into three broad categories: *equity* REITs, *mortgage* REITs, and *hybrid* REITs. Equity REITs own and operate a portfolio of real estate properties, usually focusing on a particular type of property such as office buildings. Mortgage REITs invest in, and in some cases originate, mortgage loans and mortgage-backed securities. Hybrid REITs combine the investment strategies of equity and mortgage REITs by investing in both properties and mortgages. Equity REITs dominate the REIT market, accounting for about 95% of total REIT market capitalization.

The REIT capital structure consists of secured bank loans, unsecured debt, preferred stock, and equity. Some REITs have also issued trust preferred securities (TruPS). (For more information on the mechanics of TruPS, see Chapter 8.) Unsecured REIT debt and TruPS have significant covenants to protect investors. A typical covenant package includes the following:

- Total debt cannot exceed 60% of total assets.
- Unencumbered assets must be at least 150% of unsecured debt.
- Secured debt cannot exceed 40% of total assets.
- Interest coverage must be greater than 1.5×.

Given these covenants, BBB-rated unsecured REIT debt is comparable to single-A-rated CMBS debt given the similar leverage and interest coverage levels. However, a REIT's asset portfolio, and therefore its financial ratios, can change over time, unlike the static pool of assets securing CMBS debt. Also, the REIT's debt is unsecured, while CMBS debt is secured by a pool of first mortgages. Therefore, unsecured REIT debt will likely be rated below CMBS debt that has similar leverage and interest coverage levels.

REIT securities are purchased by a variety of investors, from insurance companies, mutual funds, and CDOs to individual retail investors. REIT securities provide investors with exposure to a diversified pool of real estate-related assets with little to no negative convexity, as opposed to investments in residential mortgage-backed securities (RMBS). In addition, REITs resemble corporates more than CMBS or RMBS, which opens them up to a large investor base.

EVALUATING CREL AND CMBS

Analysis of commercial real estate investments, whether investments in B-notes or CMBS tranches, begins with an analysis of the underlying property, followed by an analysis of the loan terms. For CMBS investments, additional analysis is needed at the bond or equity level. We discuss these three types of analysis next.

Property-Level Analysis

The first step in analyzing real estate investments is a property-level analysis. Understanding the property, from the credit quality of the third floor tenant to the conditions of the local and general economies, is fundamental in assessing the financial condition of the property. Property-level analysis includes many of the elements of underwriting a loan on a property, such as property appraisals, tenant and lease review, comparable property analysis, and the like. These components are used to estimate the stabilized cash flow of the property.

A property's value can be derived from its stabilized cash flow by applying a capitalization rate appropriate for the property. A capitalization rate, or cap rate, is essentially an idealized unlevered risk-adjusted return. Embedded in the cap rate are assumptions about the relative quality of the property, the cash flow volatility common to that type of property, comparable property yields, yields on other types of investments, and so on. The value of the property is its stabilized cash flow divided by the appropriate cap rate. The lower the cap rate, the higher the resulting property value.

Loan-Level Analysis

Analyzing a CRE loan centers on two key metrics: debt service coverage ratio (DSCR) and loan-to-value (LTV). DSCR is the property's cash flow, less tenant improvements, leasing commissions, and necessary capital expenditures; divided by the debt service on the property's loans. DSCR is considered by the rating agencies to be the best indicator of default probability. The higher the DSCR, or the more cash flow a property has to cover debt service, the greater the property's ability to withstand adverse conditions before defaulting on any loan. S&P reports that the average DSCR on existing commercial mortgage loans is around 1.5×, although many loans originated today are sized at 1.2×.[2] For the second quarter of 2006, 21% of the loans in Moody's rated conduit CMBS were sized at 1.2× or less DSCR, up from just 6.3% a year earlier.[3]

---

[2] Eric Thompson, Larry Kay, and Gregory Ramkhelawan, *Defaults and Losses of U.S. Commercial Mortgage Loans: Year-End 2005 Update Reveals Improved Credit Performance*, Standard & Poor's, June 8, 2006
[3] Tad Philipp, Paulo Obias, Pamela Dent, and Dan Rubock, *U.S. CMBS and CRE CDO 2Q 2006 Review: Credit Metrics and Spreads Send Conflicting Signals*, Moody's Investors Service, July 31, 2006.

LTV is calculated as the principal loan balance divided by the estimated value of the property. Rating agencies consider the LTV to be the best indicator of loss severity in the event of default. The lower the LTV, or the lower the amount of the loan as a percentage of the property's value, the lower the odds that the loan will suffer losses in the event of default. LTVs can range from 65% to 90%+. S&P reports that the average LTV on securitized first lien commercial mortgage loans is 69%, although many loans are originated at 80% LTV.[4]

A loan's default probability and loss severity are used to determine expected losses on the loan. When rating agencies calculate expected loss, they often apply qualitative adjustments to the metrics. For example, Fitch may adjust a property's default probability upward if the property's cash flows tend to be volatile. The default probability may also be adjusted upward if the loan is floating rate, as floating rate loans introduce more variability into the debt service costs. A property's loss severity may be adjusted either upwards or downwards based on the type of loan, be it a whole loan or a mezzanine loan, the strength of the loan covenants, loan amortization, additional debt, etc. Another consideration is the thickness of the debt. A small piece of debt at the bottom of the capital structure is more likely to be wiped out, even if overall losses are small. Finally, Fitch will adjust the resulting expected losses for reserves, the quality and underwriting practices of the loan originator, potential environmental issues, and so on.

For B-notes, mezzanine loans, and whole loans that have not been securitized, prepayment risk becomes an issue. The financial condition of the property at origination plays an important role in the likelihood of loan prepayment. Most B-notes, mezzanine loans, and whole loans that end up in CRE CDOs are secured by interests in transitional properties or highly-leveraged properties. The cash flows on these types of properties tend to be more volatile, and therefore the financing costs tend to be higher. Upon stabilization, the loans can be refinanced on more favorable terms. In such cases, the loan terms tend to provide more prepayment flexibility than do the loan terms on stabilized properties.

Ideally, investors in CMBS and CRE CDOs, especially noninvestment grade and equity investors, will perform both property-level and loan-level analysis on every loan underlying the CMBS or the CDO. However, this type of in-depth analysis is not always possible, and in the case of a CDO, this is partially why investors pay management fees. Nonetheless, prudent investors will do substantial homework on the underlying properties and loans. Analysis on properties, or sponsors, that make up a large percentage of the pool backing the CMBS or CDO will give investment grade-tranche inves-

---

[4] Thompson et al., *Defaults and Losses of U.S. Commercial Mortgage Loans: Year-End 2005 Update Reveals Improved Credit Performance.*

tors some confidence in the performance of the overall pool, while analysis of the entire pool is best for non investment grade and equity investors.

CMBS Bond-Level Analysis

For CMBS investments, additional bond-level analysis is required. This includes looking at the pool of loans in a CMBS trust as a whole and assessing the collateral concentrations. Property-type, geographic, and loan-type concentrations are all important pool characteristics that impact the likelihood and correlation of defaults as well as losses. The ratings of the underlying collateral and the pool's weighted average rating are important pool characteristics, as well. In addition, the rating agencies calculate a CMBS pool's Herfindahl score, which is a measure of the effective number of assets in the pool, and accounts for concentrations due to loan size. The Herfindahl score, per Moody's, is calculated as follows for a pool consisting of N assets:

$$\text{Herfindahl score} = \frac{1}{\displaystyle\sum_{i=1}^{N} \left(\frac{\text{Principal balance of asset } i \text{ in the pool}}{\text{Aggregate principal balance of the pool}} \right)^2}$$

Rating agencies determine required credit enhancement using these pool metrics, as well as the pool's overall DSCR and LTV.

In addition to analyzing the underlying pool, bond-level analysis requires cash flow modeling. Cash flow modeling incorporates the specific structure of the CMBS, including the protective effects of overcollateralization and cash flow diversion mechanisms. With an accurate model of the CMBS tranche, cash flows can be tested for their response to various levels of default, recovery, prepayment, and other factors.

CREL HISTORICAL PERFORMANCE

Most of the historical performance data on commercial real estate loans comes from the American Council of Life Insurers (ACLI) on mortgages held by life insurance companies. However, these data are fairly difficult for the average investor to access. More readily available information comes from the CMBS market, but these data only go back 10 to 15 years. In this section, we look at the results from default studies that span 30 years of history based on data from life insurance companies. Then we focus on loan defaults and losses on CMBS loan collateral.

The loan performance data from both life insurance companies and the CMBS market focus on A-notes. Unfortunately, little information about the performance of B-notes and mezzanine loans is available, since historically these loans have been held by private investors. We extrapolate from CMBS loan collateral data to comment on the defaults and recoveries of B-notes and mezzanine loans.

Defaults and losses on CRE loans are largely determined by the state of the real estate market. But while general real estate market conditions may determine the overall level of defaults, various default studies show that seasoning and property type are important indicators of relative default probability.

Thirty Years of CRE Loan Performance

The best known default and loss study using life insurance loan data is by Mark Snyderman, first released in 1991.[5] The study has been updated several times, most recently in 2005 by Howard Esaki.[6] The performance data cover commercial mortgages held by eight large insurance companies. The 2005 study spans 1972 to 2002, and as such, covers many interest rate and business cycles, including one of the worst real estate recessions in history in the late 1980s and early 1990s.

Based on this 30-year history of CRE loan defaults, Exhibit 9.4 highlights the variability in loan performance and stresses the impact of general

EXHIBIT 9.4   Lifetime Cumulative Default Rates by Loan Amount

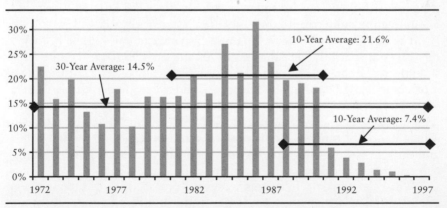

Source: UBS CDO Research and Howard Esaki and Masumi Goldman, "Commercial Mortgage Defaults: 30 Year History," *CMBS World* 6, no. 4 (Winter 2005): 21–29. Republished with permission from Commercial Mortgage Securities Association, Inc.

---

[5] Mark Snyderman, "Commercial Mortgages: Default Occurrence and Estimated Yield Impact," *Journal of Portfolio Management* 18, no. 3 (Fall 1991): 82–87.
[6] Howard Esaki and Masumi Goldman, "Commercial Mortgage Defaults: 30 Years of History," *CMBS World* 6, no. 4 (Winter 2005): 21–29.

real estate market conditions on the level of defaults. The exhibit shows life-time cumulative default rates of loans originated between 1972 and 1997. The study cuts off loans originated after 1997, so that all loan vintages in the study have at least five years of performance history. We can see the default rate variability among the vintages, ranging from a high of nearly 32% for the 1986 vintage, to a low of 0.1% for the 1997 vintage. The average lifetime cumulative default rate is 14.5%.

From the long periods of sustained high-default rates followed by peri-ods of low defaults, we can clearly see that the state of the real estate market matters. To further illustrate this relationship, we look at average lifetime default rates of loans originated over two different 10-year periods: that before the real estate bubble burst in the late 1980s, and the 10 years right after. The average cumulative default rates of loans originated before the bubble burst is nearly 21.6%, while the average of loans originated after is just 7.4%.

Differences in the market's perception of risk and loan underwriting standards account for this huge disparity. Loans originated at the market's peak were underwritten very aggressively and investors took on increas-ingly riskier loans to cash in on the booming market. This contributed to the high default rates after the real estate bubble burst. Immediately follow-ing the collapse, investors were reeling from heavy loan losses and began underwriting loans extremely conservatively. This, coupled with very strong property cash flows, has led to fewer defaults since the early 1990s, includ-ing during the more recent 2001–2003 real estate recession.

This comparison is one of the most extreme examples in the history of the real estate market. Since the late 1980s and early 1990s real estate reces-sion, the real estate market as a whole is dramatically different, especially in terms of increased information flow and standardized underwriting criteria. Some market participants believe we are unlikely to experience as severe a recession any time soon, if ever again. So, while looking at default rates over a long period of time, including the real estate recession in the late 1980s and early 1990s provides data on how things have been and how bad they can get, that is not necessarily indicative of the current market.

While default data from this extensive period of time cannot give a precise estimate for any one particular point in a real estate cycle, it can give a good sense of the timing of defaults over the life of loans. In Exhibit 9.5 we show average annual default rates by year of seasoning. The exhibit highlights the steep increase that occurs during the first seven years of a loan, particularly the first three years, and the sharply declining default rate thereafter. At the peak, defaults averaged about 2.7% per year. Thus, as a loan ages, its yearly probability of default increases until a few years before maturity, after which its probability of default is greatly reduced.

EXHIBIT 9.5   CRE Loan Average Default Curve by Loan Amount

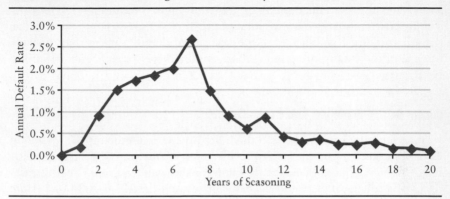

Source: UBS CDO Research and Howard Esaki and Masumi Goldman, "Commercial Mortgage Defaults: 30 Year History," *CMBS World* 6, no. 4 (Winter 2005): 21–29. Republished with permission from Commercial Mortgage Securities Association, Inc.

EXHIBIT 9.6   CRE Loan Default Curve Variability Across Vintages

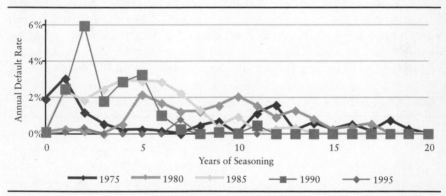

Source: UBS CDO Research and Howard Esaki and Masumi Goldman, "Commercial Mortgage Defaults: 30 Year History," *CMBS World* 6, no. 4 (Winter 2005): 21–29. Republished with permission from Commercial Mortgage Securities Association, Inc.

Yet Exhibit 9.5 shows an average default curve and tells us nothing about the *variability* in the default curve. Besides the high variability in default rates by calendar year (shown in Exhibit 9.4), there is also variability in default rates by year of seasoning. Exhibit 9.6 shows the default curve for five different loan vintages.

The default curve for the 1990 vintage (squares) peaks after just two years of seasoning at a 6% annual default rate and declines quickly afterwards. On the other hand, the default curve for the 1995 vintage (triangles) shows very few defaults until Year 7, when it hits a 1% annual default rate. The default histories of both vintages are very different from the average default curve in Exhibit 9.6. So while average default curves may provide a sense of the timing of defaults, there is nonetheless significant variability between vintages.

Recent Default History of CMBS Loan Collateral

Loan default data available from the CMBS market is on loans securitized in CMBS and focuses on the last 10 to 15 years, which may be a better indicator of future CRE loan defaults. Exhibit 9.7 shows how annual default rates on CMBS collateral increased dramatically during the 2001–2003 real estate recession. Since then, annual default rates fell as the real estate market gathered strength. The 10-year cumulative and annual default rates of CMBS loan collateral currently stand at 8.2% and 0.8%, respectively. For comparison, high-yield corporate loans have a six-year cumulative default rate of 12.5%, which annualizes to a 2.1% per year according to S&P LCD.

As we saw with the longer default history above, general real estate market conditions have a significant impact on overall default probability, even during a shorter time frame, as can be seen by default differences among loan vintages. Exhibit 9.8 shows default rates on CMBS loan collateral by vintage and by seasoning from a Fitch study of nearly 42,000 loans.[7]

EXHIBIT 9.7   CMBS Loan Collateral Historical Annual Default Rates

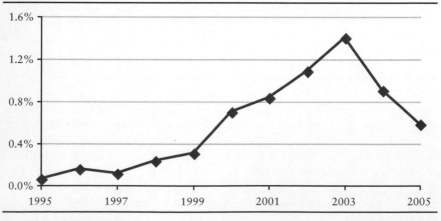

Source: FitchRatings.

[7] Patricia Bach, Robert Vrchota, and Mary MacNeill, *U.S. CMBS Loan Default Study 1993–2005*, FitchRatings, June 12, 2006.

EXHIBIT 9.8 CMBS Loan Collateral Marginal Default Rates by Vintage

Vintage	Marginal Default Rates Over Life of Loans (%)													Cumul. Default Rate (%)	Annual Default Rate (%)
	1-Yr	2-Yr	3-Yr	4-Yr	5-Yr	6-Yr	7-Yr	8-Yr	9-Yr	10-Yr	11-Yr	12-Yr	13-Yr		
1993	0.0	0.0	0.6	0.0	0.0	0.0	0.0	2.1	0.0	0.0	0.0	0.3	0.0	3.0	0.2
1994	0.0	0.0	0.9	0.0	0.0	0.2	2.0	1.5	0.0	0.3	0.0	0.0	–	4.8	0.4
1995	0.0	0.3	0.3	0.4	0.7	0.8	1.4	2.1	2.8	0.4	0.8	–	–	9.9	0.1
1996	0.0	0.3	0.9	0.7	1.0	2.3	1.7	1.3	1.4	0.3	0.0	–	–	9.9	0.9
1997	0.0	0.3	0.4	1.6	1.3	1.9	2.4	1.8	0.8	–	–	–	–	10.5	1.2
1998	0.0	0.3	0.6	0.8	1.1	1.8	1.0	0.5	–	–	–	–	–	6.0	0.8
1999	0.0	0.4	0.8	0.7	1.9	1.4	1.1	–	–	–	–	–	–	6.3	0.9
2000	0.1	0.5	1.7	2.0	1.8	1.9	–	–	–	–	–	–	–	7.9	1.3
2001	0.1	0.6	1.0	1.0	1.2	–	–	–	–	–	–	–	–	3.7	0.7
2002	0.0	0.3	0.5	0.4	0.0	–	–	–	–	–	–	–	–	1.1	0.2
2003	0.0	0.1	0.6	–	–	–	–	–	–	–	–	–	–	0.7	0.2
2004	0.0	0.1	–	–	–	–	–	–	–	–	–	–	–	0.1	0.1
2005	0.1	–	–	–	–	–	–	–	–	–	–	–	–	0.1	0.1
Average	0.0	0.3	0.7	0.7	1.0	1.3	1.4	1.5	1.0	0.2	0.3	0.2	0.0	8.6	0.7

Source: FitchRatings.

Each row of the exhibit shows the default history of CMBS loan collateral issued in a particular year. For instance, CMBS loan collateral issued in 1993 experienced no defaults until those loans reached their third year of seasoning, during which they experienced a 0.6% annual default rate. The last column shows cumulative default rate of loans from a particular vintage over the lives of the loans. For example, the 1993 vintage loans experienced a 3.0% cumulative default rate over the course of the next 13 years.

Exhibit 9.8 highlights how vintage selection can significantly impact default rates. The second to last column shows cumulative default rates of each vintage. The worst vintage is 1997, with a 10.5% cumulative default rate over nine years of seasoning.[8] The large percentage of hotel and retail loans in this vintage is the major default contributor. Hotel and retail properties were hurt most by the 2001–2003 real estate recession, although both sectors have since improved.

Looking at default rates on an annual basis also highlights the importance of vintage on default probability. The last column of Exhibit 9.8 adjusts the cumulative default rates for seasoning to better compare the default rates of difference vintages. The 2000 vintage stands out as the worst performer of all, with a 1.3% annual default rate. The cause of this abnormally poor performance is likely due to aggressive loan underwriting at the market's peak in 2000.

Property type is an important component of *relative* default probability. Different types of properties react differently to changes in the real estate cycle and are therefore likely to have different default experiences. S&P's study of nearly 30,000 CMBS loan collateral issued between 1993 and 2002 breaks down the loans by property type and year the loan collateral defaulted.[9] The results, shown as the number of defaulted loans by year of default, are in Exhibit 9.9.

Looking down the columns for the recession years of 2001 to 2003, most of the defaults that occurred were hotels and retail properties. However, defaults for both have decreased as the market has improved. This highlights the relatively high sensitivity of these two property types, especially hotels, to market conditions as compared to other property types.

---

[8] We recognize that the 3.6% cumulative default rate by Year 5 for the 1997 vintage in the Fitch study does not tie to the 0.1% 5-year cumulative default rate seen in the Esaki study. This is because loans underlying the data pool are different. They were originated for different reasons; in the Fitch study for securitizing, in the Esaki study for life insurance company holdings. Therefore, loan characteristics such as leverage, property type concentration, DSCR, and the like in the two studies differ, and have exhibited different default patterns.

[9] Thompson et al., *Defaults and Losses of U.S. Commercial Morgage Loans: Year-End 2005 Update Reveals Improved Credit Performance.*

EXHIBIT 9.9 CMBS Loan Collateral Defaults by Property Type and Year Defaulted

	1997	1998	1999	2000	2001	2002	2003	2004	2005	Total Defaults	Total Loans	Cumul. Default Rate
Health care	2	2	7	31	26	16	19	11	7	119	671	4.7%
Industrial	2	5	3	8	10	17	22	24	18	109	2,351	5.0%
Hotel	3	9	26	37	86	105	94	42	23	425	1,796	9.9%
Multifamily	11	32	28	27	37	77	115	148	116	591	9,477	10.0%
Manuf. housing		1	2	1	2	5	9	5	4	29	1,000	9.9%
Mixed use		1	3		3	4	9	3	4	27	602	6.8%
Office		1	8	8	15	31	53	45	44	205	4,429	5.4%
Retail	3	10	50	31	81	71	86	37	45	414	8,262	7.7%
Self storage		1		1	2	1	4	2	3	14	906	3.9%
Other		1	1	2	6				1	11	332	1.8%
Total defaults	19	63	128	146	268	327	411	317	265	1,944	29,826	6.5%

Source: Standard & Poor's.

Multifamily properties, on the other hand, are more sensitive than other property types to interest rates. Since 2001, loans on multifamily properties have experienced a high number of defaults relative to other property types. In fact, while overall defaults decreased in 2004 and 2005, multifamily loan defaults remained high due to poor performance. Their poor performance is largely due to the low interest rate environment that began in 2001 and extended into 2005. Low interest rates have turned more renters into home-buyers, resulting in lower occupancies for multifamily properties. However, as the housing market begins to cool, the performance of multifamily properties is improving.

Loss Severity CMBS Loan Collateral

The loss severity of defaulted CMBS loan collateral has remained relatively unchanged for the past few years, at just below 30% of original loan balance. S&P reports 2005 average loss severity of 27% for all defaulted loans originated between 1993 and 2005.[10] This loss severity is slightly higher than the typical 20% to 30% loss severity of high-yield corporate loans, but significantly lower than the 50% loss severity of high-yield bonds.[11]

Similar to default probability, overall loss severity is largely dependent the condition of the real estate market, particularly at the time when the defaulted loan is resolved. Exhibit 9.10 breaks down historical loss severities by property type (down) and year the defaulted loan was resolved (across).

As expected, loss severities are highest when defaulted loans are resolved during a real estate recession (2001 to 2003). Loss severities across almost all property types decreased in 2005, as strong property values helped limit losses. These trends confirm the dependence of loss severity on market conditions.

However, property type is also an important indicator of relative loss severity. Looking at the last column of Exhibit 9.10, we see that health care and hotel loans historically suffered the greatest losses and are a large part of why these loan types were excluded for a while from most CMBS pools. On the other hand, defaulted multifamily loans consistently experienced moderate losses, averaging less than 17%. Clearly, loans experience different relative loss severities depending on the property type underlying the loan.

[10] Thompson et al., *Defaults and Losses of U.S. Commercial Morgage Loans: Year-End 2005 Update Reveals Improved Credit Performance.*

[11] David Hamilton, Praveen Varma, Sharon Ou, and Richard Cantor, *Default & Recovery Rates of Corporate Bond Issuers: 1920–2004*, Moody's Investors Service, March 2005. David Keisman and Jane Zennario, *2003 Recovery Highlights*, Standard and Poor's, February 2004.

EXHIBIT 9.10 CMBS Loan Collateral Loss Severity Matrix by Property Type

	Year Defaulted Loan was Resolved (%)									Average Severity (%)
	1997	1998	1999	2000	2001	2002	2003	2004	2005	
Health care					2	43	65	50	22	47
Industrial		0	0	13	47	1	23	30	23	24
Hotel	0	0	0	56	40	47	47	35	34	39
Multifamily		0	4	7	22	14	18	18	19	17
Manufactured housing							23	39	15	24
Mixed use					29	0	0	17	23	17
Office				10	63	52	26	28	20	26
Retail	0	12	17	8	20	20	39	27	21	24
Self storage					0	22	25	55	1	22
Other						1	0	28	0	5
Average severity	0	1	5	10	29	29	37	29	22	27

Source: Standard & Poor's.

Defaults and Losses on B-Notes and Mezzanine Loans

The loans we have analyzed thus far in this section are mostly A-notes. While there is little historical data available to analyze the default rates and loss severities of B-notes and mezzanine loans, it would be fair to say that if the A-note defaults, the B-note and mezzanine loan have also defaulted; and if the A-note experiences a loss, the B-note and mezzanine loan lost their full principal.

So at a minimum, it can be assumed that the default rates of B-notes and mezzanine loans are at least those of the A-notes analyzed earlier. And a loss-given-A-note default is likely to be higher for B-notes and mezzanine loans than the 27% average loss severity experienced by A-notes. Figuring out how much higher default rates and loss severities have been on B-notes and mezzanine loans is tricky, but we attempt to address the issue below.

When a property's capital structure includes B-notes or mezzanine loans, it is often, but not always, fair to assume that these loans have higher LTVs than the typical A-note. So, perhaps we can extrapolate from the A-note default data, and equate a B-note or a mezzanine loan to an A-note with a high LTV.

For the most part, we believe it reasonable to assume that the default probability of B-notes is close to that of A-notes. The A- and B-notes are just pieces of the same mortgage, and the default probability of the mortgage, and therefore the default probabilities of both the A- and B-notes, is largely dependent on the sponsor's ability to refinance the entire mortgage. However, the same logic cannot be applied to mezzanine loans, since their default probability is less dependent on the refinancing of the mortgage.

Moody's looked at the relationship between leverage on A-notes and the occurrence of credit events over a 30+-year period.[12] The study found that the frequency of credit events, defined as foreclosure, restructuring, or discounted payoff, increased dramatically with higher leverage. As Exhibit 9.11 points out, the relationship between leverage and frequency of credit events is not 1:1; higher leverage raises default frequency exponentially. These results suggest that assuming that default rates of mezzanine loans are similar to A-notes may not be a fair assumption given the higher relative leverage of mezzanine loans.

In the absence of more quantitative data on B-notes and mezzanine loans, we turn to the rating agencies' methodologies for dealing with these collateral types when rating CRE CDOs. Usually, the loan collateral in CRE CDOs (whole loans, B-notes and mezzanine loans) is unrated. In such cases, the rating agencies will assign the loan a shadow rating. Moody's shadow

---

[12] Sally Gordon and Leslie Kizer, *U.S. CMBS: Case Study of Leverage and Default Over a Full Real Estate Cycle*, Moody's Investors Service, October 24, 2005.

EXHIBIT 9.11   Frequency of Credit Events by Initial LTV

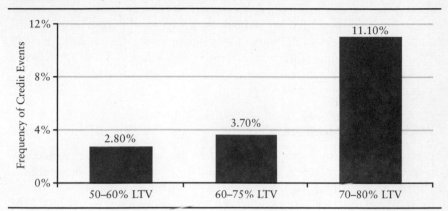

Source: Moody's Investors Service.

EXHIBIT 9.12   Example of Moody's Default and Loss Assumptions for CRE CDO Collateral

	Shadow Rating	Default Probability	Loss Severity	Resulting Expected Loss
Whole loan	B2	25%	40%	10%
B-note	B2	25%	70%	18%
Mezzanine loan	B2	25%	75%	19%
CMBS tranche	B2	25%	95%	24%

Source: Moody's Investors Service.

rating represents the bottom-dollar default probability of the loan. Therefore, the shadow rating only factors in default frequency, not loss severity. From there, Moody's determines the loan's loss severity based on the type of loan (whole, B-note, mezzanine, etc.), the LTV, and the thickness of the loan as a percent of the property's capital structure. An example of default and loss severity rates used by Moody's is shown in Exhibit 9.12.

CMBS HISTORICAL PERFORMANCE

When the CMBS market began taking off in the early to mid-1990s, the rating agencies had very little data on commercial mortgage loan performance to use to develop default, recovery, and correlation assumptions for their CMBS rating models. The rating agencies took what information they had, which included the heavy and highly correlated real estate loan losses suffered from 1990 to 1993, and came up with very conservative model assumptions. This resulted in CMBS deals with high-subordination requirements. Since then, the availability of loan performance data and the strength of the real estate market have helped lower subordination levels to what is more appropriate for the asset class. Exhibit 9.13 shows how subordination levels changed over the past 10 years.

CMBS Upgrades and Downgrades

Lower subordination levels are justified by historical CMBS upgrade and downgrade activity. Rating upgrades have long outnumbered downgrades. In 2005, 16.4% of CMBS tranches were upgraded versus 13.8% in corporate securities and 5.9% in other structured finance securities. Most CMBS tranche upgrades were due to increased credit enhancement as collateral paid off, as well as stronger than anticipated collateral performance. Only 3.5% of the CMBS tranches outstanding were downgraded, which was in line with other structured finance securities at 2%, but well outperforming corporates at 8.3%.[13]

However, strong upgrade activity is not distributed evenly across CMBS tranches. Exhibit 9.14 shows 1- and 5-year CMBS rating changes for CMBS tranches issued from 1988 to 2005. Initial tranche ratings are on the left; current tranche ratings are across the top. Percentages within the figures show rating migration from the tranche's initial rating to its current rating. For example, 99% of CMBS tranches initially rated Aaa remained Aaa after one year; 1% were downgraded to Aa after one year.

EXHIBIT 9.13   Representative CMBS Subordination Levels

	1996 (%)	2000 (%)	2006 (%)
AAA	32	23	13
AA	24	18	11
A	20	14	8
BBB	18	10	5
BB	8	5	3
B	3	3	2

Source: UBS CDO Research, Intex, Commercial Mortgage Alert.

---

[13] Julie Tung, Jian Hu, Richard Cantor, Nicolas Weill, Gus Harris, Tad Phillip, and Frederic Drevon, *Structured Finance Rating Transitions: 1983–2005*, Moody's Investors Service, February 2006.

EXHIBIT 9.14 CMBS Tranche Rating Transition Matrix 1988–2005
a. 1-Year Transition Matrix (%)

	Aaa	Aa	A	Baa	Ba	B	Caa or Below
Aaa	99	1	0	0	0	0	0
Aa	12	87	1	0	0	0	0
A	3	7	89	1	0	0	0
Baa	1	1	5	90	2	0	0
Ba	0	0	0	2	94	3	0
B	0	0	0	0	1	92	7
Caa or below	0	0	0	0	0	1	99

b. 5-Year Transition Matrix (%)

	Aaa	Aa	A	Baa	Ba	B	Caa or Below
Aaa	94	3	2	0	0	0	0
Aa	49	46	2	0	1	0	1
A	16	26	55	3	1	0	0
Baa	6	6	22	60	3	1	1
Ba	0	3	1	10	67	13	6
B	0	0	1	2	3	59	35
Caa or below	0	0	0	0	0	7	93

Source: UBS CDO Research, Moody's Investors Service.

Exhibit 9.14 shows the distribution and extremes of rating changes. It is evident that severe downgrades among any CMBS tranches are uncommon. We also point out that CMBS tranches initially rated Ba and below, the typical tranches purchased by CRE CDOs, show strong ratings stability within one year, though after five years, upgrade and downgrade activity is more varied than it is for investment-grade tranches. However, 82% of the tranches initially rated Ba and 65% of the tranches initially rated B have maintained or improved their initial ratings. This is significantly better than the upgrade and downgrade activity of all below investment grade structured finance securities, of which less than 44% have maintained or improved upon their initial ratings.

CMBS Default Rates

CMBS default studies are extremely difficult. One reason is the private nature of the securities. Another reason is that even with perfect information, it is hard to determine whether a tranche has defaulted or is certain to default in the future. For instance, it is often unclear whether a tranche is going to catch up on interest shortfalls and pay in full. Of the 185 CMBS tranches that have had interest shortfalls, substantially all of those shortfalls have been cured, resulting in a 66% payment default cure rate, which is significantly higher than the 11% average cure rate for other structured finance securities.[14] It can also be unclear whether the performing tranches of a distressed CMBS deal will pay back principal.

As a proxy for "default" we look at Moody's cumulative impairment rates.[15] Moody's defines impairment as uncured payment default (interest shortfall or principal writedown) or a downgrade to Ca or C. The impairment rate is calculated as the number of securities impaired, divided by the number of securities outstanding. Exhibit 9.15 shows the cumulative percent of impaired or "defaulted" CMBS tranches by cohort and rating for tranches issued between 1993 and 2005. For comparison, the exhibit also shows cumulative impairment rates for all structured finance securities and for RMBS.

Focusing on the first panel of the exhibit, no Aaa- or Aa-rated CMBS tranches have been impaired within the first five years of issuance. It's interesting to note the point in the CMBS capital structure at which impairment rates rise significantly, between the Ba- and B-rated tranches, revealing the bottom-weighted distribution of impairments.

Comparing CMBS cumulative impairment rates to those of all structured finance securities (second panel), we see that CMBS tranches have lower impairment rates across all cohorts and all ratings. Comparing CMBS to RMBS (third panel), we see that after five years, RMBS tranches outperform CMBS, but not by much. Over all CMBS tranches, the 5-year cumulative impairment rate is 4.9% versus 3.0% for RMBS tranches. In fact, investment grade CMBS tranches experienced a lower 5-year cumulative impairment rate than the RMBS tranches (0.5% versus 1.9%, respectively). Even more interesting, especially to CDO equity, is that while the B-rated CMBS tranches experienced higher 5-year cumulative impairment rates

---

[14] Jian Hu, Hadas Alexander, Debjani Roy, Julia Tung, Richard Cantor, Gus Harris, Detlef Scholz, and Nicolas Weill, *Default & Loss Rates of Structured Finance Securities: 1993–2005*, Moody's Investors Service, April 2006.

[15] Jian Hu, Hadas Alexander, Debjani Roy, Julia Tung, Richard Cantor, Gus Harris, Detlef Scholz, and Nicolas Weill, *Default & Loss Rates of Structured Finance Securities: 1993–2005*, Moody's Investors Service, April 2006.

EXHIBIT 9.15 Cumulative Impairment Rates by Cohort and Rating

Original Rating	CMBS (%)					All Structured Finance (%)					RMBS (%)				
	1-Yr	2-Yr	3-Yr	4-Yr	5-Yr	1-Yr	2-Yr	3-Yr	4-Yr	5-Yr	1-Yr	2-Yr	3-Yr	4-Yr	5-Yr
Aaa	0.0	0.0	0.0	0.0	0.0	0.0	0.1	0.2	0.3	0.4	0.0	0.1	0.2	0.4	0.5
Aa	0.0	0.0	0.0	0.0	0.0	0.2	0.5	1.2	2.0	2.6	0.0	0.1	0.2	0.4	0.5
A	0.0	0.2	0.3	0.3	0.3	0.2	1.0	1.8	2.6	3.4	0.3	0.7	1.0	1.0	1.1
Baa	0.3	0.7	0.8	0.9	1.1	1.2	3.5	6.8	9.7	12.9	0.9	2.5	4.4	5.9	7.1
Ba	0.6	1.5	2.7	3.4	4.3	3.8	8.8	12.9	17.1	19.5	2.1	4.5	6.7	8.2	9.4
B	2.4	6.1	11.5	17.5	23.5	5.9	11.9	17.9	22.7	26.5	3.4	6.7	9.9	11.4	12.2
IG	0.1	0.3	0.4	0.4	0.5	0.4	1.1	2.2	3.3	4.3	0.2	0.6	1.1	1.6	1.9
SG	2.1	4.8	8.4	12.5	16.5	5.6	11.1	15.9	20.5	23.5	2.9	5.7	8.3	10.0	11.1
All	0.7	1.6	2.6	3.8	4.9	1.0	2.3	3.9	5.3	6.6	0.5	1.3	2.1	2.6	3.0

Source: Moody's Investors Service.

EXHIBIT 9.16 Realized Losses for Structured Finance Securities

Original Rating	CMBS	ABS	RMBS
AAA		6.0	0.2
AA		55.1	24.3
A	3.8	56.0	10.7
BBB	20.0	66.0	19.9
BB	6.7	81.4	36.2
B	21.6	70.7	47.3
All	17.9	63.9	28.6

Source: Standard & Poor's.

EXHIBIT 9.17 Estimated Ultimate Recovery Rates for Structured Finance Securities

Original Rating	CMBS	ABS	RMBS
AAA	93.1	63.3	98.4
AA	61.5	31.7	66.8
A	52.8	23.0	58.1
BBB	46.9	17.0	52.2
BB	44.3	14.4	49.6
B	34.0	4.2	39.3

Source: Standard & Poor's.

than RMBS tranches of the same ratings, the CMBS tranche impairments were slightly more back-ended, occurring more often after Year 2.

CMBS Loss Severity

On average, loss severities of CMBS tranches tend to be lower than those of other structure finance securities. Using historical data on defaulted CMBS tranches issued from 1994 to 2001, S&P found loss severities on defaulted CMBS tranches and compared them to loss severities of other structured finance (SF) securities (see Exhibit 9.16).[16] CMBS have lower loss severities than ABS, CDO, and even RMBS across all ratings.

S&P estimates the ultimate recovery rates on SF securities, as shown in Exhibit 9.17. Their estimates are the result of regression analysis on his-

---

[16] Erkan Erturk, Peter Stavropoulos, and Thomas Gillis, *Recovery Study Reveals Behavior of Structured Finance Securities After Default*, Standard & Poor's, March 7, 2006.

torical data. The ultimate recovery rates of CMBS tranches across all rating classes don't differ much from ultimate recoveries rates on RMBS, and are actually significantly higher than ultimate recovery rates on ABS tranches.

SUMMARY

As the commercial real estate market has evolved, so have CRE investments. In this chapter, we have reviewed the different types of CRE investments from first lien mortgages to CMBS. We looked at different structures and showed how CRE loans and securities provide investors with levered exposure to price appreciating assets with the ability to customize that real estate exposure via credit enhancement and diversification. Then we discussed several factors to consider when investing in CRE, including property-level analysis, loan-level analysis, and bond-level analysis. Finally, we discussed the historical performance of commercial real estate loans and CMBS.

CHAPTER 10

Commercial Real Estate CDOs

Commercial real estate (CRE) CDOs are one of the most efficient vehicles for financing real estate investments. CRE CDOs give traditional real estate asset managers the flexibility to take advantage of relative value opportunities within the real estate market, while providing nonrecourse financing that matches the average life and interest profile of the underlying asset pool. And as managers are drawn to CRE CDOs for structural flexibility and term financing, investors benefit from exposure to a diverse portfolio of managed CRE assets.

As the CDO market continues to develop and evolve, there is an increasing number of managed CRE CDOs and CRE CDOs backed by commercial real estate loans. While this evolution brings new risks to CRE CDOs, it also provides new opportunities for investors. And as record issuance volumes continue, CRE CDOs are an important asset class that investors in CDOs and commercial mortgage-backed securities (CMBS) should consider.

In this chapter, we describe CRE CDOs, their evolution, current market trends, and historical performance. We also provide a framework for evaluating CRE CDO investments, and discuss how rating agencies rate CRE CDOs.

CRE CDO DEFINED

CRE CDOs are CDOs backed primarily by commercial real estate investments. The most common collateral in CRE CDOs includes:

- Commercial real estate loans (CREL)
  - Whole loans and A-notes
  - B-notes
  - Mezzanine loans
  - Preferred equity
- CMBS (cash and synthetic)

- REIT securities
  - Unsecured bonds
  - Trust Preferred Securities (TruPS)
- Other CRE CDOs

The collateral composition of CRE CDOs varies, from just one collateral type, such as whole loans, to a diversified mix of several collateral types. The composition is typically a function of the CDO manager's core investment competencies and investment objectives. Exhibit 10.1 shows the collateral compositions of four CRE CDOs issued in August and October 2006, and highlights potential variability among CRE CDOs.[1]

EXHIBIT 10.1   Recently Issued CRE CDOs

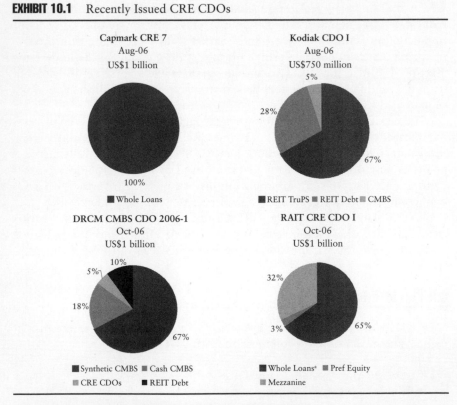

[a] The whole loans in RAIT CRE CDO I are bridge loans.
Source: Data obtained from UBS CDO Research, rating agency presale reports, and *Commercial Mortgage Alert.*

---

[1] For this chapter, we classify A-notes, bridge loans, credit tenant leases, and senior participations as whole loans, and junior participations as B-notes.

Each type of collateral has its own nuances and investment considerations. CMBS consist of whole loans and A-notes with standard terms: 10-year bullet maturities, fixed rates, and strong prepayment protection. Their risks are well understood, the most important ones being property-specific, asset-specific, and maturity extension risks. CREL, on the other hand, are generally unsuitable for CMBS securitization, and their terms and risks are far from standardized. CREL tend to be floating rate with maturities that range from months to years. They also have little to no prepayment protection.

CRE whole loans in CRE CDOs are typically high-leverage loans, or loans on transitional properties. A transitional property is an underperforming property, in which performance and value can be enhanced by improving the property through capital expenditures, waiting for an improvement in the overall real estate market, signing new tenants, or replacing the existing manager. The market values and cash flows of transitional properties tend to be more volatile and more susceptible to local market conditions than those of stabilized properties.

The B-notes and mezzanine loans in CRE CDOs are subordinate debt, typically on stabilized properties. These loans increase the overall leverage on a property. However, despite their subordinate position, B-notes and mezzanine loans on stabilized properties may have lower leverage and less cash flow volatility than whole loans on transitional properties.

CRE CDOs containing other CRE CDOs usually focus on BBB tranches. REIT debt is typically in the form of unsecured bonds issued by large, publicly-rated REITs. As explained in Chapter 8, REIT trust preferred securities (TruPS) are hybrid securities that are subordinate to all of the issuing REIT's other debt. TruPS in CRE CDOs are typically issued by large, publicly-rated REITs, but some have been issued by smaller, unrated REITs.

MARKET TRENDS

The commercial real estate market's strength this past decade has spurred demand for all CRE-related products, including CRE CDOs. While still a niche product in the overall CDO market, 2006 CRE CDO issuance is expected to double 2005 volume, growing from $21 to $40 billion, driven by both issuer and investor demand.

CMBS have historically dominated CRE CDO portfolios, but CREL allocations are growing. Exhibit 10.2 illustrates how the collateral composition of CRE CDOs has changed. Previously absent from CRE CDOs, CREL now account for nearly 50% of newly issued CRE CDOs. And the majority of CREL are floating-rate whole loans.

The trend towards CREL adds more asset diversification and more spread to CRE CDOs. However, CREL also introduce new risks, most notably, development risk and reinvestment risk. Some CRE CDOs include small allocations of construction loans, land loans, and condo-/coop-conversion loans. These loans carry high development risk, along with other third party risks.

The inclusion of riskier collateral in CRE CDOs increases an investor's dependence on the CDO manager's real estate, underwriting, and management expertise and capabilities. Furthermore, increased reinvestment risk, along with a more competitive landscape, requires that CDO managers be able to source collateral to replenish the loan pools as loans mature or prepay. More and more, CDO managers have their own in-house loan originators. This provides the CDO with a direct source for replacement collateral, access to the loan's borrower, and more control over the original terms of the loan. CDO managers such as Capmark and NorthStar Realty Finance originate their CREL collateral in-house.

We are also beginning to see more CRE CDOs backed by synthetic CMBS. As is the case with other CDOs, the use of synthetic technology allows managers to source particular vintages, originators, and servicers, taking full advantage of opportunities in the market. CDS on individual loans and other CRE CDOs, as well as property and real estate market derivatives, may further increase the use of synthetics in CRE CDOs.

EXHIBIT 10.2   CRE CDO Collateral Distribution

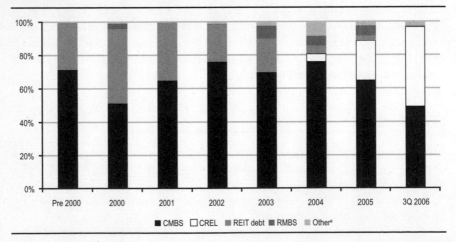

[a] Other includes: direct loans to REITs, real estate operating companies, and other retailers, ABS, and CDOs.
Note: Includes ReREMICs; excludes REIT TruPS CDOs.
Source: FitchRatings.

Finally, CRE CDOs have entered the global stage. As the spreads for U.S. commercial mortgage loans tighten, managers are looking overseas to source more collateral. European CREL are an even more diverse asset class than U.S. CREL (with respect to underwriting standards and loan terms) and thus require more thorough due diligence. Yet, Basel II requirements are making it more expensive for banks to invest in European CREL, such as B-notes and mezzanine loans. This may remove banks from the CREL market, thus providing ample supply for new CRE CDOs.

CRE FINANCE BEFORE CDOs

Traditional CMBS B-piece buyers were first to utilize CDO technology *en masse*. Before CRE CDOs, B-piece buyers would finance their CMBS tranches and other real estate subordinate debt using short-term repo financing, earning the spread between the yield on their assets and their cost of funds. However, the risks of repo financing (chiefly basis risk and margin calls) plagued B-piece buyers. The credit pullback caused by the 1998 Russian debt crisis further aggravated B-piece funding problems, forcing B-piece buyers to look for alternative financing sources.

Resecuritized Real Estate Mortgage Investment Conduit (ReREMIC) structures helped meet the financing needs of some B-piece buyers, providing high-leverage nonrecourse term financing needed to make CMBS arbitrage work. However, this financing vehicle limits B-piece buyers' investment activities. Basically, ReREMICs are static pools of CMBS. By statute, they cannot be managed pools nor contain non-CMBS assets. While this structure works for some B-piece buyers, the collateral and trading constraints of ReREMICs are too confining for others.

Enter CRE CDOs. Like a ReREMIC, CDOs provide B-piece buyers with long-term, nonmark-to-market financing, but offer much more flexibility than ReREMICs for two reasons.

First, CDOs do not have the same collateral restrictions as ReREMICs. Through a CRE CDO, an issuer can pool several different types of securities, from CMBS tranches to mezzanine loans to synthetics, taking advantage of relative value opportunities across the real estate market. This feature first caught the eye of B-piece buyers looking for nonmark-to-market financing across all the assets in their portfolios, and it is what drove issuance of static CRE CDOs.

The second reason is that CDOs can be structured as managed pools, allowing issuers to lightly trade portfolios and take advantage of market opportunities as they arise. As issuers and investors became more familiar with static CRE CDOs, managed CRE CDOs became more popular. Managed CRE CDOs are attractive to a broader base of traditional commercial real estate investors who want the flexibility to sell or buy new assets. And by retaining a significant portion of the equity and subordinate tranches of the CDO, issuers maintain control over the portfolio and the equity returns.

As the CRE CDO market continues to develop, new issuers will enter the fray, such as asset managers using the CDO structure to increase their assets under management. These managers prefer to sell CRE CDO equity to third parties to free up capital. Going forward, we expect to see more traditional real estate investors issuing CRE CDOs, as well as more asset management-oriented issuers.

TYPES OF CRE CDOs

As mentioned earlier, CRE CDOs contain an array of different types of collateral. The variability in underlying collateral, and consequently, in underlying risks, makes it difficult to generalize when discussing CRE CDOs. Nonetheless, it is helpful to think of CRE CDOs as three major types, based on dominant collateral type:

- CMBS CDOs (Cash and Synthetic)
  - Investment-grade (IG) CMBS
  - High-yield (HY) CMBS
- CREL CDOs
  - Whole loans (WL)
  - Whole loans, B-notes and mezzanine loans (WL/B/Mezz.)
- REIT TruPS CDOs

We split our first group, CMBS CDOs, into two separate subsets depending on their investment focus: *investment-grade* (IG) CMBS tranches and *high-yield* (HY) CMBS tranches, including unrated pieces. Typically, CMBS CDOs also contain 5% to 15% REIT debt allocation. We also split CREL CDOs into two subsets separate groups; those focusing on *whole loans*, typically rated loans (with a weighted average rating factor (WARF) from 1,000 to 2,700), and those with a *combination* of whole loans, B-notes and mezzanine loans, most of which are unrated (WARF from 3,000 to 6,500). REIT TruPS CDOs often contain a mix of REIT TruPS and REIT bonds.

In Exhibit 10.3, we categorize 37 CRE CDOs issued between September 2005 and September 2006, and show their weighted average ratings and average collateral compositions by principal amount.

Each type of CRE CDO has a different underlying motivation. IG and HY CMBS CDOs capitalize on the strong historical performance of CMBS

EXHIBIT 10.3 CRE CDO Characteristics

	IG CMBS	HY CMBS	WL	WL/B/ Mezz.	REIT TruPS
Volume	$4,600	$6,100	$4,600	$3,400	$4,300
Avg. deal size	$500	$770	$650	$500	$720
Avg. WARF	260–1,000	2,000–5,600	1,000–2,700	3,000–6,700	1,250–2,000
Collateral ratings	BBB+/BBB–	BB/Unrated	BB+/B	B/Unrated	BB/B

Collateral	IG CMBS	HY CMBS	WL	WL/B/ Mezz.	REIT TruPS
CMBS	78%	85%	6%	6%	6%
REIT debt	10%	0%	0%	0%	11%
CRE CDO	6%	4%	0%	1%	0%
Whole loans	0%	1%	79%	31%	0%
B-notes	1%	5%	9%	29%	0%
Mezzanine	0%	6%	6%	32%	0%
RMBS	4%	0%	0%	0%	0%
TruPS	0%	0%	0%	0%	83%
Other	0%	0%	0%	1%	0%
Total	100%	100%	100%	100%	100%

Note: $ amounts in USD millions; CMBS includes cash and synthetic securities.
Source: UBS CDO Research, rating agency presale reports.

by levering up CMBS tranche investments to create arbitrage. CREL CDOs contain loans with less liquidity, less transparency, and greater risk than loans underlying CMBS. Typically, CREL investors must be prepared to become the owner of the underlying property, should the property's performance decline. Therefore, CREL CDO managers leverage their real estate expertise to identify and create value. REIT TruPS CDOs exploit the limited primary and secondary markets for REIT TruPS to generate excess spread.

CRE CDO PERFORMANCE

As of October 2006, no CRE CDO tranche has ever been downgraded by S&P. Between 2004 through October 2006, Fitch did not downgrade any post-2002 issued CRE CDO tranche. The eight older CRE CDO tranches

Fitch downgraded were from vintages that contained asset-backed security (ABS) collateral. These downgrades were due to the CRE CDOs' manufactured housing bucket. Manufactured housing (MH) collateral has since been "black balled" from virtually all 2005 and 2006 vintage CDOs and CMBS.

Between 2004 through October 2006, Fitch upgraded 265 of the nearly 800 CRE CDO tranches it rates. This strong performance is largely attributed to strong performance and upgrade activity of underlying CMBS tranches. Fitch cautions that CRE CDOs backed by 2005 and 2006 vintage CMBS will not experience the same positive ratings migration as those backed by earlier vintages, since CMBS subordination levels have decreased due to strong collateral performance.

It is tough to predict future rating performance of CREL CDOs. Estimating default and recovery rates of B-notes, mezzanine loans, and transitional whole loans is difficult, given a paucity of historical data. The last real estate downturn was the third quarter of 2001, before CDOs began including B-notes, mezzanine loans, and transitional whole loans. So CREL CDO performance is unproven in a difficult environment.

INVESTORS

Exhibit 10.4 breaks down typical CRE CDO investors by tranche. CRE CDO debt investors are similar to investors of other types of CDOs. Real money investors, financial institutions, insurance companies, and the like,

EXHIBIT 10.4 Typical CRE CDO Investors

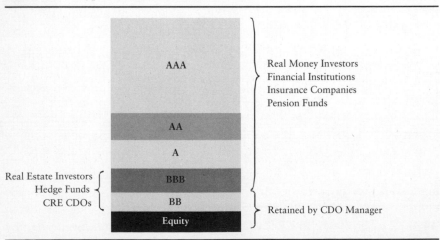

Source: UBS CDO Research.

tend to buy investment grade tranches. Hedge funds and other CDOs, particularly CRE CDOs, buy mezzanine tranches. Many of the portfolio managers that invest in CRE CDOs have traditionally invested in commercial real estate investments (i.e., CMBS), rather than other types of CDOs such as collateralized loan obligations (CLOs).

The equity tranche of a CRE CDO is almost always retained by the CDO manager, especially in the case of CREL CDOs. One reason is that by retaining equity, the manager's interests are aligned with those of CDO debt holders. In the event of a loan default, a manager who retained the CDO's equity has a greater incentive to resolve the defaulted loan in a manner that will minimize losses to the CDO.

The real answer is that many CRE CDO managers are experienced real estate investors who are using the CDO structure as a financing tool to enhance returns on their real estate portfolio. So they want to retain the equity. In the case where the manager is a REIT, they are required to retain all of the CDO tranches rated below investment grade in order for the CDO's collateral, which appears as assets on the REIT's balance sheet, to qualify as REIT-eligible assets.[2]

However, managers using the CDO structure to increase their assets under management and to generate origination fees are more likely to sell the equity tranche. This is common in CMBS CDOs, where the main motivation for using the CDO structure is arbitrage.

CDO Investors: Same Game/New Collateral

Structurally, CRE CDOs are the same as other types of CDOs, but they differ with respect to their collateral, which is unfamiliar to traditional CDO investors. Because of the single industry focus, CRE CDO portfolios have historically been considered highly correlated. However, CRE CDOs have considerable diversification in the types of loans and securities they hold, and in the underlying property types, tenant concentrations, and geographic locations of their assets. Bottom line, the underlying collateral is physical, (hopefully) price-appreciating, real estate properties. This point is very appealing to investors.

The trick for CDO investors is to understand the underlying collateral and/or be comfortable with the CDO manager's capabilities. The level of understanding and comfort is typically a function of the tranche an investor buys: the lower the credit rating of the tranche, the more due diligence the investor should do. We discuss the credit analysis of CRE CDOs in the next topic section of this chapter.

---

[2] To qualify as a REIT, at least 75% of the REIT's asset must be REIT-eligible.

CMBS Investors: New Game/Same-ish Collateral

While a full comparison of CRE CDOs and CMBS/ReREMIC trusts is beyond the scope of this chapter, we highlight a few key points here. CDOs are similar to CMBS and ReREMIC trusts in that they all use subordination as a means of credit support. However, in a CDO, credit protection does not stop there. CDOs have cash flow diversion triggers, such as interest coverage and overcollateralization tests (IC and OC tests, respectively). These triggers protect the senior tranches from credit and cash flow issues before they become major problems by diverting principal and interest away from junior tranches to senior tranches.

However, the quality and real estate expertise of the issuer/manager is even more important in CRE CDOs than it is in CMBS and ReREMICs. A CRE CDO manager not only selects the initial collateral pool, but can also lightly trade within the CDO (usually limited to 15% of the pool per year), and can reinvest principal prepayments in new collateral for the first 3 to 5 years. (We discuss additional considerations regarding managers that a CRE CDO investor should take into account in the next section.) Finally, as we have mentioned previously, the collateral underlying CRE CDOs and CMBS/ReREMICs is not identical and carries different risks.

CRE CDO CREDIT ANALYSIS

First and foremost, analysis of a CRE CDO begins with a thorough understanding of the underlying collateral. We described this collateral in the previous chapter. Ideally, investors in CRE CDOs will review every security underlying the CDO. But that level of analysis is not always possible, and investors pay fees to the CDO manager to perform that analysis.

Nonetheless, prudent investors do substantial homework on the underlying properties and loans. Analysis on properties or sponsors that make up a large percentage of the CDO collateral pool give investors some confidence in the performance of the overall pool. Looking at the debt service coverage ratio (DSCR) and loan-to-value (LTV) ratio of the underlying loans provides insight into the pool's credit quality. For CDOs containing CMBS tranches, reviewing the performance history, including loan delinquencies and defaults, tranche upgrade and downgrade history, as well as the largest and riskiest loans in the underlying CMBS portfolio is suggested.

At the bond-level, CRE CDO investors look at all the loans and securities in a CDO pool in aggregate, and assess the collateral concentrations. Property-type, tenant, geographic, and loan-type concentrations are all important pool characteristics impacting the likelihood and correlation of defaults and the severity of default losses.

The ratings of the underlying collateral and its WARF are important pool characteristics, as well. In addition, rating agencies calculate a CDO pool's Herfindahl score, which measures the effective number of assets in the pool, accounting for concentrations due to loan size.[3] Pool characteristics, WARF and the Herfindahl score, in conjunction with the pool's overall DSCR and LTV, give indications of the default probabilities, loss severities, and correlations of the underlying pool.

Bond-level analysis also requires cash flow modeling. Cash flow modeling incorporates the structure of the CDO, including the impact of overcollateralization tests and fast pay amortization structures. Default and recovery assumptions, as well as default timing, play an important role in cash flow analysis and can significantly alter the bond's expected cash flows.

For investors familiar with CMBS analysis, the collateral underlying some CRE CDOs will involve additional considerations. Default and recovery assumptions of CREL differ from those of typical A-note CMBS collateral. Additionally, prepayment risk and interest rate risk, virtually non-existent in CMBS, are factors in some CRE CDOs.

Finally, CRE CDO analysis is incomplete without reviewing the CDO manager. A CRE CDO manager should have strong collateral underwriting practices and, in the event of default, be capable of working out a defaulted loan, or taking control of a poorly performing property. To minimize losses, a manager may need to provide additional funding to turn around a property or cure/buy-out the existing senior debt, so access to capital is also important.

Furthermore, a managed CDO's collateral pool changes over time. Looking at trading limitations and collateral concentration limitations helps investors understand how much the portfolio can change. A good manager uses trading as an opportunity to improve the collateral pool's quality and risk management. It is also important for the CDO's allowable collateral concentrations to be consistent with the core competencies of the manager. For example, if the CDO has a 15% synthetic bucket, the manager should have some expertise in such instruments. And finally, investors should also consider the ability to source replacement collateral in the future, as competition for good quality CRE-related securities is likely to increase.

RATING CRE CDOs

Overall, the methodology used by the rating agencies to rate CRE CDOs is similar to that used for other CDOs. Simulation models generate portfolio

---

[3] The Herfindahl score, per Moody's, is calculated by dividing (i) one by (ii) the sum of, for each asset in the pool, the square of, (a) the principal balance of each asset in the pool, divided by (b) the aggregate principal balance of the assets in the pool.

default scenarios which, together with recovery rates and other portfolio assumptions, feed into cash flow models to determine required credit support. Before assigning tranche ratings, additional consideration is given to manager quality.

However, determining model inputs is where CRE CDO rating methodology differs from rating other types of CDOs. In fact, analyzing CRE CDO collateral is more similar to analyzing CMBS loan collateral. The rating agencies perform loan-level analysis on a majority (40% to 100%) of assets in the underlying pool and assess fundamental real estate risk. Through cash flow analysis, the rating agencies calculate a property's "stabilized" net cash flow (NCF) and apply a "stabilized" capitalization rate appropriate for the property to determine the property's value.[4]

Using the property's value and NCF, a stabilized DSCR and LTV is calculated. Fitch regards DSCR as the best indicator of a loan's probability of default, and LTV the best indicator of loss severity. Exhibit 10.5 shows how Fitch translates DSCR and LTV into default probability and loss severity. Fitch uses those two indicators, and other loan-specific factors such as interest rate risk, amortization, debt thickness,[5] borrower quality, and so on, to determine a loan's expected loss.

EXHIBIT 10.5 Fitch Default and Loss Curves for CMBS Loan Collateral
A. Default Probability Curve

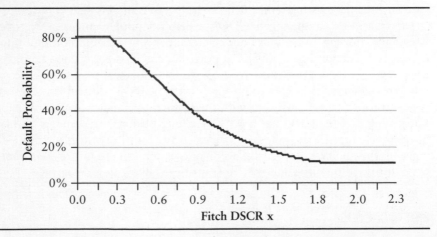

---

[4] The value of a property is estimated by dividing the NCF by the property's capitalization rate.
[5] Debt thickness is the loan's percentage of the property's value. In the event of loan default, a thin debt tranche will likely experience a higher proportionate loss severity than a thicker debt tranche.

EXHIBIT 10.5 (Continued)
B. Loss Severity Curve

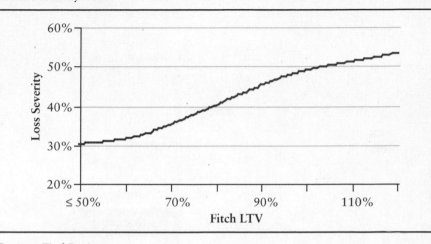

Source: FitchRatings.

Moody's and S&P use cash flow analysis to assign a "shadow rating" to a loan. Moody's shadow rating represents the bottom-dollar default probability of the loan. Therefore, shadow ratings reflect default frequency, not expected loss, as Moody's other ratings address.

Hypertranching

In determining a loan's shadow rating (especially for high LTV loans), a property's capital structure is "hypertranched," which is similar to the rating methodology used when rating large loan CMBS. When a loan is hypertranched, it is split into tranches, each with its own rating. For example, as shown in Exhibit 10.6, a whole loan with a Baa2 rating can be split into 4 tranches, with ratings ranging from Aaa down to Baa2.

Exhibit 10.7 shows how Moody's analyzes large loan CMBS. The first two columns show a large loan's LTV and resulting rating. For example, a loan with a 65% LTV would have a Baa2 rating. The next few columns show the loan hyper-tranched into multiple tranches, some rated higher than the entire loan. A Baa2 loan can be hypertranched into four separate tranches: the first 63% would be rated Aaa, the next 12% would be A2, the next 12% A2, the remaining 12% Baa2.

CRE CDOs benefit from the hypertranching rating approach, since some of the underlying loans have high LTVs. Without hypertranching, a high LTV loan (greater than 85% LTV) would be rated Caa or below. And

EXHIBIT 10.6 Hypertranching Example

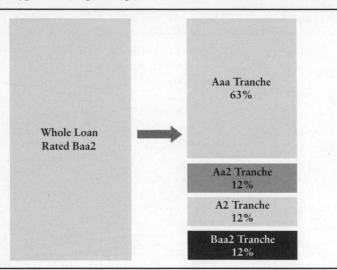

Source: UBS CDO Research.

EXHIBIT 10.7 Moody's Hypertranching for CMBS Large Loans

Loan LTV	Loan Rating	Hypertranching Treatment of Loan as CDO Asset (%)						
		Aaa	Aa2	A2	Baa2	Baa3	Ba2	B2
46%	Aaa	100						
53%	Aa2	85	15					
60%	A2	73	13	13				
65%	Baa2	63	12	12	12			
67%	Baa3	60	12	12	12	4		
75%	Ba2	51	11	11	11	4	13	
85%	B2	41	9	9	9	4	12	15

Source: UBS CDO Research Calculations from Moody's Investors Service *LTV Tranching Parameters for Large Loan CMBS.*

low and unrated assets have a significant impact on a CDO's subordination levels. However, by hypertranching a high LTV loan, portions of the loan can be treated as rated assets in the CDO's collateral pool, thus lessening the negative impact of the high LTV loan. The hypertranching methodology also serves as a proxy for shadow rating subordinate property debt such as B-notes and mezzanine loans.

Collateral Recovery Rates

A loan's recovery rate is based on the type of loan (whole, B-note, mezzanine), property type, and the thickness of the loan as a percent of the property's capital structure. In general, Moody's uses recovery rates of 40% to 60% for whole loans, depending on property type. The recovery rates used for CMBS, B-notes and mezzanine loans vary with the rating and the thickness of the tranche or loan. For example, the recovery rate on a Ba2 rated B-note with a 20% thickness would be 35%, while a Ba2 B-note with a 5% thickness would only have a recovery rate of 20%.

S&P's recovery rates on all CREL are independent of the loan's shadow rating. We show the recovery rates used by S&P in Exhibit 10.8. The recovery rates for CMBS tranches are dependent on the CRE CDO and CMBS tranches' ratings, and are shown in Exhibit 10.9.

EXHIBIT 10.8 S&P CREL Recovery Rates

	Recovery Rate (%)
Whole loans	50
B-notes	
Senior B-note	35
First-loss B-note	30
Mezzanine loans	25

Source: Standard & Poor's.

EXHIBIT 10.9 CMBS Assumed Recovery Rates

CMBS Rating	CDO Liability Rating (%)						
	AAA	AA	A	BBB	BB	B	CCC
AAA	80	85	90	90	90	90	90
AA	70	75	85	90	90	90	90
A	60	65	75	85	90	90	90
BBB	45	50	55	60	65	70	75
BB	35	40	45	45	50	50	50
B	20	25	30	35	35	40	40
CCC	5	5	5	5	5	5	5
NR	0	0	0	0	0	0	0

Source: Standard & Poor's.

EXHIBIT 10.9   CMBS Assumed Recovery Rates

CMBS	CDO Liability Rating (%)						
Rating	AAA	AA	A	BBB	BB	B	CCC
AAA	80	85	90	90	90	90	90
AA	70	75	85	90	90	90	90
A	60	65	75	85	90	90	90
BBB	45	50	55	60	65	70	75
BB	35	40	45	45	50	50	50
B	20	25	30	35	35	40	40
CCC	5	5	5	5	5	5	5
NR	0	0	0	0	0	0	0

Source: Standard & Poor's.

The collateral recovery rates, combined with collateral shadow ratings (or in the case of Fitch, the loan-level expected losses), are aggregated and fed into simulation models, as are correlation assumptions, to determine portfolio default rates. S&P assumes 10% correlation between CMBS, REITs and CREL. Intra-sector, S&P assumes 30% correlation for CMBS and REITs, and 15% correlation for CREL.

Simulation model results serve as inputs into the CDO's cash flow model. After running stressed cash flow scenarios to determine minimum subordination requirements, the rating agencies adjust the final CDO subordination levels based on their assessment of the CDO manager's quality.

SUMMARY

In this chapter, we discussed CRE CDOs, looking at their history, evolution and characteristics. We also provided a framework for how investors should evaluate their CRE CDO investments and how rating agencies rate CRE CDOs. The CDO structure provides efficient financing for commercial real estate-related investments, benefiting both issuers and investors. While the shift in collateral towards more commercial real estate loans increases risks and uncertainty in CRE CDOs, it also increases access to a new and diverse asset class.

CHAPTER 11

CRE CDO Relative Value Methodology

In the previous chapter, we discussed commercial real estate (CRE) CDOs. We explained how CRE CDOs are a heterogeneous group, containing an assortment of different CRE investments from whole loans to CMBS tranches, with collateral ratings ranging from single A to single B to unrated. We also classified CRE CDOs into three major groups according to their primary underlying collateral type: (1) commercial mortgage-backed (CMBS) CDOs; (2) commercial real estate loan (CREL) CDOs; and (3) REIT TruPS CDOs. We further divided these major classes into groups according to their investment focus: (1) investment-grade (IG) CMBS CDOs; (2) high-yield (HY) CMBS CDOs; (3) whole loan (WL) CREL CDOs; (4) whole loan, B-note, and mezzanine loan (WL/B/Mezz.) CREL CDOs; and (5) REIT TruPS CDOs.

In this chapter, we suggest a methodology to analyze relative value in CRE CDOs. The methodology involves comparing spreads, subordination levels, and total credit enhancement of CRE CDOs with those of CDOs backed by high-yield corporate loans and CDOs backed by structured finance securities. In Exhibit 10.3 of the previous chapter, we categorize 37 CRE CDOs issued between September 2005 and September 2006 into the groups we have classified. The exhibit shows the weighted average ratings and average collateral compositions of these CDOs by principal amount. In the description and application of our methodology, we use the average characteristics of the CDOs shown in that exhibit to determine relative value.

WHOLE LOAN CREL CDOs VERSUS HIGH-YIELD CLOs

Let us begin the description of our methodology by performing a relative value analysis on whole loan (WL) CREL CDOs and CDOs backed by high-yield corporate loans (HY CLOs). Intuitively, it makes sense to compare WL CREL CDOs and HY CLOs because the performance of most commercial real estate properties is closely tied to the credit quality of the properties' corporate tenants. Consequently, both WL CREL CDOs and HY CLOs have corporate exposure. Further, whole loans are generally secured, as are senior loans underlying HY CLOs. The credit quality of the underlying collateral is also comparable: HY CLOs have a weighted average rating factor (WARF) of 2,250 while WL CREL CDOs' average WARF is 2,200.

Spreads and Subordination Levels

We begin by comparing spreads and subordination levels of WL CREL CDOs with those of HY CLOs issued between September 2005 and September 2006 in Exhibit 11.1 Looking first at the spreads, we see that on average, WL CREL CDOs and HY CLOs have priced inline with one another at the AAA and AA level. At A and below, however, WL CREL CDOs can price considerably tighter than HY CLOs, especially at the BBB and BB tranches, though most BB WL CREL CDOs are retained by the manager.

The last two columns of Exhibit 11.1 shows the subordination levels of WL CREL CDOs and HY CLOs.[1] The two CDO types have relatively similar subordination levels across all rating cohorts. This suggests that the rating agencies view the underlying collateral of WL CREL CDOs and HY CLOs similarly. However, the tighter spreads in the lower tranches of WL CREL CDOs suggest that the market believes that those tranches are overprotected relative to HY CLO tranches of the same rating. We next explore whether investor enthusiasm for WL CREL CDOs, as manifested by tighter spreads, is justified.

EXHIBIT 11.1   WL CREL CDO and HY CLO Spreads and Subordination

	Spreads, Basis Points		Subordination Levels (%)	
	WL CREL CDOs	HY CLOs	WL CREL CDOs	HY CLOs
Sr. AAA	26–32	23–25	26–46	25–30
Jr. AAA	30–35		28–33	
AA	37–47	38–45	19–36	18–22
A	56–80	65–80	15–26	12–15
BBB	120–170	145–175	9–15	9–12
BB	250–350	350–425	5–11	6–9

Source: UBS CDO Research.

---

[1] CRE CDOs typically have many more tranches than are shown here. In general, CRE CDOs are tranched similar to CMBS transactions, customarily with AAA, AA+, AA, AA–, A+, A, A–, BBB+, BBB, BBB–, BB+, BB, and BB– tranches. We only show the Senior AAA, Junior AAA, AA, A, BBB and BB tranches here for ease of comparison.

Scenario Default Rates and Recovery Stresses

Subordination is an important source of credit enhancement, but it does not tell the whole credit support story. CDO tranches also receive credit support from the diversion of excess spread. To get a better picture of a tranche's total credit support, one can look at the tranche's S&P Scenario Default Rate (SDR). SDR is the cumulative collateral default rate that S&P demands a tranche be able to withstand and still pay full principal and interest. S&P demands different SDRs to obtain different ratings; higher SDRs for higher ratings and lower SDRs for lower ratings. S&P also requires different SDRs for CRE CDOs and HY CLOs. For example, from the first row of Exhibit 11.2, S&P requires an average of 28% SDR for WL CREL CDOs to obtain a BBB rating. In comparison, S&P only requires an average of 25% SDR for HY CLOs to obtain the same BBB rating.

As shown in the second row the exhibit, S&P makes different recovery assumptions for collateral in WL CREL CDOs (46% recovery) and HY CLOs (55% recovery). Combining S&P's default and recovery assumptions, the third row of Exhibit 11.2 shows that to obtain a BBB rating, S&P requires that a WL CREL CDO tranche survive the loss of 15% of its collateral and still pay principal and interest and a HY CLO tranche survive the lost of 11% of its high-yield loan (HYL) collateral portfolio.

This shows that S&P believes the default and loss severities of WL CREL CDO collateral are likely higher than the default and loss severities of HY CLO collateral. Therefore, S&P requires that WL CREL CDOs provide more credit support to its tranches to protect against collateral losses than they require of HY CLOs. But is that assessment justified? We explore that question next.

Historical Results

What is the actual default and loss experience of WL CREL CDO and HY CLO collateral? Exhibit 11.3 details our estimates from historical studies. The default and recovery assumptions for the WL CREL collateral are based on the historical data from Moody's, S&P, and Fitch reviewed in Chapter 9

EXHIBIT 11.2   S&P BBB CDO Required Collateral Loss Rates

	WL	HYL
Avg. S&P SDR	28%	25%
Avg. S&P recovery rate	46%	55%
S&P required BBB loss rate	15%	11%

Source: UBS calculations from S&P Presale Reports.

EXHIBIT 11.3　WL CREL CDO and HY CLO Collateral Historical Default and Recovery Rates

WL CREL CDO	CDO	Annual CDR	Recovery Rates
CMBS	6%	0.2%	75%
Whole loans	79%	1.1%	60%
B-notes	9%	1.1%	50%
Mezzanine	6%	3.2%	30%
Total/Blended avg.	100%	1.1%	58%

HY CLO	CDO	Annual CDR	Recovery Rates
High-yield loans	100%	2.1%	70%

Source: UBS CDO Research; FitchRatings; Moody's Investors Service.

EXHIBIT 11.4　WL CREL and HYL Collateral Historical and S&P BBB Required Loss Rates

	WL	HYL
Avg. annual CDR	1.1%	2.1%
5-Yr. cumul. default rate	5.6%	10.5%
Avg. recovery rate	58%	70%
Historical loss rate	2.4%	3.2%
S&P required BBB loss rate	15%	11%
Difference	6.5×	3.6×

Source: UBS CDO Research calculations from rating agency data.

with slight adjustments. For instance, we have very little historical data on mezzanine loan defaults and losses. So in our analysis, we assume that, given their higher leverage, default rates of mezzanine loans are higher and recovery rates lower than those of whole loans. We use historical default data derived from S&P LCD to arrive at a 2.1% annual historic default rate for high-yield loans. The 70% recovery assumption for high-yield loans comes from Moody's study of senior secured loan recovery rates from 1982 to 2005.[2]

Using historical default and recovery rates, we convert average annual constant default rates (CDRs) into 5-year cumulative default rates and multiply them by one minus average recovery rates to arrive at the historical loss rates for WL CREL and HYL collateral, as shown in the first four rows of Exhibit 11.4.

---

[2] See Kenneth Emery et al, *Syndicated Bank Loans: 2005 Global Review and Outlook*, Moody's Investors Service, February 2006.

Comparing the historical loss rates, we see that WL CREL collateral has lower loss rates than HYL collateral by a measure of 2.4% to 3.2%. Yet, S&P BBB required loss rates are higher for the former by 15% to 11%. In all, BBB WL CREL CDOs have 6.5× coverage against historical losses while HY CLOs have 3.6× coverage. Since WL CREL CDOs are better protected against historical losses, their tighter BBB tranche spreads seem justified.

Are We Missing Anything?

If we rely solely on our results above, we would likely conclude that WL CREL CDOs have far more credit enhancement than appropriate for their collateral. However, we have only focused on *average* historical performance and not considered potential *variability* in performance over time. If loss rates on WL CREL collateral are more volatile year to year than those of HYL collateral, higher WL CREL BBB CDO loss requirements might be justified.

In Exhibit 11.5, we show *annual collateral default rates* of CMBS loan and HYL collateral for the 8-year period 1998 to 2005. We use the performance of CMBS loan collateral as it is the only comprehensive historical performance data available on WL CREL. Over this period, HYL collateral has experienced significantly more volatility in annual default rates (ranging 1% to 7%), than did those on CMBS loan collateral (ranging 0.2% to 1.4%).

Besides annual default rates, we also compare the *cumulative default rates* of CMBS loan collateral and HYL collateral in Exhibit 11.6. Not only is the *average* cumulative default rate of CMBS loan collateral lower than that of HYL collateral (3.7% versus 9.5%, respectively), but the *volatility* of the default rate has been significantly lower, by a standard deviation of 3.1% to 9.0%. In all, the annual and cumulative default data show that

EXHIBIT 11.5   Annual Default Rates of CMBS Loan Collateral and HYL Collateral

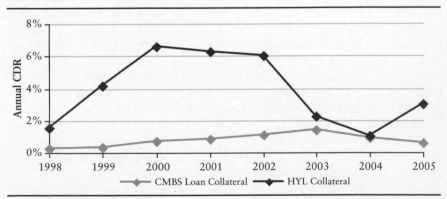

Source: S&P LCD, FitchRatings.

EXHIBIT 11.6   Cumulative Collateral Default Rates of CMBS Loan and HYL Collateral

Vintage	CMBS Loan Collateral (%)	HYL Collateral (%)
1998	6.0	19.1
1999	6.3	16.4
2000	7.9	21.0
2001	3.7	5.3
2002	1.1	3.6
2003	0.7	1.0
2004	0.1	0.2
Average	3.7	9.5
Standard deviation	3.1	9.0

Source: S&P LCD, FitchRatings.

WL CREL collateral is not more volatile than HYL collateral, suggesting that the higher S&P BBB tranche loss protection level in WL CREL CDOs is unnecessary.

However, there are two problems with this comparison. First is the time frame problem. The real estate market tends to move in longer cycles than corporate credit. If we looked back further, we would see that annual and cumulative default rates on commercial mortgage loans have ranged as high as 10.3% and 32% respectively in the 1986 vintage.[3] That is quite a bit higher than the 0.8% average annual CDR and the 3.7% cumulative default rate we have seen over the past eight years. The second problem is that using annual default rates of CMBS loan collateral as a proxy for the historical annual default rates of WL CREL collateral is not necessarily reasonable, especially for low-rated WL CREL collateral. While CMBS loan collateral is generally whole loans, and at 79% WL CREL CDOs are made up primarily of whole loans, whole loans in CMBS are often different than the whole loans in WL CREL CDOs. The other 21% of the collateral in WL CREL CDOs is even more different than CMBS. As mentioned earlier, WL CREL collateral tends to be riskier, in terms of leverage and underlying property performance, than CMBS loan collateral. Therefore, historical default rates of CMBS loan collateral likely *underestimate* the volatility we would expect in WL CREL collateral default rates.

To match the volatility seen in HYL collateral, however, the default rate volatility of WL CREL collateral would have to be nearly 300% higher than

[3] Howard Esaki and Masumi Goldman, "Commercial Mortgage Defaults: 30 Years of History," *CMBS World* 6, no. 4 (Winter 2005): 21–29.

the volatility of CMBS loan collateral. Despite the differences between WL CREL collateral and CMBS loan collateral, we find this level of incremental volatility unlikely. Therefore, we believe WL CREL collateral has less credit volatility than HYL collateral and higher credit volatility does not explain S&P's higher BBB WL CREL CDO tranche loss requirements.

Aside from collateral performance volatility over time, our analysis also fails to account for differences in the *diversity* within WL CREL CDOs and HY CLOs. HY CLOs have very diverse collateral pools, averaging around 200 different loans. The large number of individual loans dampens the impact of any single loan default. Additionally, the corporate credits securing the loans come from a broad range of industries, adding to the overall diversity.

By contrast, WL CREL CDOs are not nearly as diverse. The average Herfindahl score[4] for the WL CREL CDOs in our study is 23. The Herfindahl score is the CRE CDO equivalent of a diversity score, and measures the effective number of assets in the pool, accounting for concentrations in loan size. A Herfindahl score of 23 means that the average WL CREL CDO effectively contains only 23 distinct assets when adjusted for size. So if one loan defaults, it has a larger impact on the overall CDO than if any of the 200 loans in a HY CLO defaults. And not only are there fewer effective assets in a WL CREL CDO collateral pool, but all loans are secured by the same type of collateral: commercial real estate.

Yet, if we look a bit deeper, default risk in WL CREL CDOs is not nearly as concentrated as it may first appear. Cash flows underlying most loans in a WL CREL CDO are very diverse in and of themselves. Take, for example, a loan on a commercial office building. The building's cash flows come from rents paid by the property's occupants, which are typically a number of different corporations. Therefore, the cash flows from the property, and by extension the principal and interest payments due on the loan, are tied to a number of different corporate credits.

So while the CDO receives cash flow from a single loan, the cash flows of that single loan are a function of *multiple* different cash flows, with different corporate credit risks. However, WL CREL CDOs still have single-asset event risk. If anything should seriously impair cash flows from the property securing a loan (i.e., local economic problems), it would have a considerable impact on the loan's and the WL CREL CDO's cash flows.

WL CREL CDOs also have a higher degree of variability *between* deals. Not only do WL CREL CDOs contain many different types of securities, but property-type concentrations, rating distributions, borrower concentrations, etc. can also vary. For example, for two WL CREL CDOs made up

---

[4] The Herfindahl score, per Moody's, is calculated by dividing (i) one by (ii) the sum of, for each asset in the pool, the square of, (a) the principal balance of each asset in the pool, divided by (b) the aggregate principal balance of the assets in the pool.

of 100% whole loans, one CDO might contain more multifamily property loans; the other more office property loans. This difference in property-type concentration alone could lead to very different relative portfolio performance. In contrast, differences between HY CLO portfolios tend to be more subtle given their greater portfolio diversity.

However, even though WL CREL CDOs have more concentrated risks, there are benefits to managing a concentrated pool. WL CREL CDO managers typically have significant expertise in the specific types of properties and markets underlying the loans. Further, they generally have direct contact with the loan's borrower, and in many cases, they even originate the loan themselves. HY CLO managers, who manage larger loan pools, may not have as much expertise in or control over every loan as WL CREL CDO managers typically have. Therefore, our relative methodology would suggest that differences in collateral volatility or pool diversity justify the higher level of credit protection offered by WL CREL CDOs. Accordingly, the methodology suggests BBB WL CREL CDOs deserve their tighter spreads as compared to BBB HY CLOs.

INVESTMENT-GRADE CMBS CDOs VERSUS MEZZANINE STRUCTURED FINANCE CDOs

We next perform the same relative value analysis between investment-grade (IG) CMBS CDOs and mezzanine structured finance (Mezz. SF) CDOs as we did between WL CRE CDOs and HY CLOs. IG CMBS CDOs and Mezz. SF CDOs have similar investment considerations, as both are secured by asset-backed securities. We also compare these CDOs because their average WARFs (320 for Mezz. SF CDOs; 600 for IG CMBS CDOs) are more similar as compared to HG SF CDOs (100 WARF) and HY CMBS CDOs (4,400 WARF).

Spreads and Subordination Levels

In Exhibit 11.7, we show the spreads and subordination levels of IG CMBS CDOs and Mezz. SF CDOs. Across virtually all rating levels, the IG CMBS CDOs have priced significantly tighter than Mezz. SF CDOs. IG CMBS CDOs also have more subordination at every rating level.

The difference in subordination levels reflects S&P's perception of differences in underlying collateral pools. Part of the reason IG CMBS CDOs have higher subordination is their higher collateral WARFs. Yet, the tighter spreads of IG CMBS CDOs suggest that the market believes IG CMBS CDOs are overprotected relative to Mezz. SF CDOs.

EXHIBIT 11.7   IG CMBS CDO and Mezz. SF CDO Spreads and Subordination Levels

	Spreads (bps)		Subordination Levels (%)	
	IG CMBS	Mezz. SF CDOs	IG CMBS	Mezz. SF CDOs
Sr AAA	27–28	30–32	18–39	27–32
Jr AAA	32–38	42–45	19–31	19–27
AA	38–50	50–55	13–22	12–16
A	60–85	125–145	9–17	7–9
BBB	140–200	295–330	6–12	4–5
BB	350–500	600–650	3–6	3–4

Source: UBS CDO Research.

EXHIBIT 11.8   S&P BBB CDO Required Collateral Loss Rates

	IG CMBS	Mezz. SF
Avg. S&P SDR	13%	9%
Avg. S&P recovery rate	51%	47%
S&P required BBB loss rate	6%	5%

Source: UBS calculations from S&P Presale Reports.

Loss Rates

We calculate the S&P required loss rates for BBB IG CMBS and Mezz. SF CDOs in Exhibit 11.8. Given the loss rates, let's look at the historical performance of the collateral underlying IG CMBS and Mezz. SF CDOs. The historical default and recovery rates in Exhibit 11.9 are blended average rates. Our default and recovery estimates for IG CMBS CDO collateral are based on historical data from the rating agencies reviewed in Chapter 9, again, slightly adjusted. We use Baa rated CMBS default and recovery rates for the CMBS underlying IG CMBS CDOs.[5] For Mezz. SF CDOs, we assume the underlying SF collateral is made up of a mix of 90% RMBS and home equity securities and 10% other structured finance securities such as ABS, CMBS, CDOs. We used an average rating of Baa for the underlying SF collateral.

---

[5] For structured finance securities (CMBS, RMBS/HEL, ABS), it is difficult to determine if a tranche has defaulted, so as a proxy for "default" we use Moody's impairment rates. "Impairment" is defined by Moody's as uncured payment default (interest shortfall or principal writedown) or a downgrade to Ca or C. The impairment rate is the number of securities impaired, divided by the number of securities outstanding. Jian Hu, Hadas Alexander, *et al.*, *Default & Loss Rates of Structured Finance Securities: 1993–2005*, Moody's Investors Service, April 2006.

EXHIBIT 11.9   IG CMBS and Mezz. SF Collateral Historical Default and Recovery Rates

IG CMBS CDO	CDO	Annual CDR	Recovery Rates
CMBS	78%	0.2%	75%
REIT debt	10%	2.1%	70%
CRE CDO	6%	0.5%	50%
B-notes	1%	1.1%	50%
Mezzanine	0%	3.2%	30%
RMBS	4%	0.6%	70%
Total/Blended avg.	100%	0.5%	72%

Mezz. SF CDO	CDO	Annual CDR	Recovery Rates
RMBS/HEL	90%	0.6%	67%
Other ABS	10%	2.0%	50%
Total/Blended avg.	100%	0.8%	65%

Source: UBS CDO Research, FitchRatings, Moody's Investors Service.

EXHIBIT 11.10   IG CMBS and Mezz. SF Collateral Historical and Required Loss Rates

	IG CMBS	Mezz. SF
Avg. annual CDR	0.5%	0.8%
5-Yr. cumul default rate	2.3%	3.9%
Avg. recovery rate	72%	65%
Historical loss rate	0.6%	1.4%
S&P required BBB loss rate	6.1%	4.6%
Difference	9.6×	3.4×

Source: UBS CDO Research from rating agency data.

We calculate the historical loss rates for IG CMBS CDOs and Mezz. SF CDOs shown in Exhibit 11.10 and compare them to S&P required loss rates from Exhibit 11.8. BBB IG CMBS must withstand over nine times more losses than historically experienced, whereas Mezz. SF CDOs only have to withstand three and a half times their historical loss rate. In other words, BBB IG CMBS CDOs have nearly 300% more protection against expected losses than do BBB Mezz. SF CDOs. Therefore, based on our methodology it appears that the IG CMBS CDO spread premium over Mezz. SF CDOs is reasonable.

Are We Missing Anything?

Again there are additional factors we must consider before concluding that IG CMBS CDOs are overprotected relative to Mezz. SF CDOs. For instance, fundamental risks underlying CMBS CDOs versus SF CDOs are very different. Similar to CREL CDOs, CMBS CDOs are exposed to diversified *corporate* credit. SF CDOs, on the other hand, are exposed to diversified *consumer* credit. Thus spread differences between CMBS CDOs and SF CDOs may reflect investors' market views in addition to comparable credit protection.

Aside from the collaterals' fundamental risk differences, we must also consider the variability in collateral performance over time. We compare lifetime cumulative default rates of 1999–2003 vintage IG CMBS and Mezz. SF collateral in Exhibit 11.11. The former are blended averages of the cumulative default rates of the underlying collateral: 78% Baa CMBS, 10% REIT debt, and the like, as shown in Exhibit 10.3 in the previous chapter. For the latter cumulative default rates we use a blended average of 90% RMBS/HEL and 10% other ABS (excluding HEL and Manufactured Housing). Not only is the average cumulative default rate for IG CMBS (2.2%) lower than the average cumulative default rate for Mezz. SF securities (3.7%), but the volatility of IG CMBS, as measured by the standard deviation of life cumulative loss is lower (2.2% versus 3.1%). Therefore, it would seem that IG CMBS CDOs provide much more protection against expected collateral losses than Mezz. SF CDOs.

As another measure of performance volatility, we look at historical ratings transitions. Exhibit 11.12 shows the 5-year historical transitions matrices for CMBS and RMBS/HEL rating cohorts. Initial tranche ratings are on the left; ratings after five years are across the top. Percentages within the matrices show the rating migration from the tranche's initial rating to its

EXHIBIT 11.11 IG CMBS and Mezz. SF Lifetime Cumulative Default Rates by Vintage

Vintage	IG CMBS (%)	Mezz. SF (%)
1999	2.1	6.9
2000	5.6	6.1
2001	2.8	4.8
2002	0.5	1.0
2003	0.2	0.0
Average	2.2	3.7
Standard deviation	2.2	3.1

Source: UBS CDO Research, FitchRatings, Moody's Investors Service.

rating after five years. For example, 94% of CMBS tranches initially Aaa remained Aaa after five years; 3% were downgraded to Aa and 2% to A.

Looking across the Aa rating, we see that 95% of Aa-rated CMBS tranches maintained or improved their Aa rating after five years, versus 92% for Aa RMBS/HEL. In fact, for collateral most common in IG CMBS and Mezz. SF CDOs, Aa through Ba level, CMBS is more likely to maintain or improve its ratings over five years than the RMBS/HEL collateral. These data suggest that CMBS performance is more stable relative to RMBS/HEL performance.

Given the default rate volatility and comparable tranche rating performance, BBB IG CMBS CDOs are better protected from losses in its underlying collateral than are BBB Mezz. SF CDOs. The methodology would therefore suggest that IG CMBS CDOs should be priced tighter than similarly rated Mezz. SF CDOs, as they are.

EXHIBIT 11.12 Structured Finance 5-Year Rating Transition Matrices

	CMBS (%)						
	Aaa	Aa	A	Baa	Ba	B	Caa or below
Aaa	94	3	2	0	0	0	0
Aa	49	46	2	0	1	0	1
A	16	26	55	3	1	0	0
Baa	6	6	22	60	3	1	1
Ba	0	3	1	10	67	13	6
B	0	0	1	2	3	59	35
Caa or below	0	0	0	0	0	7	93

	RMBS/HEL (%)						
	Aaa	Aa	A	Baa	Ba	B	Caa or below
Aaa	98	1	0	0	0	0	0
Aa	26	67	5	2	0	0	1
A	11	13	64	6	2	1	2
Baa	3	3	10	61	7	5	11
Ba	2	1	6	10	57	5	19
B	3	0	1	6	4	65	21
Caa or below	0	0	0	0	1	0	99

Source: UBS CDO Research calculations from Moody's data.

Assumption Sensitivity

Even after considering differences in volatility, diversification, and risk, it is hard to dismiss the apparent disconnect between the required credit enhancement and the historical loss rates of CRE CDOs as compared to other types of CDOs. But then again, not everyone will necessarily agree with the default and recovery assumptions we used in our analysis. Furthermore, since our analysis is based on historical default and loss data, it is admittedly backward looking. So we will next look at the sensitivity of loss rates to assumptions on the underlying CDO collateral.

Exhibit 11.13 shows matrices of loss rates for WL CREL CDOs and HY CLOs. The first column shows recovery rates. Across the top are various annual constant default rates (CDRs). We vary the annual CDRs as multiples of their historical averages (0.5×, 1×, 2×, 5×, and 10×). In the body of the figure are the resulting loss rates. For instance, for a WL CREL CDO, a 20% recovery rate and a 0.6% annual CDR (0.5 times the historical average CDR of 1.1%) creates a 2% loss rate.

Using different recovery rates and different multiples of historical default rates, collateral loss rates range from 1% to as high as 84%. In the matrices, we have shaded in where collateral losses exceed S&P BBB required loss rates.

Depending on recovery rate, BBB WL CREL CDOs can withstand more than five times their historical average default rate before they exceed S&P's required loss rate. BBB HY CLOs, however, break their required loss rate at just two times their historical average default rate. In fact, at five times their historical default rate, BBB HY CLOs reach their required loss rate even

EXHIBIT 11.13 WL CREL and HYL Collateral Loss Rate Sensitivity Matrices

		WL					HYL				
Annual		0.5×	1×	2×	5×	10×	0.5×	1×	2×	5×	10×
CDR		0.6%	1%	2%	6%	11%	1%	2%	4%	11%	21%
Recovery Rate	20%	2%	4%	9%	22%	45%	4%	8%	17%	42%	84%
	30%	2%	3%	7%	17%	34%	4%	7%	15%	37%	74%
	40%	2%	3%	7%	17%	34%	3%	6%	13%	32%	63%
	50%	1%	3%	6%	14%	28%	3%	5%	11%	26%	53%
	60%	1%	2%	4%	11%	22%	2%	4%	8%	21%	42%
	70%	1%	2%	3%	8%	17%	2%	3%	6%	16%	32%
	80%	1%	1%	2%	6%	11%	1%	2%	4%	11%	21%

Source: UBS CDO Research.

if recoveries are as high as 80%. BBB WL CREL CDOs are therefore less sensitive to comparative changes in default rates than are BBB HY CLOs. Along with required subordination levels, the difference in default rate sensitivity further supports our assertion that WL CREL CDOs have better protection from underlying collateral losses than HY CLOs.

We show the same sensitivity matrices for IG CMBS CDOs and Mezz. SF CDOs in Exhibit 11.14. Again, the first column shows recovery rates while the top two rows vary annual CDR from the historic average.

Using different recovery rates and different multiples of historic default rates, collateral loss rates range from 0% to 68%. Again, we shade in where collateral losses exceed S&P BBB stress loss rates. The shaded regions contrast how much more sensitive BBB Mezz. SF CDOs are than BBB IG CMBS CDOs to comparative changes in default rates. This further supports the early findings of our methodology that IG CMBS CDOs have better protection from underlying collateral losses than SF CDOs.

RELATIVE VALUE AMONG CRE CDOs

Now that we have demonstrated how the methodology can be used to perform relative value analysis *across* CDOs, we turn to our methodology for relative value analysis *among* CRE CDOs. We compare spreads of the different types of CRE CDOs issued between September 2005 and September 2006 in Exhibit 11.15. We see that on average, WL CREL CDOs have priced tighter than other types of CRE CDOs. The difference is most dramatic at the BBB and BB levels. With the exception of REIT TruPS CDOs,

EXHIBIT 11.14   IG CMBS and Mezz. SF Collateral Loss Rate Sensitivity Matrices

	Annual CDR	\multicolumn 5 IG CMBS					\multicolumn 5 Mezz. SF				
		0.5×	1×	2×	5×	10×	0.5×	1×	2×	5×	10×
		0.2%	0.5%	0.9%	2%	5%	0.4%	0.8%	2%	4%	8%
Recovery Rate	20%	1%	2%	4%	9%	18%	3%	7%	14%	34%	68%
	30%	1%	2%	3%	8%	16%	3%	6%	12%	30%	59%
	40%	1%	1%	3%	7%	14%	3%	5%	10%	25%	51%
	50%	1%	1%	2%	6%	12%	2%	4%	8%	21%	42%
	60%	0%	1%	2%	5%	9%	2%	3%	7%	17%	34%
	70%	0%	1%	1%	3%	7%	1%	3%	5%	13%	25%
	80%	0%	0%	1%	2%	5%	1%	2%	3%	8%	17%

Source: UBS CDO Research.

EXHIBIT 11.15   CRE CDO Spreads (basis points)

	IG CMBS	HY CMBS	WL	WL/B/Mezz.	REIT TruPS
Sr AAA	27–28	28–35	26–32	31–37	35–40
Jr AAA	32–38	34–40	30–35	35–45	48–55
AA	38–50	38–55	37–47	40–55	70–90
A	60–85	68–85	55–80	75–95	140–160
BBB	140–200	150–205	120–170	150–230	260–350
BB	350–500		250–350	325–350	475

Source: UBS CDO Research.

EXHIBIT 11.16   CRE CDO Subordination Levels (%)

	IG CMBS	HY CMBS	WL	WL/B/Mezz.	REIT TruPS
Sr AAA	18–39	70–80	26–46	48–74	48–55
Jr AAA	19–31	60–70	28–33	40–43	33–43
AA	13–22	51–70	19–36	33–60	22–30
A	9–17	43–63	15–26	27–53	13–17
BBB	6–12	35–46	9–15	21–43	7–11
BB	3–6	18–28	5–11	14–32	3–4

Source: UBS CDO Research.

CREL CDOs backed by a combination of whole loans, B-notes and mezzanine loans have priced wider than all other types of CRE CDOs. IG and HY CMBS CDOs fall in the middle, pricing in line with one other.

Exhibit 11.16 shows CRE CDO subordination levels. The different types of CRE CDOs have significantly different subordination levels across all rating cohorts. The large difference in subordination levels reflects how differently the rating agencies view the various types of underlying collateral pools.

However, given that different types of CRE CDOs have priced differently, it appears the market believes that some CRE CDO tranches offer more protection than other equally rated CRE CDO tranches. Are these pricing differences justified? We look at this next.

Loss Rates

As we have said before, subordination alone does not tell the whole credit enhancement story of a CDO. To better compare credit enhancement, we calculate S&P required loss rates for the various types of CRE CDOs in Exhibit 11.17.

EXHIBIT 11.17   S&P BBB CRE CDO Required Collateral Loss Rates

	IG CMBS	HY CMBS	WL	WL/B/Mezz.
Avg S&P SDR	13%	43%	28%	50%
Avg S&P Recovery Rate	51%	20%	46%	33%
S&P Required BBB Loss Rate	6%	34%	15%	34%

Source: UBS CDO Research calculations from S&P Presale Reports.

S&P required loss rates vary dramatically across different types of CRE CDOs. For a BBB rating, S&P requires HY CMBS and WL/B/Mezz. CREL CDO tranches to withstand 34% collateral losses, while BBB IG CMBS CDOs need only withstand 6% losses. This indicates that S&P believes the default and loss severities of HY CMBS and WL/B/Mezz. collateral are likely to be much higher than those of IG CMBS collateral. Therefore, S&P demands that HY CMBS and WL/B/Mezz. CREL CDOs provide additional credit support to their tranches to protect against losses, as evidenced by their higher subordination levels. We next consider whether these distinctions in CRE collateral are justified.

Exhibit 11.18 shows our estimates from historical default and recovery studies. As described earlier, the default and recovery assumptions in the exhibit are based on historical data reviewed in Chapter 9, slightly adjusted where we felt it necessary. We split CMBS into two collateral types to correspond with the types of CMBS in CRE CDOs. For investment grade (IG) CMBS, we used Baa tranche historical default and recovery rates. For high yield (HY) CMBS, we used a blended average of Ba, B and Caa historical default and recovery rates. The CMBS historical data comes from Moody's study of structured finance defaults and losses from 1993 to 2005.

Using the historical default and recovery rates, we calculated historical loss rates for the four types of CRE CDOs as shown in Exhibit 11.19. Comparing historic loss rates, we see that BBB expected loss rates vary for the different types of CRE collateral, ranging from 0.6% for IG CMBS to 4.9% for HY CMBS. That's to be expected, given the different default and loss histories of their underlying collateral.

While all BBB CRE CDOs can withstand losses numerous multiples higher than what the underlying collateral has historically experienced, the difference is greatest for BBB IG CMBS CDOs, which S&P require to withstand losses more than nine times higher than their collateral has historically experienced. Therefore, IG CMBS CDOs appear to have better protection against defaults and losses than do other types of CRE CDOs, despite having the lowest subordination levels of the group (6% to 12% for BBB IG CMBS CDOs versus 9% to 43% for other BBB CRE CDOs). Yet when comparing spreads, BBB

EXHIBIT 11.18 CRE CDO Collateral Default and Recovery Estimates

	Annual CDR (%)	Recovery Rates (%)
IG CMBS	0.2	75
HY CMBS	1.6	40
REIT debt	2.1	70
CRE CDO	0.5	50
Whole loans	1.1	60
B-Notes	1.1	50
Mezzanine	3.2	30
RMBS	0.6	70
Other	1.1	60

Source: UBS CDO Research, FitchRatings, Moody's Investors Service.

EXHIBIT 11.19 CRE CDO Collateral Historical and Required Loss Rates

	IG CMBS	HY CMBS	WL	WL/B/Mezz.
Avg. annual CDR	0.5%	1.6%	1.1%	1.7%
5-Yr. cumul default rate	2.3%	8.2%	5.6%	8.4%
Avg. recovery rate	72%	40%	58%	48%
Historical loss rate	0.6%	4.9%	2.4%	4.4%
S&P-required BBB loss rate	6%	34%	15%	34%
Difference	9.6×	7.1×	6.5×	7.6×

Source: UBS CDO Research calculations from rating agency data.

IG CMBS CDOs have priced inline with the other BBB CRE CDOs. In fact, BBB IG CMBS CDOs priced *wider* than most WL CREL CDOs. Based on our methodology, it therefore seems that BBB IG CMBS CDOs offer better value than other BBB CRE CDOs, particularly BBB WL CREL CDOs.

Are We Missing Anything?

Relying solely on our results above, we would likely conclude that IG CMBS CDOs have far more credit enhancement than appropriate for the collateral, relative to other CRE CDOs. But as we have said before, other factors should be considered, such as potential variability in performance over time. If default rates of IG CMBS prove much more volatile year to year than those of other CRE collateral, it would be reasonable to demand that IG CMBS CDOs be able to withstand a greater range of collateral losses.

EXHIBIT 11.20 CMBS CDO Collateral Cumulative Default Rates, by Vintage

Vintage	IG CMBS (%)	HY CMBS (%)
1999	2.1	12.8
2000	5.6	14.3
2001	2.8	13.1
2002	0.5	2.5
2003	0.2	0.5
Average	2.2	8.6
Standard deviation	2.2	6.6

Source: UBS CDO Research, FitchRatings, Moody's Investors Service.

First, we compare the loss volatility of IG CMBS and HY CMBS. Intuitively, it seems obvious that the volatility of HY CMBS would exceed that of IG CMBS. CMBS, like CDOs, are structured to provide additional credit support to the senior tranches, thereby reducing the performance volatility of IG CMBS relative to HY CMBS. Nonetheless, we prove the higher volatility of HY CMBS with data in Exhibit 11.20. The exhibit shows historical cumulative default rates of 1999 to 2003 vintage CMBS. The cumulative default rates shown are blended averages of the cumulative default rates of the underlying collateral (CMBS, REIT debt, whole loans, etc.).

From Exhibit 11.20, we see that HY CMBS have higher cumulative default rates than IG CMBS (8.6% versus 2.2%, respectively). The volatility of HY CMBS is also significantly higher than the volatility of IG CMBS, as measured by the standard deviation (6.6% versus 2.2%). We illustrate the impact of this volatility in Exhibit 11.21. For HY CMBS, defaults would have to be around seven standard deviations above their historical average or 57% before a BBB HY CMBS CDO breaks its 34% required loss rate, assuming a 40% recovery. For IG CMBS, defaults would have to be nine standard deviations above their historical average, or 21% before a BBB IG CMBS CDO breaks its 6% required loss rate, assuming 72% recovery. Therefore, it would seem that IG CMBS CDOs provide more protection against expected collateral losses than HY CMBS CDOs.

Next, we compare the volatility of IG CMBS and CREL collateral. Exhibit 11.22 shows the historical cumulative default rates of IG CMBS and CREL collateral.[6] The IG CMBS cumulative default rates are blended averages of the cumulative default rates of the underlying collateral, as we

---

[6] We recognize that the cumulative impairment rates for HY CMBS shown in Exhibit 11.20 are actually higher than the cumulative default rates that we show in Exhibit 11.22 for CMBS loan collateral for the 2001 and 2002 vintages. This difference is likely due to differences in data sources (*Moody's* for CMBS *impairment* rates; *Fitch*

EXHIBIT 11.21 IG CMBS and HY CMBS Collateral Default Rate Volatility and Loss Rates

	IG CMBS	HY CMBS
Avg. cumul. default rate	2.2%	8.6%
Standard deviations	9	7
Cumul default rate	21%	57%
Recovery rate	<u>72%</u>	<u>40%</u>
Resulting loss rate	6%	34%
S&P-required BBB loss rate	6%	34%

Source: UBS CDO Research calculations from rating agency data.

EXHIBIT 11.22 IG CMBS CDO and CREL CDO Collateral Cumulative Default Rates, by Vintage

Vintage	IG CMBS (%)	CREL (%)
1999	2.1	5.9
2000	5.6	7.6
2001	2.8	3.7
2002	0.5	1.0
2003	<u>0.2</u>	<u>0.6</u>
Average	2.2	3.8
Standard deviation	2.2	3.0

Source: UBS CDO Research, FitchRatings, Moody's Investors Service.

did above. For CREL collateral, we use cumulative default rates that are a blended average of 94% CREL and 6% CMBS. As historical default performance data for CREL is not readily available, we use CMBS loan collateral as a proxy for historical performance. Comparing the relative volatility of the cumulative default rates, as measured by the standard deviation in the final row of Exhibit 11.23, we see that the volatility of WL CREL collateral is greater than the volatility of IG CMBS (3.0% versus 2.2%).

Again, as shown in Exhibit 11.23, defaults would have to be nine standard deviations above their historical average, or 21% before a BBB IG CMBS CDO breaks its stressed loss rate, assuming 72% recovery. By comparison, using the CREL historical default data, CREL defaults would have to be *11* standard deviations above their historical average, or 36% before a BBB WL CREL CDO breaks its 15% required loss rate, assuming 58%

for CMBS loan collateral *default* rates). Nonetheless, we believe the differences in volatility as measured by the standard deviation are valid for comparison.

EXHIBIT 11.23   IG CMBS and CREL Collateral Default Rate Volatility and Loss
Rates

	IG CMBS	WL	WL/B/Mezz.
Avg. cumul default rate	2.2%	3.8%	3.8%
Standard deviations	9	11	15
Cumul. default rate	21%	36%	65%
Recovery rate	72%	58%	48%
Resulting loss rate	6%	15%	34%
S&P-required BBB loss rate	6%	15%	34%

Source: UBS CDO Research calculations from rating agency data.

recovery. For WL/B/Mezz., defaults would have to be *15* standard deviations above their historical average shown in Exhibit 11.21, or 65% before a BBB WL/B/Mezz. CREL CDO breaks its 34% required loss rate, assuming 48% recovery. Given these results, we might conclude that CREL CDOs, especially WL/B/Mezz. CREL CDOs offer a higher level of credit protection relative to their underlying collaterals' historical performance.

However, the cumulative default rates in Exhibits 11.22, which are for CMBS loan collateral, underestimate the cumulative defaults and volatility of CREL, especially WL/B/Mezz. CREL collateral. It is difficult to judge, however, just how much higher the default rates of CREL are compared to CMBS loan collateral. Using a Moody's study on the effects of leverage on default rates, we estimate that the default rates of WL CREL collateral are likely to be 30% higher than CMBS loan collateral, and WL/B/Mezz. CREL collateral default rates nearly 300% higher, due to the higher leverage and higher risk associated with these types of collateral.[7] As such, the additional credit protection provided by CREL CDOs, especially WL/B/Mezz. CREL CDOs, as compared to the credit protection provided by IG CMBS CDOs is justified.

Another factor to consider is diversity. A CDO with low diversity has concentrated risk. Performance of a single loan in a low diversity CDO or a downturn in a particular market where several of the underlying properties are located can greatly impact a CDO's overall performance. If IG CMBS CDOs were less diverse than CREL CDOs, then IG CMBS CDOs would have to withstand a greater range of collateral losses relative to CREL CDOs. Since CMBS are already diversified pools of commercial real estate loans, the additional amount of diversification created by pooling CMBS securities that are themselves already diversified is questionable. Moody's

[7] Sally Gordon and Leslie Kizer, *U.S. CMBS: Cash Study of Leverage and Default Over a Full Real Estate Cycle*, Moody's Investors Service, October 24, 2005.

argues that most of the loan diversity in underlying CMBS is already captured in the CMBS tranche's rating.

CMBS CDOs may also contain multiple tranches of the same CMBS transaction, thus reducing underlying diversification. The presence of pari passu notes in CMBS is another concern. The A-note of a large loan on a single property can be split into multiple pari passu notes that are placed into multiple CMBS pools. If that single property defaults on the A-note, the default will impact several different CMBS pools at once. If several of the underlying CMBS in a CDO contain the same pari passu notes, then default risk may be more concentrated than assumed. Nonetheless, diversification among vintages, originators, servicers, and CMBS tranches increase a CMBS CDO pool's diversity.

CREL, however, clearly benefits from pooling. CREL risks are very concentrated, centering on a specific property, market, borrower, and the like. Pooling the risks of 20 or more individual loans greatly increases diversity across all risk measures. And since most CREL CDOs contain only 20 to 30 loans, there is virtually no collateral overlap within or across CREL CDOs.

However, there is a potential for collateral overlap in CREL CDOs that contain CMBS. A property securing a B-note or mezzanine loan in a CREL CDO may also be the property securing one of the A-notes underlying a CMBS tranche which is also in the CREL CDO. Additionally, a CREL CDO's cash flows depend on the performance of just 20 to 30 properties, whereas cash flows from a CMBS CDO draw on performance of hundreds of properties. Yet, we do not believe that the pooling benefits enjoyed by CREL CDOs make them any more diverse than IG CMBS pools.

Even after accounting for collateral volatility and diversification, we still see IG CMBS CDOs as better protected from underlying collateral losses relative to other CRE CDOs.

SUMMARY

In this chapter we present and illustrate a methodology for analyzing the relative value of CRE CDOs. The methodology involves comparing the spreads, subordination levels, and collateral loss rates of CRE CDOs and other types of CDOs. It also requires analyzing the sensitivity of a CDO's loss rates to default and recovery rate assumptions. We demonstrate how the methodology can be use to analyze relative value across CRE CDOs.

For the time period studied and based on historical defaults and losses used in applying the methodology, our findings suggest that despite differences in the underlying collateral, investors receive better credit protection in CRE CDOs than they do in other types of CDOs, Further, the methodology suggests that IG CMBS CDOs provide the highest level of credit protection relative to other CRE CDOs.

However, the relative analysis methodology employed does not account for differences in types of CDOs (diversity, performance volatility, fundamental risk, etc.). These are tough to quantify, and could cause significantly different portfolio performances. Our methodology suggests that these differences are not enough to justify the differences in required credit enhancement, thereby supporting tighter spreads for CRE CDOs, particularly IG CMBS CDOs.

PART Four

Other CDO Topics

CHAPTER 12

Rating Agency Research on CDOs

The rating agencies publish reports on a wide range of topics that are important to CDO investors. In this chapter, we discuss an important study by Moody's on the use of corporate rating watches and outlooks to improve default predictions, focusing on the implications for CDO investors. Then we review changes in rating methodologies by S&P and Moody's to illustrate the often unintended consequences of rating agency actions.

USING RATING WATCHES AND OUTLOOKS TO IMPROVE
THE DEFAULT PREDICTION POWER OF RATINGS

A 2005 study by Moody's demonstrated that the predictiveness of its corporate ratings can be improved by utilizing the credit's *outlook status*.[1] A corporate credit's outlook status is whether its ratings are on watch for an upgrade or downgrade and if its long-term ratings outlook is positive, negative, or stable. Using historical default and ratings data from 1995 through 2005, the study shows that *outlook status* is, in fact, a crucial factor in predicting a credit's default likelihood.

The implications of this study are useful for using ratings to evaluate the credit quality of corporate debt, bearing directly upon CDO portfolios composed of corporate credits. In this chapter, we focus on some of the most significant aspects of the study.

Rating Watches, Rating Outlooks, and Historical Default Rates

Moody's believes that a change in an issuer's rating should reflect a fundamental and permanent shift in its credit quality. As a result, ratings usually change gradually. To signal information regarding the likely direction and

---

[1] David T. Hamilton and Richard Cantor, *Rating Transitions and Defaults Conditional on Rating Outlooks Revisited: 1995–2005*, Moody's Investors Service, December 2005.

timing of future rating changes, however, Moody's developed the concepts of rating watches and outlooks.

Rating watches for downgrades and upgrades are announcements by the agency that it is actively considering changing a credit's rating. Watches are usually resolved in three months, either by a rating change in the indicated direction of the watch or by a confirmation of the rating at its current level. Rating outlooks are long-term projections of 12 to 18 months indicating whether a credit's rating is more likely to be upgraded, downgraded, or remain stable. Rating outlook designations are "positive," "stable," or "negative."

Moody's new study provides 1- to 5-year historical default rates from 1995 through 2005 by senior unsecured rating and by rating watch and outlook status. We produce two tables from Moody's data in Exhibits 12.1 and 12.2.

The results show great differences in default rates by senior unsecured rating when rating watches and outlooks are taken into account. For example, Exhibit 12.1 demonstrates that no credit that has been placed on watch for an upgrade, all the way down to a Ba3 rating, has ever defaulted within one year. But A2 credits, even with stable ratings outlooks, *have* defaulted within a year. Among B3 credits, 1-year historical default rates range from 0% to 28%, depending on rating watch and outlook status.

Exhibit 12.2 indicates that few credits that are rated between Aa1 and Baa1 and are either on watch for an upgrade or boast a positive outlook have defaulted within five years. However, some credits rated Baa1 and above, holding stable and negative ratings outlooks, or on watch for a downgrade, *have* defaulted within five years. Five-year default rates for B3 credits range from 31% to 74%.

Results in the tables are remarkably consistent in that default rates generally *increase* (1) as one goes *down* the charts and therefore in senior unsecured rating and (2) as one goes to the *right* of the charts and therefore down in rating watch and outlook status. Clearly, rating watch and outlook status make a difference in historical default rates. The message of these tables to a user of credit ratings is clear: *Considering only a credit's unsecured rating ignores important information contained in rating watches and outlooks.*

Distinguishing Relative Credit Quality

The downward and rightward trend of default rates in Exhibits 12.1 and 12.2 poses tough questions about the trade-off between a rating and its outlook status. For example, over five years, would one rather own a Baa2 on watch for downgrade or a B2 on watch for upgrade? Both have about the same 7% historical probability of default in the Moody's study.

EXHIBIT 12.1   One-Year Default Rates by Ratings and Rating Outlook Status

Rating	Upgrade (%)	Positive (%)	Stable (%)	Negative (%)	Downgrade (%)
Aaa	NA	NA	—	—	—
Aa1	—	—	—	—	—
Aa2	—	—	—	—	—
Aa3	—	—	—	—	—
A1	—	—	—	—	—
A2	—	—	0.07	0.20	0.10
A3	—	—	0.11	—	0.23
Baa1	—	—	0.27	0.23	0.76
Baa2	—	—	0.12	0.21	1.28
Baa3	—	0.15	0.37	0.78	2.12
Ba1	—	—	0.35	0.26	3.19
Ba2	—	—	0.59	1.71	2.62
Ba3	—	0.09	1.02	0.86	5.97
B1	0.73	0.33	2.27	4.68	8.44
B2	2.78	0.36	4.03	8.41	22.80
B3	—	1.76	5.96	13.72	28.44
Caa1	5.19	5.64	7.37	21.50	45.74
Caa2	14.52	0.66	16.62	30.59	43.70
Caa3	12.00	22.64	20.79	29.95	53.01
Ca-C	—	3.81	29.58	51.22	44.44
Investment grade	—	0.02	0.12	0.20	0.54
Speculative grade	1.11	0.62	3.69	13.18	15.18
All rated	0.45	0.32	1.53	6.32	5.45

Source: Exhibit 14 in David T. Hamilton and Richard Cantor, *Rating Transitions and Defaults Conditional on Rating Outlooks Revisited: 1995–2005*, Moody's Investors Service, December 2005, pp. 14–16.

In response to this question, Moody's reiterates advice from a 2004 study on how to aggregate corporate credits into groups of homogeneous default probability. It recommends the following adjustments to a corporate's senior unsecured rating:

EXHIBIT 12.2 Five-Year Default Rates by Ratings and Rating Outlook Status

Rating	Upgrade (%)	Positive (%)	Stable (%)	Negative (%)	Downgrade (%)
Aaa	NA	NA	—	—	—
Aa1	—	—	—	—	—
Aa2	—	—	—	—	—
Aa3	—	—	—	—	—
A1	—	—	0.08	0.57	—
A2	0.40	1.66	0.10	1.85	0.58
A3	—	—	2.19	1.65	0.66
Baa1	—	—	1.76	0.44	2.90
Baa2	2.42	0.72	1.17	0.82	6.84
Baa3	0.49	3.24	3.88	5.79	8.11
Ba1	4.71	0.95	4.22	3.68	7.30
Ba2	2.13	1.38	4.79	17.54	16.07
Ba3	6.38	4.53	11.58	15.97	29.09
B1	8.35	7.62	23.52	22.33	36.98
B2	6.65	11.47	27.92	33.10	45.96
B3	45.26	31.10	35.98	44.59	73.83
Caa1	56.64	50.59	54.52	56.85	75.86
Caa2	32.20	44.06	53.87	57.03	74.69
Caa3	30.86	—	77.95	55.11	56.25
Ca-C	60.17	73.66	60.81	66.87	100.00
Investment grade	0.56	0.83	1.19	1.43	2.14
Speculative grade	12.23	10.32	23.57	34.17	35.78
All rated	4.40	5.49	10.64	16.27	12.53

Source: Exhibit 14 in David T. Hamilton and Richard Cantor, *Rating Transitions and Defaults Conditional on Rating Outlooks Revisited: 1995–2005*, Moody's Investors Service, December 2005, pp. 14–16.

- Credits on downgrade watch should be pushed down two rating notches.
- Credits on upgrade watch should be bumped up two rating notches.
- Credits on negative ratings outlook should be pushed down one rating notch.

- Credits on stable ratings outlook should remain at their official ratings.
- Credits on positive ratings outlook should be bumped up one ratings notch.[2]

Using these adjustments, Exhibit 12.3 shows credits with approximately the same default probability (per Moody's). The combinations of ratings and outlook status in the exhibit are considered to have lower default probability than the next grouping of credits: Baa1 on downgrade watch, Baa2 with negative outlook, Baa3 with stable outlook, Ba1 with positive outlook, and Ba2 on upgrade watch.

In making recommendations, Moody's was guided by a statistic called the *accuracy ratio*. In brief, an accuracy ratio measures the ability of ratings to differentiate between defaulters and nondefaulters. The ratio ranges between 0 and 1, with a ratio of 1 representing a perfect default predictor. For example, if 10 out of 100 rated credits default, and the 10 that defaulted had the worst ratings of the 100 credits, the accuracy ratio would be 1. If the 10 credits that defaulted had the best ratings of the 100 credits, the accuracy ratio would be 0.

Moody's adjustments increase the accuracy ratio of its credit ratings in predicting defaults from 66.2% to 71.1% over a 5-year time horizon. In the 1-year time frame, different adjustment scenarios increase the accuracy of the ratings even more. For example, pushing a credit down one notch for a negative ratings outlook and up three notches for a positive ratings outlook increases the 1-year accuracy to 84.1%. However, Moody's questions whether this more aggressive notching would remain optimal in the long run.

Additionally, the rating agency believes that symmetric adjustments are more convenient for investors. We feel, however, that Moody's suggestions are also driven by a desire not to adjust a credit's relative default-rate grouping too far from its official rating.

EXHIBIT 12.3   Equivalent Default Probabilities

A3 Downgrade watch
Baa1 Negative outlook
Baa2 Stable outlook
Baa3 Positive outlook
Ba1 Upgrade watch

---

[2] David T. Hamilton and Richard Cantor, *Rating Transitions and Defaults Conditional on Watchlist, Outlook and Rating History*, Moody's Investors Service, February 2004.

An Alternative Default Rate Equivalents

We created our own arrangement of ratings, watches, and outlooks, which honor current ratings less than Moody's recommendations. We group ratings, watches, and outlooks according to historical default rates on a 1-year and 5-year basis in Exhibits 12.4 and 12.5, resulting in a more homogenous grouping than Moody's recommendation.

Exhibit 12.4 shows our rearrangement of ratings, watches, and outlooks to form more homogeneous 1-year historical default-rate categories. The historical default rates fall into distinct ranges, with a few judgment calls to account for discontinuities in the data. For example, over a 1-year period, B3 credits on upgrade watch experienced no defaults. However, B2 credits on upgrade watch show a 2.8% default rate over the same time frame.

So, instead of showing the B3 credits in a lower default-rate category than the B2 credits, we group them together in the 1.3% to 2.8% default-rate category. As a result, some of our groupings are more conservative than what the historical data suggests.

These groupings are not intended to suggest that an investor should be indifferent between holding, for example, a 1-year maturity Aa1 bond on credit-watch upgrade or a 1-year maturity Ba3 bond on credit-watch upgrade. Nor are we saying that an investor should demand the same coupon for those two investment alternatives. What we are saying is that, from 1995 through 2005, the timespan of the Moody's study, there was absolutely no difference in their 1-year default experience. And a Ba3 credit

EXHIBIT 12.4 UBS Stratification of Unsecured Rating, Rating Watch, and Rating Outlook, 1-Year Default Rates

Default Rate Range (%)	Average Default Rate Range (%)	Upgrade	Positive	Stable	Negative	Downgrade
0.0–0.0	0.0	Aa1–Ba3	Aa1–Baa2	Aaa–A1	Aaa–A1	Aaa–A1
0.1–1.0	0.6	B1	Baa3–B1	A2–Ba3	A2–Ba1	A2–Baa1
1.3–2.8	2.1	B2–B3	B2–B3	B1	Ba2–Ba3	Baa2–Baa3
3.2–4.7	4.0			B2	B1	Ba1–Ba2
5.9–6.0	6.0			B3		Ba3
8.4–8.5	8.5				B2	B1
13.7	13.7				B3	
22.8–28.4	25.6					B2–B3

EXHIBIT 12.5 UBS Stratification of Unsecured Rating, Rating Watch, and Rating Outlook, 5-Year Default Rates

Default Rate Range (%)	Average Default Rate Range (%)	Upgrade	Positive	Stable	Negative	Downgrade
0.0–0.0	0.0	Aa1–A1	Aa1–A1	Aaa–Aa3	Aaa–Aa3	Aaa–Aa3
0.1–2.4	1.3	A2–Baa3	A2–Baa2	A1–Baa2	A1–Baa2	A1–A3
2.9–4.8	3.9	Ba1–Ba2	Baa3–Ba2	Baa3–Ba2		Baa1
5.8–6.8	6.3	Ba3	Ba3		Baa3–Ba1	Baa2
7.6–8.4	8.0	B1–B2	B1			Baa3–Ba1
11.5–11.6	11.6		B2	Ba3		
16.0–17.5	16.8				Ba2–Ba3	Ba2
22.3–29.0	25.7			B1–B2	B1	Ba3
31.1–46.0	38.6	B3	B3	B3	B2–B3	B1–B2
73.8	73.8					B3

on watch for upgrade has historically been as good a bet as a A1 credit on watch for downgrade.

Exhibit 12.5 shows our rearrangement of ratings, watches, and outlooks to form more homogeneous 5-year historical default rate categories. Again, in the exhibit, we are not saying that an investor should be indifferent between holding, for example, a 5-year maturity Aa1 bond on upgrade watch or a 5-year maturity A1 bond on upgrade watch. Nor are we saying that an investor should demand the same coupon for those two investment alternatives. What we are pointing out, again, is that from 1995 through 2005, there was no difference in their 5-year default experiences. And a A1 credit on watch for upgrade has historically been as good a bet as a Aa3 bond on watch for downgrade.

Whether one sticks with Moody's scheme for adjusting ratings by rating watches and outlooks, or our more radical adjustments, as shown in Exhibits 12.4 and 12.5, the gist of the recommendations are the same. One can get more information from Moody's credit analysis by looking beyond their official ratings and by considering rating watches and rating outlooks.

How Good Are Rating Watch and Will They Continue to Produce Accurate Results?

Given this improved way of using rating agency opinions, should CDO investors stop doing credit analysis or stop subscribing to services that provide alternative sources of default predictions? In short, no. Of course, we appreciate the improved default-predicting performance of combining ratings and rating watches and outlooks, but we consider this to be just another instrument in the credit analyst's toolbox, rather than a replacement for methods already used.

Moody's findings also highlight how slow rating agencies are to change their ratings. If their ratings were up to date, outlooks would contain no additional default-prediction information. In our view, these nonrating signals from the agencies will be useful in predicting defaults unless (or until) they are incorporated into investment guidelines and capital requirements. Then, if regulatory capital or compulsory sales ever become driven by rating outlooks, rating agencies will slow the pace of outlook changes in order to again give investors adequate warning. It is already worrisome that issuing a rating watch or changing a rating outlook now requires mustering a full rating committee rather than being decided by a simple agreement between an analyst and a managing director.

Should outlooks actually become part of regulatory frameworks, however, the solution is simple—outlooks on outlooks!

CHANGES IN RATING METHODOLOGIES

In this section, we discuss changes in rating methodologies by S&P and Moody's. These changes have been met with confusion and fear in the CDO market in 2006. Ironically, the intent behind the changes from both agencies was simply to improve the accuracy of their ratings. It seems S&P confused CDO structurers by changing part of its rating methodology without fully explaining the changes they were going to make in the rest of their CDO rating methodology. Moody's sparked fear in the CLO market with the seemingly benign offer to raise their ratings on leveraged loans. The move took the market by surprise, even though Moody's had begun discussing this potential change over a year prior to its announcement.

S&P's New Collateral Assumptions

In December 2005, S&P announced new collateral assumptions with respect to default probabilities. The new assumptions, the rating agency said, were due to the availability of more and better historical data. In comparison to their previous default assumptions, S&P lowered default probability for collateral rated AAA to BBB+ and raised default probability for collateral rated BBB and below. Another change in S&P's new collateral assumptions was to model interindustry default correlation at 5% and intraindustry default correlation at 15%.

These collateral assumptions drive the cumulative default scenarios that come out of S&P's CDO Evaluator 3.0 model. To rate a CDO, these defaults must be put into a cash flow model of the particular CDO. The cash flow model must incorporate S&P's assumptions about the timing of defaults, interest rates, and collateral prepayments, among other factors.

However, at the same time that S&P announced its new collateral assumptions, the rating agency also announced that it would be changing its cash flow modeling assumptions—in the future. This caused confusion, as some CDO structurers tried to figure out how the new collateral assumptions would affect cash flow CDOs. Using the combination of new collateral assumptions and old cash flow assumptions, some CDO structurers predicted wholesale downgrades of existing CLOs and mezzanine structured finance CDOs and much higher levels of subordination for new CDOs to reach their rating targets. Structurers wondered what types of deals they were going to be able to create under S&P's new criteria when both halves of the methodology were finalized. S&P tried to allay concerns that the final rating methodology would not be punitive and, in fact, not change very much for the vast majority of deals.

S&P's new collateral assumptions applied immediately to synthetic CDOs that do not use cash flow mechanisms such as overcollateralization (OC) and interest coverage (IC) triggers for cash diversion. Following the announcement on December 19, 2005, S&P put 28 U.S. synthetic CDOs on watch for downgrade and nine European CDOs on watch for upgrade. Synthetic CDOs in Asia saw rating actions in both directions. Under the new collateral default assumptions, the pattern of watches followed the fortunes of collateral in the CDO portfolios. In general, CDOs with higher-rated collateral were subject to upgrades while CDOs with lower-rated collateral were subject to downgrades.

The U.S. downgrades received particular criticisms from normally very thoughtful commentators. Ignoring the European upgrades, it was suggested that the necessity of the downgrades demonstrated the weakness of the single-rated CDO synthetic market, and S&P's ratings in particular. But one could make a more persuasive case that the 95.4% of U.S. synthetic CDO ratings that did not change showed S&P's continued confidence in their ratings.

When S&P finally released both halves of their rating methodology, the results were ho-hum:

1. The vast majority of S&P's existing cash flow CDO did not change and the vast majority of new cash flow CDOs did not require extra credit enhancement to meet their desired ratings.

2. The types of CDOs that might require increase credit enhancement are:

- CLOs with very low-rated collateral or CLOs with barbell portfolios.
- CBOs backed by high-yield bonds.
- CLOs with substantial amounts of second lien loans.
- ABS CDOs with substantial amounts of BBB and lower collateral.

3. On the other hand, some high-grade SF CDOs with BBB+ or higher portfolios were candidates for upgrades.

Our view of S&P's new collateral assumptions is that it was done for two reasons. First, to counter annoying criticism, such as that from the default correlation fetishers. Second, to tighten up rating criteria for specific problematic types of collateral. We do not think S&P ever wanted the bulk of their outstanding cash flow CDO ratings or required credit enhancements to change. Rather, they achieved rating stability by tweaking their cash flow assumptions.

Moody's Higher Loan Ratings

Moody's seemingly benign proposal, in January 2006, to raise its ratings on leveraged loans also caused fear in the CLO market. Who does not like higher ratings? Many parties, as Moody's plan for a wholesale increase in bank loan ratings set off a ministorm of protest. The protest caught Moody's loan raters by surprised, as the upgrades had been foreshadowed as in a series of 2004 research reports.

Moody's impetus to raise loan ratings derived from solid analytical grounds. Their default and recovery studies of high-yield bonds and loans showed that on an expected loss basis, loans perform much better than bonds of the same rating. Studies showed, for example, that loans default about half as often as bonds of the same rating and recover about twice as much. Moody's thought that one-to-two rating notch upgrades for bank loans would equalize the expected losses for bonds and loans.

One concern of CLO structurers, managers, and investors was that loan spreads would tighten as a result of upgrades. Some market participants predicted tightening of 25 to 50 basis points and a wave of loan prepayments and recouponings. If so, this tightening would occur despite the fact that the inherent credit risk of loans remained the same. The only thing that would change is the loan's ratings, after all, not their true credit risk. But tight loan spreads were already a problem for outstanding CLOs, and the fear was that at higher ratings loans would be more attractive to new investors and the action of the new marginal investor would tighten spreads.

The other thing that worried the CLO market was the effect loan rating changes would have on new CLO structures. Wouldn't higher ratings on loan collateral result in higher leverage in CLOs? If so, would CLO leverage go up just as loan collateral was becoming more risky, as measured by leverage multiples and weakened covenant protections?

After delays, Moody's loan raters did go ahead and raise ratings on well-secured loans. The average rating increase was a notch and a half. But Moody's CLO raters deftly changed their CLO requirements so that the increased ratings had little effect on CLO ratings or CLO leverage. As with the S&P two-step release of their new rating requirements, the CDO rating results were managed to near stasis.

CONCLUSIONS

In this chapter, we discussed the findings and implications of a 2005 study by Moody's suggesting that the predictiveness of its corporate ratings can be improved by utilizing the credit's outlook status. In addition, we proposed a default-rate equivalent arrangement of ratings, watches, and outlooks, which honor current ratings less than Moody's recommendations. What Moody's proposes, as well as our rearrangement, are simply another instrument in the credit analyst's toolbox.

We then discussed two changes that Moody's and S&P made in their rating methodologies and the confusion and concern they sowed in the CDO market. The first was the two-step implementation process S&P employed in announcing new rating criteria. The second was Moody's loan raters' decision to upgrade senior secured loans. Ironically, in the end, CDO rating changes were basically left the same in both cases.

It is in the interest of the CDO market (and all the capital markets) to maintain or improve the quality of rating agency ratings. Investor and regulator confidence in the credibility of ratings is vital. Thus, while the rating agencies will continue to refine their CDO rating methodologies, it is important that rating agencies realize they are effectively in partnership with CDO managers, investors, and structurers. Coordination and communication are vital. Rating agencies need to better foresee where their actions will cause discomfort and give appropriate warnings. Market participants who use those ratings need to pay better attention to the warnings that are issued by the rating agencies.

CHAPTER 13

Collateral Overlap and Single-Name Exposure in CLO Portfolios

Investors in collateralized loan obligations (CLOs) may get the feeling that they have seen a CLO's collateral portfolio before. That is because they have. CLO portfolios, even from CLOs issued in different years, tend to have a lot of underlying borrower names in common. This situation is the result of loan prepayments, which cause CLO managers to continually buy loans for their CLOs. Thus portfolio differences due to CLO vintage are muted. Additionally, CLO managers commonly allocate loan purchases across all the CLOs they manage. This also causes collateral overlap among CLOs managed by the same manager.

At the same time, however, small loan allocations and the necessity of filling several CLOs with collateral keep single-name concentrations within individual CLO portfolios from being large. For example, for the sample of CLOs that we studied and whose results are reported in this chapter, the average number of separate credits in the CLOs is 233.

How do these two phenomena—greater collateral overlap and smaller individual exposures—shake out for CLO debt investors? Using our measure of the risk of single-name exposure, it turns out that CLO debt investors, especially CLO subordinate debt investors, are better off. With respect to concentration risk across CLO portfolios and within a particular CLO portfolio, the positive effect of smaller exposures swamps the negative effect of collateral overlap.

In this chapter, we use a sample of 32 CLOs to assess collateral overlap and single-name risk. We begin by looking at collateral overlap between individual CLOs, between CLO managers, and between CLO vintages. We then look at the most common credits across CLOs and across CLO managers. Finally, we look at the risk of the 10 most common CLO credits in each of the 32 CLOs we study.

COLLATERAL OVERLAP IN U.S. CLOs

To study collateral overlap among managers and vintages, we selected 32 CLOs from seven different managers, spanning vintages from 2001 through 2005, as shown in Exhibit 13.1. The collateral portfolios of these CLOs range from $300 million to $1.1 billion. None of the CLOs in our study has ever experienced a downgrade and one, Dryden III, was called after we collected data for our study.

EXHIBIT 13.1 CLOs in Study by Vintage

Vintage	Manager	CLO
2001	Octagon Investment Partners	Octagon Investment Partners IV
2001	Sankaty Advisors	Race Point CLO
2002	Deerfield Capital Management	Bryn Mawr CLO
2002	Sankaty Advisors	Castle Hill I - INGOTS
2002	Sankaty Advisors	Castle Hill II - INGOTS
2002	American Express Asset Management	Centurion VI
2002	Prudential Investment Management	Dryden II
2002	Prudential Investment Management	Dryden III
2002	Deerfield Capital Management	Rosemont CLO
2003	Sankaty Advisors	Avery Point CLO
2003	David L Babson & Company	Babson CLO 2003-I
2003	Sankaty Advisors	Castle Hill III CLO
2003	Prudential Investment Management	Dryden IV
2003	Prudential Investment Management	Dryden V
2003	Deerfield Capital Management	Forest Creek CLO
2003	Octagon Investment Partners	Octagon Investment Partners V
2003	Octagon Investment Partners	Octagon Investment Partners VI
2003	Sankaty Advisors	Race Point II CLO
2003	Invesco	Sagamore CLO
2004	David L Babson & Company	Babson CLO 2004-I
2004	American Express Asset Management	Centurion VII 2004
2004	Invesco	Champlain CLO
2004	Prudential Investment Management	Dryden VII
2004	Deerfield Capital Management	Long Grove CLO
2004	Octagon Investment Partners	Octagon Investment Partners VII
2004	Invesco	Saratoga CLO I
2005	David L Babson & Company	Babson CLO 2005-I
2005	David L Babson & Company	Babson CLO 2005-II
2005	American Express Asset Management	Centurion IX
2005	American Express Asset Management	Centurion VIII 2005
2005	Prudential Investment Management	Dryden VIII
2005	Octagon Investment Partners	Octagon Investment Partners VIII

Source: UBS CDO Research.

To *determine* whether two CLOs contain the same credit, we first looked to the "Issuer" data field in INTEX's asset detail. INTEX provides the most up-to-date asset detail, current as of the CLO's last trustee report, which in our study was typically December 2005 or January 2006. Unfortunately, as INTEX relies on trustee-reported data, it does not have a single unique issuer identifier across all CLOs. Nor does it group affiliated legal entities, such as holding companies and their subsidiaries. To aid in grouping affiliated entities, we used data from MarkIt, Bloomberg, and Loan Pricing Corporation.

To quantify single-name risk, we look at the percent of a CLO portfolio, by par amount, that is made up of obligations of the same credit. For a particular credit, collateral overlap between two CLOs is defined as the average percentage of that single name in the two portfolios. Because Charter Communications makes up 0.8% of Centurion IX's portfolio and 1.0% of Centurion VII's portfolio, the collateral overlap of Charter between the two CLOs is calculated as 0.9%. The total collateral overlap between Centurion IX and Centurion VII is the sum of these single-name collateral overlaps, or 83%, as shown in the top left cell of Exhibit 13.2.[1]

Exhibit 13.2 shows the collateral overlaps among 32 CLOs. In the exhibit, CLOs are grouped by manager. The average overlap between any two CLOs in our sample is 46% and the range is from 21% to 91%. The far right column in Exhibit 13.2 shows the average collateral overlap between a particular CLO and the other 31 CLOs.

Exhibit 13.3 summarizes the findings of Exhibit 13.2 by manager, averaging the collateral overlap of CLOs from different managers. For example, the average collateral overlap between CLOs managed by American Express and CLOs managed by Babson is 49%. The diagonal of the exhibit shows the collateral overlap among CLOs managed by the same manager. For example, Amex-managed CLOs have an average 85% collateral overlap with one another. The "average" column at the far right of the exhibit measures each manager's overlap against all the other managers.

---

[1] There are two ways to do the overlap calculation. The first way, and the one we employ, is to *average* the two CLOs' exposures to a credit; the second that is followed by some researchers is to take the *minimum* of the two CLOs' exposure to the credit. A simple example shows the correctness of the first approach. Suppose CLO A and CLO B own the same 50 credits, but not in the same amounts. For 25 credits, CLO A has 3% exposure, while CLO B has 1% exposure. For the other 25 credits, CLO A has 1% exposure while CLO B has 3% exposure. With the second approach, one would measure each collateral overlap as 1% and sum all 50 to get 50% collateral overlap. The first approach measures each collateral overlap at 2% and sum all 50 to get 100% collateral overlap and is the correct approach for the following reason. If all the credits in CLO A default, 100% of the credits in CLO B would default, and vice versa. For the CLOs in the study discussed in this chapter, the second approach would underestimate collateral overlap by 13%.

EXHIBIT 13.2 Percent of Collateral Overlap—Borrowers Common to Any Two CLOs Grouped by Manager

	Amex				Babson				Deerfield				Invesco			Octagon					Prudential						Sankaty						Average
	CENTUR9	CENTUR6	CENTUR7	CENTUR8	BABS031	BABS041	BABS051	BABS052	BRYNMAWR	FORESTCR	LONGRV	ROSEMONT	CHAMPLN	SAGAMORE	SARATOGA	OCTAGON4	OCTAGON5	OCTAGON6	OCTAGON7	OCTAGON8	DRYDN022	DRYDN032	DRYDNO43	DRYDN5	DRYDN7	DRYDN8	AVERYPT	CASTHILL1	CASTHILL2	CASTHILL3	RACEPOIN	RACEPNT2	
CENTUR9		84	83	88	46	46	54	53	49	49	52	52	53	60	63	44	48	44	46	49	38	26	42	38	39	37	53	53	51	46	54	57	52
CENTUR6			87	85	47	48	52	50	50	51	54	53	56	61	64	46	49	47	49	49	38	29	43	39	38	36	55	54	50	47	54	56	52
CENTUR7				84	45	47	52	49	50	50	54	53	55	60	63	45	50	46	49	48	38	28	43	37	37	37	54	54	50	46	53	56	52
CENTUR8					45	43	53	50	49	48	52	51	52	56	59	42	46	45	47	46	37	27	43	37	38	38	54	54	51	47	54	56	51
BABS031						60	63	65	42	40	44	44	45	48	49	39	41	41	38	39	35	24	37	35	34	40	47	45	45	41	46	47	44
BABS041							61	62	41	40	43	44	47	50	52	36	35	34	41	38	30	21	32	28	33	31	41	41	38	34	41	43	41
BABS051								72	43	41	45	44	52	54	56	41	41	40	47	45	35	25	37	32	37	51	44	46	43	41	45	47	46
BABS052									44	44	48	46	49	52	53	38	39	38	41	43	33	24	35	32	33	37	46	46	44	39	46	47	45
BRYNMAWR										86	86	87	45	52	52	34	37	37	36	40	35	23	42	36	38	39	48	42	44	38	47	48	46
FORESTCR											85	85	44	50	51	36	40	38	38	38	36	26	44	38	39	35	47	41	46	37	45	46	46
LONGRV												87	47	54	54	39	42	41	40	44	38	26	45	39	41	42	51	46	48	41	49	52	49
ROSEMONT													46	52	53	37	41	39	39	42	37	26	42	37	39	39	50	46	49	40	50	52	48
CHAMPLN														79	80	43	42	40	46	46	35	29	40	34	36	41	47	51	47	43	47	50	47
SAGAMORE															90	48	45	43	48	50	37	30	47	37	43	43	52	52	50	46	53	55	52
SARATOGA																49	47	45	51	52	41	34	47	37	43	42	53	52	51	48	55	56	53

EXHIBIT 13.2 (Continued)

	Amex				Babson				Deerfield				Invesco			Octagon					Prudential						Sankaty						Average
	CENTUR9	CENTUR6	CENTUR7	CENTUR8	BABS031	BABS041	BABS051	BABS052	BRYNMAWR	FORESTCR	LONGRV	ROSEMONT	CHAMPLN	SAGAMORE	SARATOGA	OCTAGON4	OCTAGON5	OCTAGON6	OCTAGON7	OCTAGON8	DRYDN022	DRYDN032	DRYDN043	DRYDN5	DRYDN7	DRYDN8	AVERYPT	CASTHLL1	CASTHLL2	CASTHLL3	RACEPOIN	RACEPNT2	Average
OCTAGON4																	80	80	77	68	32	28	30	34	35	31	45	43	41	39	44	47	44
OCTAGON5																		84	77	70	34	28	33	35	36	29	46	43	45	40	45	47	46
OCTAGON6																			76	70	34	27	32	37	34	29	49	43	45	40	45	48	45
OCTAGON7																				69	33	24	29	31	32	31	45	42	40	38	43	46	45
OCTAGON8																					29	24	29	30	30	35	46	43	41	38	45	47	45
DRYDN022																						42	53	50	48	37	37	36	31	29	37	39	37
DRYDN032																							40	35	38	29	28	30	30	26	29	31	29
DRYDN043																								52	55	46	40	38	35	34	39	41	40
DRYDN5																									54	41	37	32	30	25	34	35	36
DRYDN7																										46	39	34	34	27	37	37	38
DRYDN8																											40	39	32	31	40	41	38
AVERYPT																												79	77	70	85	89	52
CASTHLL1																													78	73	81	83	50
CASTHLL2																														77	75	78	48
CASTHLL3																															68	71	44
RACEPOIN																																91	51
RACEPNT2																																	53

Source: UBS, Intex, MarkIt, Bloomberg, and LPC.

EXHIBIT 13.3   Collateral Overlap Among Managers

Manager	Amex	Babson	Deerfield	Invesco	Octagon	Prudential	Sankaty	Average
Amex	85	49	51	58	47	37	53	49
Babson		64	43	51	40	33	43	43
Deerfield			86	50	39	37	46	44
Invesco				83	46	39	44	48
Octagon					75	31	44	41
Prudential						44	34	35
Sankaty							78	44

Source: UBS, Intex, MarkIt, Bloomberg, and LPC.

EXHIBIT 13.4   Collateral Overlap Among Vintages

Vintage	2001	2002	2003	2004	2005	Average
2001	44	45	51	46	46	47
2002		43	45	45	43	45
2003			45	46	45	47
2004				47	49	46
2005					50	45

Source: UBS, Intex, MarkIt, Bloomberg, and LPC.

Exhibit 13.3 shows that, by far, the greatest collateral overlap occurs among the CLOs managed by the same manager. CLOs managed by Deerfield Capital have the highest average overlap at 86%, while the average overlap between CLOs managed by the same manager is 74%. The average overlap between CLOs managed by different managers is 44%. These findings suggest that owning two CLOs managed by the same manager does not provide the same collateral diversification as owning CLOs from different managers. Interestingly, Prudential has only a 44% collateral overlap across six of its Dryden CLOs, which is the lowest among the managers. We understand that it is Prudential's policy to limit collateral overlap across their CLOs. At 35%, Prudential also has the lowest overlap with other CLO managers.

Exhibit 13.4 also summarizes the findings from Exhibit 13.2, but this time by vintage. In this exhibit, we average the collateral overlap of CLOs across different vintages. For example, the average collateral overlap between 2001 vintage CLOs and 2002 vintage CLOs is 45%. The diagonal of the exhibit shows the collateral overlap of CLOs within the same vintage. For example, 2001 vintage CLOs have an average of 44% collateral overlap with one another. The "average" column at the far right of the exhibit measures each vintage's overlap against all the other vintages.

The average collateral overlap of CLOs from the same vintage is 46%, with all results in a tight range from 43% to 50%. The average collateral overlap of CLOs from different vintages is also 46%. Therefore, CLOs from different vintages have the same collateral overlap as CLOs from the same vintage. Furthermore, it appears that having the same manager produces higher collateral overlap between CLOs than does being in the same vintage year.

Favorite CLO Credits

There are 873 unique borrowers represented in the 32 CLO portfolios we examined, so that across all CLOs, the average par exposure to any particular credit is 0.1%. But Exhibit 13.5 shows the 10 highest single-name exposures across the 32 CLOs. The biggest common holding across all of our sampled CLOs is R. H. Donnelley. On average, it comprises 1.2% of each CLO's portfolio and it is present in all 32 CLOs. The top 10 credits average between 0.7% and 1.2% of each CLO portfolio.

Exhibit 13.6 lists the highest single-name exposures across CLOs from the seven managers. The most popular names for any given manager are generally in the top 10 or 15 across all managers, with a few exceptions. For example, Capital Automotive makes up 1.8% of Deerfield's CLO assets. While Capital Automotive is present in 14 non-Deerfield CLOs, it has a

EXHIBIT 13.5 Most Common Borrowers in Sampled CLOs

Rank	Borrower	Average (%)	CLOs with Exposure	Managers with Exposure
1	R. H. Donnelley	1.2	32	7
2	Metro-Goldwyn-Mayer Inc.	1.1	32	7
3	Charter Communications	1.0	26	7
4	Solar Capital Corp (Sungard)	1.0	30	7
5	General Growth Properties Inc.	0.9	29	7
6	Graham Packaging Co.	0.9	28	7
7	United Pan-Europe Communications N.V.	0.8	29	6
8	Insight Communications Co.	0.8	29	7
9	Time Warner	0.7	27	7
10	Rockwood Specialties Group Inc.	0.7	27	7

Source: UBS, Intex, MarkIt, Bloomberg, and LPC.; CLO portfolio data as of December 2005 and January 2006 trustee reports.

EXHIBIT 13.6 Most Common Borrowers by Manager

Rank	Amex	Percent	Babson	Percent
1	Penn National Gaming	0.9	Metro-Goldwyn-Mayer	1.3
2	Huntsman	0.9	Solar Capital (Sungard)	1.2
3	Graham Packaging	0.9	United Pan-Europe Communications	1.1
4	Charter Communications	0.8	Rockwood Specialties Group	1.1
5	Metro-Goldwyn-Mayer	0.8	R. H. Donnelley	1.0
6	DaVita	0.8	Insight Communications	0.9
7	Jarden	0.8	Celanese	0.9
8	Reliant Energy	0.8	Warner Chilcott	0.9
9	Wynn Las Vegas LLC	0.7	Smurfit-Stone Container	0.9
10	Goodyear Tire & Rubber	0.7	Invensys International Holdings	0.8
	Total number of borrowers	367	Total number of borrowers	378
	Avg. number of borrowers per CLO	303	Avg. number of borrowers per CLO	269
	Avg. CLO size ($ million)	$729	Avg. CLO size ($ million)	$546

Rank	Deerfield	Percent	Invesco	Percent
1	Capital Automotive	1.8	R. H. Donnelley	1.1
2	General Growth Properties	1.4	Reliant Energy	0.9
3	Fidelity National Information Services	1.2	General Growth Properties	0.9
4	Solar Capital (Sungard)	1.2	Celanese	0.9
5	Metro-Goldwyn-Mayer	1.2	Calpine	0.8
6	Regal Cinemas	1.1	Metro-Goldwyn-Mayer	0.8
7	Charter Communications	1.1	PanAmSat	0.7
8	Targa Resources	1.1	Dole Food Company	0.7
9	United Pan-Europe Communications	1.0	NRG Energy	0.7
10	PanAmSat	1.0	LifePoint Hospitals	0.7
	Total number of borrowers	295	Total number of borrowers	421
	Avg. number of borrowers per CLO	252	Avg. number of borrowers per CLO	260
	Avg. CLO size ($ million)	$344	Avg. CLO size ($ million)	$347

Rank	Octagon	Percent	Prudential	Percent
1	R. H. Donnelley	1.7	Metro-Goldwyn-Mayer	1.4
2	Charter Communications	1.4	Solar Capital (Sungard)	1.4
3	Huntsman	1.4	Rockwood Specialties Group	1.2
4	Graham Packaging	1.4	R. H. Donnelley	1.2
5	Metro-Goldwyn-Mayer	1.3	Vought Aircraft Industries Inc	1.1
6	Solar Capital (Sungard)	1.1	United Pan-Europe Communications	1.1
7	Boyd Gaming	1.1	Insight Communications	1.0
8	Rockwood Specialties Group	1.1	Celanese	1.0
9	Celanese	1.0	Neiman Marcus Group	0.9
10	Berry Plastics	1.0	ON Semiconductor Corp	0.9
	Total number of borrowers	308	Total number of borrowers	311
	Avg. number of borrowers per CLO	180	Avg. number of borrowers per CLO	128
	Avg. CLO size ($ million)	$368	Avg. CLO size ($ million)	$367

EXHIBIT 13.6 (Continued)

Rank	Sankaty	Percent
1	General Growth Properties	1.5
2	R. H. Donnelley	1.3
3	Charter Communications	1.2
4	Springer Group	1.2
5	Metro-Goldwyn-Mayer	1.1
6	United Pan-Europe Communications	1.1
7	Capital Automotive	1.1
8	Eastman Kodak	1.0
9	Bresnan Communications	1.0
10	Time Warner	1.0
	Total number of borrowers	285
	Avg. number of borrowers per CLO	236
	Avg. CLO size ($ million)	$444

Source: UBS, Intex, MarkIt, Bloomberg, and LPC.

significant presence ($25 million in total) across all four Deerfield-managed CLOs.

The bottom three rows of each panel in Exhibit 13.6 show the total number of borrowers across all the CLOs managed by a single manager, the average number of borrowers per CLO, and the manager's average CLO size. The exhibit shows that Prudential has the lowest number of borrowers per CLO than any other manager. Prudential CLOs, as you recall, also have the lowest collateral overlap with other CLOs. Prudential's CLOs are apparently comprised of a smaller number of more unique names than other CLOs.

SINGLE-NAME RISK AND TRANCHE PROTECTIONS

Now that we have quantified collateral overlap across CLOs and collateral diversification within CLOs, what do we make of it? How do we combine these factors and measure single-name risk? And how can we measure and compare single-name risk for CLO tranches at *different points* in the CLO capital structure? For example, an investor's CLOs might own $15 million of Charter and $30 million of R. H. Donnelley. Does the CLO investor bear twice the risk to R. H. Donnelley as to Charter? Not necessarily. Suppose that investor owns senior tranches of CLOs that hold R. H. Donnelley, but subordinate tranches of CLOs that hold Charter. An R. H. Donnelley default might have less of an impact on senior CLO tranches than the default of Charter would have on subordinate tranches.

This discrepancy in the dollar amount and significance of exposure might arise even if an investor consistently purchased CLO tranches of the same seniority. This would be the case if Charter-owning CLOs happen to suffer more collateral losses than CLOs owning R. H. Donnelley, thus making the former more sensitive to future collateral losses. The collateral overlap problem can be summarized as follows: How does a CLO investor weigh the amount of exposure a CLO has to a single name against the credit protection a tranche has against that single name? And, even more difficult, how does a CLO investor aggregate the balance of exposure and protection to a single name across a portfolio of CLOs?

Our suggestion is to look at the CLO's excess overcollateralization.

EXCESS OVERCOLLATERALIZATION AND EXCESS OVERCOLLATERALIZATION DELTA

A tranche's *excess* overcollateralization (OC) is the excess of collateral par over the outstanding par amount of that tranche plus all the tranches *above* it in seniority. For a CLO with $100 of collateral, $70 of Tranche A, $10 of Tranche B, and $10 of Tranche C, excess OC for Tranches A and C are:

$$\text{Tranche A Excess OC} = \text{Collateral} - \text{Tranche A} = \$100 - \$70 = \$30$$

$$\begin{aligned}\text{Tranche C Excess OC} &= \text{Collateral} - \text{Tranches A, B, and C}\\ &= \$100 - \$90 = \$10\end{aligned}$$

An intuitive interpretation of excess overcollateralization is that it is the amount of par the CLO could lose before the tranche is collateralized exactly 100%. Note that excess OC increases with the par amount of collateral and decreases with the outstanding par amount of the tranche and more senior tranches.

Now suppose that this CLO has a $2 investment in Charter Communications. Each tranche's excess OC delta with respect to Charter is the amount its excess OC would decrease if Charter suddenly defaulted without any recovery. To calculate each tranche's excess OC delta with respect to Charter, we compare the par amount of Charter to that tranche's excess OC:

$$\text{Tranche A excess OC Charter Delta} = \$2/\$30 = 6.7\%$$

$$\text{Tranche C excess OC Charter Delta} = \$2/\$10 = 20.0\%$$

The excess OC deltas show that Tranche A would lose 6.7% of its excess OC if Charter defaulted without recovery while Tranche C would lose 20%

of its excess OC. In other words, because of the difference in tranche subordination, Tranche C is 3 times as exposed to Charter as is Tranche A (20.0% versus 6.7%). Note that excess OC delta increases with the dollar amount of the single-name risk and decreases with the amount *of* the tranche's excess OC. In this manner, excess OC delta takes into account both single-name concentration *and* the amount of protection the tranche has from over-collateralization.

Senior tranche and subordinate tranche excess OC deltas are comparable. Thus, if an investor holds tranches of different seniorities, excess OC delta allows summarizing exposure to a particular name across different CLO tranches. The concentration of a particular credit across different CLO tranches can be gauged by averaging the credit's excess OC deltas or by looking at the range of the credit's excess OC deltas.

Senior and Subordinate Excess OC Deltas

Exhibit 13.7 shows senior tranche excess OC deltas for each of the most common names in the CLOs we examined, excluding Champlain CLO.[2] The first row of the exhibit, for R. H. Donnelley, shows how much senior tranche excess OC would decline if R. H. Donnelley defaulted without any recovery. The decline in excess OC varies from 1.2% to 13.6% and averages 5.8%. The bottom row of Exhibit 13.6 shows the decline in excess OC if *all 10* credits defaulted without any recovery. The amounts for the different CLOs range from 22.5% to 73.9% and average 44.9%.

Exhibit 13.7 neatly combines the effects of collateral overlap across CLO portfolios with the effect of single-name concentration *within* a particular CLO. Collateral overlap is addressed because we are looking at the ten most common credits across all CLOs. Single-name concentration is addressed because we are looking at the concentrations of those names within each individual CLO portfolio.

It is obviously a remote possibility that all 10 credits in Exhibit 13.7 would default and almost an impossibility that all 10 credits would default with zero recovery. Yet, even in this latter scenario, senior tranche excess OC would not be completely eaten through for any of the CLOs. Each senior tranche would still have greater than 100% OC coverage. Exhibit 13.7 also does not capture protection from the diversion of excess spread to protect the senior tranche. We therefore find it very difficult to get excited about single-name risk at the senior tranche level for healthy CLOs.

Exhibit 13.8, in contrast, shows much more severe excess OC deltas for the subordinate tranches of these same CLOs. The excess OCs for R. H.

---

[2] We exclude Champlain CLO in our senior and subordinate excess OC deltas analysis because this CLO has a revolving senior tranche in its capital structure, which makes it hard to calculate its excess OC.

EXHIBIT 13.7 Senior Tranche Excess Overcollateralization Deltas (%)

	AVERYPT	BABS031	BABS041	BABS051	BABS052	BRYNMAWR	CASTHLL1	CASTHLL2	CASTHLL3	CENTUR9	CENTUR6	CENTUR7	CENTUR8	DRYDN022	DRYDN032	DRYDN043
R. H. Donnelley	6.5	7.5	3.8	4.6	7.4	5.3	7.1	7.6	4.6	3.7	4.6	3.4	2.4	4.1	13.6	4.8
Metro-Goldwyn-Mayer Inc.	5.0	3.3	3.0	4.5	4.5	5.6	5.1	8.0	9.2	5.4	2.1	4.8	3.2	6.4	6.8	7.5
Solar Capital Corp (Sungard)	4.1	0.0	3.0	4.7	5.5	3.3	4.6	2.4	0.0	3.8	2.9	3.5	3.5	6.4	6.0	6.7
Charter Communications	4.9	1.1	0.0	3.7	5.5	3.5	9.1	8.2	3.9	4.4	2.8	5.0	4.0	2.5	0.0	0.0
General Growth Properties Inc.	3.7	4.0	2.5	4.6	7.5	7.2	3.7	4.4	4.8	1.7	3.3	3.9	3.4	0.0	0.0	4.2
Graham Packaging Co.	4.5	3.3	2.0	3.4	3.9	0.0	6.3	7.7	8.7	5.5	2.8	4.3	4.2	4.5	0.0	6.7
United Pan-Europe Communications	2.2	2.3	2.0	3.8	3.3	5.2	3.7	4.3	4.0	2.8	2.1	2.5	2.5	5.1	6.8	6.0
Insight Communications Co.	3.0	0.0	2.7	1.6	2.2	5.5	7.9	6.6	2.7	2.4	2.1	0.7	1.7	5.1	6.8	5.9
Time Warner	7.3	2.4	3.5	0.0	5.5	4.1	0.0	0.0	4.6	3.6	2.9	2.9	3.0	1.2	6.7	5.9
Rockwood Specialties Group Inc.	3.7	0.0	0.0	0.0	3.3	4.5	3.7	0.0	0.0	2.1	2.0	2.4	4.8	6.4	8.5	5.9
Total	44.8	23.8	22.5	30.9	48.7	44.2	51.3	49.3	42.5	35.6	27.6	33.4	32.7	41.8	55.3	53.4

EXHIBIT 13.7 (Continued)

	DRYDN5	DRYDN7	DRYDN8	FORESTCR	LONGRV	OCTAGON4	OCTAGON5	OCTAGON6	OCTAGON7	OCTAGON8	RACEPOIN	RACEPNT2	ROSEMONT	SAGAMORE	SARATOGA	Average
R. H. Donnelley	3.3	9.2	2.3	8.0	3.4	6.0	8.5	13.4	1.2	5.5	4.1	5.0	4.3	7.2	8.8	5.8
Metro-Goldwyn-Mayer Inc	5.8	9.5	6.0	9.0	6.1	5.7	5.6	7.9	7.4	3.7	2.8	3.6	6.1	7.6	6.8	5.8
Solar Capital Corp (Sungard)	5.8	7.9	6.4	9.0	5.8	2.9	2.4	5.6	4.5	6.0	4.6	5.4	9.5	6.4	5.7	4.8
Charter Communications	0.0	0.0	4.6	0.0	7.2	6.8	4.7	6.7	7.4	5.6	8.1	7.4	11.6	7.8	6.0	4.6
General Growth Properties Inc.	2.3	0.0	3.1	13.8	6.2	6.8	6.3	9.0	8.5	7.4	2.5	2.4	6.3	3.2	2.9	4.5
Graham Packaging Co.	4.6	4.7	0.0	1.3	0.7	5.1	6.3	3.4	6.7	0.0	4.7	5.2	1.7	7.0	8.1	4.1
United Pan-Europe Communications	4.7	4.7	4.6	7.1	4.8	5.2	6.4	9.0	6.7	3.7	1.5	1.3	6.4	0.0	0.0	4.0
Insight Communications Co.	4.5	10.9	0.0	6.6	6.0	1.1	3.9	6.6	0.0	3.2	3.7	5.0	4.5	2.6	3.8	3.9
Time Warner	4.6	0.0	0.0	5.0	3.6	5.7	2.4	5.6	5.9	4.7	7.6	6.4	3.4	2.6	3.9	3.7
Rockwood Specialties Group Inc.	5.8	6.3	3.7	3.8	4.0	3.1	5.6	6.7	5.9	0.5	4.0	3.4	3.2	7.1	4.8	3.7
Total	41.3	53.2	30.6	63.7	48.0	48.4	52.0	73.9	54.2	40.3	43.6	45.2	56.9	51.6	50.7	44.9

Source: UBS, Intex, MarkIt, Bloomberg, and LPC.

EXHIBIT 13.8 Subordinate Tranche Excess Over-Collateralization Deltas (%)

	AVERYPT	BABS031	BABS041	BABS051	BABS052	BRYNMAWR	CASTHILL1	CASTHILL2	CASTHILL3	CENTUR9	CENTUR6	CENTUR7	CENTUR8	DRYDN022	DRYDN032	DRYDN043
R. H. Donnelley	21.1	24.4	12.4	15.0	31.9	18.9	10.5	11.5	—	14.6	13.6	12.7	9.0	18.6	38.9	15.2
Metro-Goldwyn-Mayer Inc.	16.3	10.7	10.0	14.5	19.2	19.9	7.6	12.1	—	21.2	6.3	18.0	11.9	29.4	19.6	23.7
Solar Capital Corp (Sungard)	13.5	0.0	9.9	15.3	23.9	11.6	6.8	3.6	—	15.1	8.7	12.8	13.1	29.3	17.1	21.3
Charter Communications	15.9	3.6	0.0	12.0	23.8	12.4	13.5	12.4	—	17.4	8.2	18.5	15.0	11.6	0.0	0.0
General Growth Properties Inc.	12.0	13.0	8.2	15.0	32.6	25.3	5.5	6.6	—	6.8	9.7	14.4	12.7	0.0	0.0	13.2
Graham Packaging Co.	14.7	10.6	6.6	10.9	16.8	0.0	9.3	11.6	—	21.9	8.4	16.1	15.9	20.4	0.0	21.2
United Pan-Europe Communications	7.1	7.5	6.6	12.2	14.4	18.3	5.4	6.5	—	11.0	6.3	9.4	9.5	23.6	19.6	19.0
Insight Communications Co.	9.9	0.0	8.9	5.3	9.5	19.5	11.7	9.9	—	9.4	6.2	2.5	6.3	23.4	19.5	18.7
Time Warner	23.7	7.8	11.4	0.0	23.9	14.7	0.0	0.0	—	14.4	8.7	10.8	11.4	5.6	19.2	18.6
Rockwood Specialties Group Inc.	12.1	0.0	0.0	0.0	14.4	15.9	5.5	0.0	—	8.3	5.8	9.0	18.2	29.3	24.3	18.9
Total	146.2	77.6	74.0	100.1	210.4	156.5	75.8	74.0	—	140.1	81.9	124.3	123.0	191.3	158.1	169.8

EXHIBIT 13.8 (Continued)

	DRYDN5	DRYDN7	DRYDN8	FORESTCR	LONGRV	OCTAGON4	OCTAGON5	OCTAGON6	OCTAGON7	OCTAGON8	RACEPOIN	RACEPNT2	ROSEMONT	SAGAMORE	SARATOGA	Average
R. H. Donnelley	15.7	17.2	5.0	18.8	11.8	30.2	24.0	29.2	2.4	21.3	9.9	12.6	18.5	20.9	25.4	17.7
Metro-Goldwyn-Mayer Inc.	27.9	17.8	12.9	21.3	21.0	28.9	15.8	17.3	14.9	14.4	6.9	9.1	26.5	22.2	19.7	17.2
Solar Capital Corp (Sungard)	27.8	14.8	13.9	21.3	19.9	14.4	6.7	12.3	8.9	23.4	11.4	13.7	41.2	18.5	16.5	15.6
Charter Communications	0.0	0.0	9.9	0.0	24.8	34.3	13.3	14.6	14.8	21.6	19.9	18.7	50.1	22.6	17.3	14.2
General Growth Properties Inc.	11.0	0.0	6.7	32.7	21.3	34.4	17.9	19.6	16.9	28.5	6.1	6.0	27.3	9.4	8.4	14.0
Graham Packaging Co.	22.2	8.9	0.0	3.2	2.5	25.9	17.9	7.4	13.3	0.0	11.4	13.2	7.2	20.5	23.4	12.0
United Pan-Europe Communications	22.3	8.9	10.0	16.8	16.6	26.0	18.0	19.8	13.4	14.4	3.8	3.3	27.5	0.0	0.0	12.6
Insight Communications Co.	21.7	20.5	0.0	15.7	20.6	5.8	11.0	14.5	0.0	12.4	9.0	12.6	19.5	7.4	11.0	11.4
Time Warner	21.9	0.0	0.0	11.8	12.4	28.6	6.6	12.2	11.7	18.1	18.6	16.3	14.6	7.6	11.3	12.1
Rockwood Specialties Group Inc.	27.8	11.8	7.9	9.0	13.8	15.8	15.7	14.7	11.8	1.8	9.8	8.5	13.8	20.7	13.9	12.0
Total	198.3	99.8	66.3	150.5	164.5	244.4	146.9	161.6	108.2	156.0	106.9	114.1	246.2	149.9	146.9	138.8

Source: UBS, Intex, MarkIt, Bloomberg, and LPC.

Donnelley across all the CLOs vary from 2.4% to 38.9% and average 17.7%. Subordinate tranche excess OC would be significantly reduced by the default of R. H. Donnelley.

The loss of all ten credits at 100% severity would cause most of the subordinate tranches in the 31 CLOs to lose all their excess OC. Over-collateralization of each subordinate tranche would therefore fall below 100%. Again, it is obviously a remote possibility that all 10 credits would default and almost an impossibility that all 10 credits would default with zero recovery. The subordinated notes of Rosemont, the CLO with the highest subordinated tranche excess OC, would still be covered, even if all 10 credits defaulted, as long as they had a 60% recovery.

Equity Tranches and Distressed Tranches

Exhibit 13.8 also has applicability to the equity tranches of these CLOs. Excess OC for the subordinate debt tranche is also the *residual amount of par* available for the equity tranche after all the debt tranches are satisfied. Thus, each excess OC delta in the exhibit shows the reduction in residual par available to the equity tranche if the credit defaults without any recovery. For example, for Babson 2004-1, the default of all 10 names without recovery would reduce the subordinate tranche's excess OC by 100%, but it would eliminate principal to the equity tranche.

Whereas excess OC delta for the subordinate debt tranche quantifies the potential deterioration of *coverage above 100%*, for the equity tranche, the same statistic quantifies the potential deterioration of *par otherwise applicable to equity*. This same analysis is valid for any distressed CLO tranche that does not have 100% par coverage and therefore no excess par coverage.

SUMMARY

CLOs have more and more of the same underlying credits in common. The average collateral overlap among the 32 CLOs we studied is 46% of par. The average overlap among CLOs from the same vintage is also 46%, and the average collateral overlap among CLOs managed by the same manager is 74%. But the average CLO has grown to include 233 credits. This means that while a particular name is more likely to be in different CLOs, that same name is likely to be a smaller component of any particular CLO. The 10 most common credits make up 0.7% to 1.2% of each CLO.

We used excess OC delta to measure the combined effect of these two phenomena. Senior and subordinate OC deltas are relatively small and subordinate OC deltas have shrunk over the last year. With respect to concentration risk across CLO portfolios and within a particular CLO portfolio, the smaller size of credits in CLOs has more than offset the prevalence of the same names across different CLOs.